THE C

SIMPLE YET PROFOUND

NEIL CULLAN McKINLAY

Published by WEEMAC Publishing

September 2022

"The secret of the Lord is with those who fear Him, and He will show them His covenant" (Psa. 25:14).

CONTENTS

PART THREE: The Covenant of Grace

Special thanks to D. Rudi Schwartz for his ongoing encouragement for me to see this project through, and for his many helpful suggestions. And to my elder brother Fearghas MacFhionnlaigh for his input and interactions with me throughout the writing of this book, and to my other brother, Stuart McKinlay, and John Swift for engaging me in very helpful discussion.

INTRODUCTION

This book is intended for all Christians. Those who have only a rudimentary understanding of the gospel, as one would expect, will find some portions more difficult than others. And, conversely, those with a mature knowledge, will perhaps find some portions simplistic (and perhaps a little repetitive!). Regardless, I have written this book about covenant theology especially with the layman in mind. Indeed, as will be demonstrated, this book is really about the gospel by another name. But let's not get too far ahead of ourselves.

Speaking of the gospel, when attempting to share it with a non-Christian, have you ever experienced anything like the following? There you are explaining who Jesus is and what He was doing on the cross, only to notice the eyes of the person you're talking to begin to glaze over? Of course, that may mean that, somehow, you've made the gospel presentation rather boring! Or it could mean that the other party is not in the least bit interested. Perhaps because they have their own opinions and preconceived ideas about things. Perhaps they may even think that they have heard it all before. Whatever the reason, they simply switch off.

Then there're those robust discussions that Christians sometimes have with non-Christians. You say your piece, and they say their piece to counter what you have said. Then after maybe a few back and forths, never the twain shall meet! The famous Welsh preacher Martin Lloyd Jones provides the following insightful comment,

Is [this] not, generally, the trouble in most arguments? You watch the next time you see two people having an argument! If you just sit and listen to them, you will notice that neither is really listening to the other; he is waiting for the other to stop; indeed he is ready to interrupt him. And that is what so many people do with the Scriptures. They have never really allowed the Scriptures to speak to them; they are so anxious to give their opinion.[1]

Yes, some non-Christians may "switch off" to the gospel. But what about some Christians shutting off at the mere mention of covenant theology? Will their eyes glaze over? Perhaps because they may have preconceived ideas (often erroneous) of what covenant theology is? Therefore, let's state it as simply and as clearly as possible: covenant theology is about the gospel. But, unlike Jonah's gourd (Jon. 4:6-9), covenant theology did not spring up overnight and wither as quickly. It has always been the teaching of the Bible. Yes, like the gospel itself, it is sometimes popular, and sometimes less popular. This book seeks to make it popular again.

At its simplest, covenant theology is about the New Adam doing what the Old Adam failed to do, how He did it, and the promised reward He then received from God for a job well done. In short,

---

[1] D. Martyn Lloyd-Jones, *Romans, Exposition of Chapter 9, God's Sovereign Purpose*, The Banner of Truth Trust, Edinburgh, Scotland, 1991, 128.

before the foundation of the world (1 Pet. 1:20), God the Father promised God the Son (i.e., Christ) an uncountable amount of people (Psa. 2:8; John 17:9), and a place (i.e., the world, as in the renewed Heavens and the renewed Earth) for them to live in along with Him forever (Rev. 21:1).

The Bible is the infallible record of the progressive revelation of God regarding His covenant promise. The Old Testament reveals what the Old Adam did, and the consequences for his breaking the covenant. The New Testament reveals what the New Adam did, and the reward He received for His perfectly keeping the covenant and paying its threatened penalty on behalf of all the people He represented. R. Scott Clark provides a useful summary of what we are talking about here where he says,

> The law demands perfect obedience, and the gospel announces Christ's perfect obedience to that law, His death and His resurrection for His people.[2]

Some perhaps shun covenant theology because of their own preconceived and perhaps alternate definition of the word covenant. Indeed, there are different types of covenants in the Bible. According to The NIV Study Bible these are commonly referred to as Royal Grant *(unconditional)*, Parity *(between equals)*, and Suzerain-vassal

---

[2] R. Scott Clark, *The History of Covenant Theology*, Ligonier Ministries, 2006, The History of Covenant Theology by R. Scott Clark (ligonier.org)

(conditional).[3] So far, so good. However, the study Bible says the following,

> Commitments made in these covenants were accompanied by self-maledictory oaths (made orally, ceremonially or both). The gods were called upon to witness the covenants and implement the curses of the oaths if the covenants were violated.[4]

As will become clearer later, it is hard to see from this how any covenant (regardless of type) can possibly be construed as "unconditional" (as suggested above in the "Royal Grant" type of covenant). There must always be a *condition* attached to a covenant. Otherwise, there can be no understanding of the supposed agreement. Whatever else a covenant may be, there needs to be an agreement at its heart to secure the bond. Notice the synonymous use of words covenant and agreement in the following, in what is known technically as a *parallelism*, "We have made a *covenant* with death, and with Sheol we have an *agreement*" (Isa. 28:15).

In modern times, even if you were to sign up for some service app or other online, you must first read (does anyone actually do this?!) and then sign or at least acknowledge that you have read the "terms of agreement" before you can make use of the product. If you do not acknowledge the terms of the

---

[3] *The NIV Study Bible*, Zondervan, Grand Rapids, Michigan, 1985, 19.
[4] Ibid., 19.

agreement, then you have not "bonded" with the provider, and may not use their product.

A royal grant, even if made by God, still requires your agreement or belief in the covenant with its stipulations (i.e., its "terms of agreement"), for it to have any meaning. E.g., where Jesus says, "The time is fulfilled, and the kingdom of God is at hand. Repent, and believe in the gospel" (Mark 1:15). To not repent and believe in the gospel is to not fulfill the conditions of the royal grant (i.e., of salvation from being punished by God for your sins). The law (summarised in the Ten Commandments) shows us what to repent of, and the gospel (the life, death, resurrection, and ascension of Christ Jesus) shows us what to believe in.

To be sure, according to covenant theology, and more importantly according to Scripture, God graciously grants certain people repentance AND gives them the gift of faith to believe in the gospel (Acts 11:18; 2 Tim. 2:25; Eph. 2:8-9.) Thus, though it is a "royal grant", the conditions of that grant remain, and they need to be met, even if they are met by God's grace.

One of the reasons some people shy away from the profitable study of the covenant of works and more broadly covenant theology, is because the word 'covenant' does not appear in the Bible until God mentions it to Noah in Genesis 6:18. J.V. Fesko says,

> Genesis is an organic part of the Pentateuch and ... no one book was supposed to be isolated from the four other books. In other

words, critics … read Genesis 1-3 as if the rest of the Pentateuch did not exist, which is ironically similar to higher-text critical readings. They bypass the literary context of the first three chapters and read it in chronological succession as if the reader was not supposed to peer over the wall of the third chapter to see what follows. Hence, if the term *covenant* does not appear in the first three chapters, then the idea must not exist.[5]

Pact, treaty, agreement, testament, bargain, confederation, contract, compact, alliance, oath, and promise etc., are all features of covenants. Therefore, why let simple semantics risk your missing out on the order and cohesiveness that covenant theology brings to the whole of Scripture, to the inner workings of the triune God, and to His relationship with humanity? Let us agree that, in its simplest form, a covenant at the very least is a bond. With this mutual understanding, let us begin to strengthen this bond. The following quote from J. V. Fesko sums up the intention of this book,

> Reformed Orthodoxy and classic covenant theology still have much to offer. The threefold covenant scheme (redemption, works, and grace) offers the best explanation of the biblical data.[6]

---

[5] J.V. Fesko, *Adam and the Covenant of Works*, Mentor Imprint by Christian Focus Publications Ltd., Geanies House, Fearn, Ross-shire, 2021, 197.

[6] J.V. Fesko, *The Trinity and the Covenant of Redemption*,

PART ONE
The Covenant of Redemption

"Yes, He shall build the temple of the LORD.
He shall bear the glory,
And shall sit and rule on His throne;
So He shall be a priest on His throne,
And the counsel of peace shall be between them
both" (Zech. 6:13).

Mentor Imprint by Christian Focus Publications Ltd., Geanies House, Fearn, Ross-shire, 2016, *xviii*.

COVENANT BOND

Introduction

Having seen that a covenant is essentially a type of bond, in the following we shall consider how that bond is *conditional* by nature.

The bond in question is God's covenant. (Hebrew בְּרִית *berith*, Greek διαθήκη, *diatheke* = covenant.) It is a *conditional* promise. E.g., note that when God cut a covenant with Abraham, the father of all believers (Gen. 15:7-21; Gal. 2:6-9), God, by His Spirit, was giving His Word, (and His Word is His bond!), that if He were to break His eternal covenant, He would no longer be the triune God.

We see this self-maledictory oath fully illustrated when God was cutting His covenant with Abraham as He moved through dismembered animals. "And it came to pass, when the sun went down and it was dark, that behold, there appeared a smoking oven and a burning torch that passed between those pieces" (Gen. 15:17; cf. Jer. 34:18-19). God here was saying in effect, "May what was done to these animals be done to Me should I ever break My covenant." This, too, points us to Christ. Says Hermann Witsius,

> God likewise signified ... that all the stability of the covenant of grace was founded on the sacrifice of Christ, and that the soul and body of Christ were one day to be violently separated asunder.[7]

---

[7] Herman Witsius, *Economy of Covenants Between God and Man*, 2 Vols, Book I, Chapter I, VII, (First published 1677,

It also gives insight into what happens to man, body and soul and spirit, as a result of Adam, our covenant representative, breaking God's pre-fall covenant. Says Kenneth Gentry,

> Covenants are not casual, informal, and inconsequential arrangements. They are established in a most solemn manner by means of designated symbolic actions. The manner in which they are established is quite significant. For instance, in Genesis 15 God sovereignly and graciously established His covenant with Abram by passing alone between the pieces of the animals Abram had sacrificed (Gen. 15:8-17). The symbolic covenantal action represented to Abram was a graphic 'pledge-to-death' by God. He solemnly promised that He would perform His covenant promise, or else be 'destroyed' (as were the sacrificial animals). Thus, in the Hebrew language the phrase 'to make a covenant' may be translated literally 'to *cut* a covenant.'[8]

Abraham, by God's grace alone, had already beforehand met the condition of this cutting of the covenant: "And he believed in the LORD, and He accounted it to him for righteousness" (Gen. 15:6; Rom. 4:3,9,22). The righteousness that God

reprinted 1822, Kindle version 2014), 37.
[8] Kenneth L. Gentry, *The Greatness of the Great Commission*, Institute for Christian Economics, Tyler, Texas, 1993, 6.

accounted to Abraham belongs to Abraham's promised Seed, i.e., Jesus Christ who was going to be sacrificed (1 Pet. 1:20; Rev. 13:8b).

God now applies His covenant's benefits to all who believe "according to the eternal purpose which He accomplished in Christ Jesus our Lord" (Eph. 1:11).

The Eternal Bond Between the Father & the Son

Whether made pre-fall with Adam, or post-fall with Noah or Abraham or Moses or David, all of God's covenants throughout the Bible from beginning to end are ultimately made with Christ. How so? "For no matter how many promises God has made, they are 'Yes' in Christ" (2 Cor. 1:20a). Therefore, even when God says, "I set My rainbow in the cloud, and it shall be for the sign of the covenant between Me and the earth' (Gen. 9:13), the rainbow points us to Christ. Says Louis Berkhof,

> A surety is one who engages to become responsible for it that the legal obligations of another will be met. In the covenant of redemption Christ undertook to atone for the sins of His people by bearing the necessary punishment, and to meet the demands of the law for them. And by taking the place of delinquent man He became the last Adam, and as such also the Head of the covenant, the Representative of all those whom the Father has given Him.[9]

---

[9] Louis Berkhof, *Systematic Theology*, The Banner of Truth Trust, Edinburgh, Reprinted 2000, 267.

God's eternal bond is with Christ, who wears as it were God's covenant rainbow coat of many colours. Christ is the surety, the surety-bond, i.e., the guarantor guaranteeing the performance of God's contracts and covenant obligations. In short, Jesus Christ is the fulfillment in time of all of God's promises from eternity. Hence, we are positing the idea that God's eternal (and in time variously and differently administered) covenant is *conditional* because every time we see it in the Bible we are being pointed to Jesus Christ. In a foreword to a book, Sinclair B. Ferguson says,

> For ultimately God's covenant with his people is not only *found in* Jesus Christ; it is Jesus Christ. The new covenant, the final covenant, the covenant in which is experienced the fullness of God's promise 'I will be your God and you will be my people' is made in him. In him all the (covenant) promises of God find their 'yes!' So when we rightly speak of 'Christ and the covenant,' this is ultimately the same as speaking of 'Christ who *is* the covenant.'[10]

Jesus said to some Jews that were trying to kill Him, "You search the Scriptures, for in them you think you have eternal life; and these are they which testify of Me. But you are not willing to come to Me

---

[10] Cornelis P. Venema, *Christ and Covenant Theology: Essays on Election, Republication, and the Covenants*, Phillipsburg, NJ, P&R Publishing, 2017, xi.

that you may have life" (John 5:39-40). Thus, the whole Bible (Old and New Testaments) is revelation about Christ, the One in whom the eternal covenant of God is revealed and ultimately is fulfilled.

The blood He shed to give life to those who come to Him is "the blood of the everlasting covenant" (Heb. 13:20b). This everlasting or eternal covenant is also known as the covenant of redemption, (Latin, *pactum salutis*). Says J.V. Fesko,

> When Zechariah speaks of the council of peace between Yahweh and the Branch, which Paul echoes in Ephesians 2:14, 'he himself is our peace,' this covenanted peace originates before the foundations of the world. When the psalmist writes of the covenant, the decree, "The LORD said to me, 'You are my Son; today I have begotten you,'" this covenantal utterance originates before the foundation of the world, as the elect are chosen in the Anointed, the Messiah, the Christ. The second person of the Trinity was identified as the Christ before the foundation of the world, not merely in history. His pre-temporal designation as the Messiah unfolds in history.[11]

We are here dealing with the triune God and His covenant of redemption, with its administration first in the covenant of works and then in the covenant of grace. If we assume that each clause in

---

[11] J.V. Fesko, *The Trinity and the Covenant of Redemption*, Mentor Imprint by Christian Focus Publications Ltd., Geanies House, Fearn, Ross-shire, 2016, 111-112.

the following verse is referring to a different person in the Trinity, we will be able to understand that though each person does not operate to the exclusion of the others, each has a particular role in the Godhead: "For from him and through him and to him are all things. To him be glory forever. Amen" (Rom. 11:36). Thus, the Trinity in unity. As lawgiver, the Father legislatively decreed everything that comes to pass, including redemption. As executor, the Son obediently enforces what the Father has decreed. And, as judiciary, the Spirit applies to believers the redemption that the Father has decreed and the Son has purchased (Isa. 33:22; John 5:22, 27, 16:8). In the covenants of redemption (Father), works (Son), and grace (Spirit), we also see Scriptural basis for the three aspects of government found in Western liberal democracies, viz., *legislative, executive, and judicial* branches.

The trinitarian council of peace is the covenant of redemption. The covenant of redemption was partially revealed and applied to the pre-fall Adam as the covenant of works, and, of course, when redemption was needed, was more fully revealed to him post-fall as the covenant of grace. It may help to think of it as the law ultimately pointing to Christ as revealed in the gospel, (*cf.,* Gal. 3:24.) This pre-fall bond with Adam goes by various names, e.g., creational covenant, Edenic covenant, covenant of nature, etc. (It will become clear later why we prefer to call it the covenant of works.)

The Westminster Standards, to which this book subscribes, consist of the Westminster Confession of Faith, the Westminster Larger and

Shorter Catechisms, the Directory for the Publick (sic) Worship of God, and the Form of Church Government. Says Ligon Duncan,

> [T]he covenant made with humanity before the fall is identified by the Westminster Standards as a covenant of *works* (respecting terms and conditions; WCF 7.2), a covenant of *life* (respecting its goal or end; WLC 20) a covenant with *Adam* (respecting its party or representative; WLC 22; and *first* covenant (respecting its chronological priority and indicating that there is a successor; WCF 7.2). All four names are apt descriptors of the same prefall covenant and are aspects essential to it.[12]

In this administration of God's eternal covenant, Adam was promised eternal life. But if Adam were to break the everlasting covenant (as the covenant of redemption applied to him in the pre-fall covenant of works), he would forfeit the eternal life he (and his posterity in him) had been, albeit conversely, promised, (which promise was signified by the tree of life), and instead would receive the threatened penalty, which is death. For God gave Adam, as the federal representative or covenant head of humanity, an outward test: "And the LORD God commanded the man, saying, 'Of every tree in the garden you may freely eat, but of the tree of the knowledge of good and evil you shall not eat, for in

---

[12] Guy Prentiss Waters, J. Nicholas Reid, and John R. Muether, *Covenant Theology: Biblical, Theological, and Historical Perspectives*, Crossway, Wheaton, Illinois, 2020, 28.

the day you eat of it you shall surely die'" (Gen. 2:16-17). Says John Calvin,

> We must therefore look farther, because the prohibition of the tree of knowledge of good and evil was a test of obedience [*obedientiae examen*], that Adam might prove his willing submission to the divine government. And the name itself shews that the precept was given for no other purpose than that he might be contented with his condition, and not aim with criminal cupidity at any higher. But the promise [*promissio*] which authorised him to expect eternal life, as long as he should eat of the tree of life, and on the other hand, the dreadful denunciation of death, as soon as he should taste of the tree of knowledge of good and evil, were calculated for the probation [*probandam*] and exercise of his faith. Hence it is easy to infer, by what means Adam provoked the wrath of God against him. Augustine indeed properly observes, that pride was the first of all evils: because if ambition had not elated man beyond what was lawful and right, he might have continued in his honourable situation.[13]

Adam, by his rebellious disobedience dissolved God's bond as it was administered at that time. However, Adam's breaking of the bond's

---

[13] Calvin, J., & Allen, J, (1816), *Institutes of the Christian Religion*, II.1.4, (Vol. 1, pp. 260–261). Hezekiah Howe; Philip H. Nicklin.

conditions did not sever the Father's eternal covenant (of redemption) with His Son who would at a future point go on to keep the covenant (of works) that Adam broke.

The Gospel Covenant

The covenant of grace is the gospel by another name. Immediately after Adam had broken the covenant of works (by instead bonding with Satan against God and eating the forbidden fruit), God began to reveal another aspect of the eternal covenant of redemption, viz., the covenant of grace. This He did by announcing the gospel promise, cursing the serpent Satan, and saying to him, "And I will put enmity between you and the woman, and between your seed and her Seed; He shall bruise your head, and you shall bruise His heel" (Gen. 3:15.) God then clothed Adam and Eve with animal skin, (presumably from a sacrificed lamb?), symbolizing what Jesus "the Lamb of God who takes away the sin of the world" (John 1:29) would do in the future.

As per the gospel-promise, in time the Seed of the Woman figuratively inflicted a fatal head-wound when He bruised or crushed the serpent's head at Golgotha, the Place of the Skull. In this He had His own heel (as opposed to His head) bruised (Isa. 53:5), thus receiving at the cross a fatal (but temporary) physical wound (by the hand of God), which would (as we shall see later) fulfill, activate, and release the "last will and testament" aspects of the covenant.

Christ is "the Lamb slain from the foundation of the world" (Rev. 13:8b), meaning that the event of the cross was decreed by God in eternity past.

Sometimes called "the counsel of peace" (Zech. 6:13), as already mentioned, this decree is usually referred to as the *pactum salutis*, which is the covenant of redemption (Psa. 2:7; 110:1; Eph. 1; 2 Tim. 1:9-10). Therefore, it was God who had it in mind to sacrifice His own Son (as pre-figured by Abraham's figurative sacrifice of his (only) son Isaac (Heb. 11:17-19), when he, Abraham, under direction from God, substituted a ram that's head had been caught in a thicket (Gen. 22).

The promised Seed, i.e., Christ, was to come from the loins of the aged Abraham and his (barren) wife, Sarah (Gen. 18). Jesus is the son of Abraham (Matt. 1:1). Like Abraham's ram whose head was caught in the thicket, with a crown of thorns He is our substitute sacrifice (2 Cor. 5:21).

The gospel-promise was made earlier to Abraham where God says, "In you all the families of the earth shall be blessed" (Gen. 12:3b). This blessing flows through and from Christ, the Word, who is the promised Seed, (Gal. 3:16). It is also worth noting at this point that "The Word of the LORD came to Abram in a vision, saying, 'Do not be afraid, Abram. I am your shield, your exceedingly great reward" (Gen. 15:1). And, as the pre-incarnate Christ, i.e., "the Word of the LORD" that came to Abram, i.e., the One who is his "shield and exceedingly great reward", says after He had become also flesh, "Your father Abraham rejoiced to see My day, and he saw it and was glad" (John 8:56). The outpouring of the Holy Spirit on all peoples is bringing to fulfilment God's promise to Abraham that all the families or nations on earth would be blessed through him.

Abraham behaved very much like a man who had heard good news, i.e., the gospel. Indeed, Scripture testifies that Abraham heard the gospel. E.g., "And the Scripture, foreseeing that God would justify the Gentiles by faith, preached the gospel to Abraham beforehand saying, 'In you all the nations of the earth shall be blessed'" (Gal. 3:8).

Before the time of Moses, i.e., from Adam onward, God's people saw the gospel when they made animal sacrifices to God (Gen. 4:4; Heb. 11:4). By the time of Moses, the people of God were seeing the gospel depicted in the ceremonial law, i.e., the sacrificial system, the ark of the covenant, the tabernacle and then the temple etc. Jesus Christ is the fulfilment of everything depicted by, in, and through all of these. These all were types. He is the great antitype. Thus, the Old Testament is full of the gospel! Says Edmund P Clowney,

> Christ revealed Himself in the types of Old Testament symbolism. Through the Old Testament story we hear not only about the presence of the Lord but also about the coming of the Servant of the Lord, foreshadowed in those who served in His covenant. The elaborate symbolism of the ceremonial law no longer offers a handbook for ritual since Christ has come. Rather, we are drawn from the shadows into His light, the light of His presence.[14]

---

[14] Edmund P Clowney, *Preaching Christ in All of Scripture*, Crossway Books, Wheaton, Illinois, 2003, 53-54.

If we are going to carry Bibles and not simply pocket Testaments, we should surely be using the Old Testament more than we do. The missionary Bible of the apostolic church was the Old Testament Scripture. Our Lord in the synagogue of Nazareth (Luke 4), Peter at Pentecost (Acts 2), Paul in the synagogues of Asia Minor and Greece – these all preached the gospel from the Old Testament. During the time which the apostolic witness to Christ was still being recorded, the Old Testament was the Scripture from which the church preached Christ.[15]

The covenant of grace was differently administered in the Old Testament. Thus, Circumcision and Passover were pictures of the gospel, the good news. These blood sacraments became the unbloody New Testament sacraments of Baptism and the Lord's Supper respectively. Circumcision and Baptism have the same covenantal meaning, (i.e., regeneration, the removal of sin, cleansing by the shed blood of the promised Messiah, etc.) (Col. 2:11-12). And Passover and the Lord's Supper both speak of "the Lamb that takes away the sin of the world."

---

[15] Edmund P. Clowney, *Preaching*, *The Preacher and Preaching in the Twentieth Century*, Edited by Samuel T Logan, Presbyterian & Reformed Publishing, Phillipsburg, New Jersey, 1986, 163.

Covenant Types & Theophanies

Then there were the various Old Testament theophanies. We have already mentioned that the preincarnate Christ came to Abraham announcing, "Do not be afraid Abram, I am your shield, your exceedingly great reward" (Gen. 15:1). The pillar of fire and pillar of cloud, the appearances of the Angel of the LORD, are theophanies. Theophanies are God appearances (from the Greek *theos* God, and *phainein* to show). These showings or appearances took place in the Old Testament. (They could also be called Christophanies, i.e., Christ appearances, where the preincarnate Christ made appearances before His incarnation.)

Perhaps the most well-known theophany in the Bible is when Israel, after God had set them free from their Egyptian captivity, was being led by Him through the wilderness. "Then the Angel of God, who had been traveling in front of Israel's army, withdrew and went behind them. The pillar of cloud also moved from in front and stood behind them, coming between the armies of Egypt and Israel. Throughout the night the cloud brought darkness to the one side and light to the other side; so neither went near the other all night long" (Exod. 14:19-20; cf. Acts 7:38). This Angel of God is the same Angel who delivered the Ten Commandments to Moses on Mount Sinai, a mountain that was burning with fire, darkness, gloom, and storm (Heb. 12:18). "He [Moses] was in the assembly in the wilderness, with the Angel who spoke to him on Mount Sinai, and with our ancestors; and he received living words to pass on to us" (Acts 7:38). Of theophanies Meredith Kline says,

So it was perceived by eyes supernaturally opened and so transcribed in prophetic words. Seen by the natural eye, it was a heavenly phenomenon of light and clouds. Adapting its form to its function, it appeared in the varied modes of the sky, now a clear firmament or sheltering canopy, now a whirlwind or thunderhead of terrifying trumpet and flashing arrow.

The theophanic glory was expressed as light, at whatever dimensional level it was perceived or whatever guise the divine epiphany assumed in other respects. The appearance of the Glory was the appearance of light as of fire or the sun, the light of divine glory that no man can approach. This theophanic light appeared at times as a rainbow radiance expressive of the holy beauty of the Lord in his temple; at times, as the illuminating light of wisdom and truth, penetrating the darkness in the service of judicial righteousness to expose the works of darkness; and again as an effective energy, executing judgment whether to bless or curse, whether as a sun of righteousness rising with healing in its wings or as a light like the blinding, searing glare of the burning oven.[16]

[16] Meredith G. Kline, *Images of the Spirit*, Eugene, OR, Wipf and Stock Publishers, 1999, 18.

Now, God covered our first parents with skin for protection before expelling them from the garden of Eden. Presumably they observed God (in whatever form He appeared to them) sacrifice and then carve up the animal (a sheep?) by shedding its blood and removing its skin to clothe them (Lev. 17:11, Heb. 9:22). This symbolized what the promised Redeemer was coming to do, i.e., to make a sacrifice that would crush the serpent's head (Gen. 3:15, 21). Adam no doubt passed on this gospel knowledge to his son Abel who was a keeper of sheep of which he would make sacrificial offerings to God (Gen. 4:1-4; Heb. 11:4) typifying the promise of the gospel.

Now, the Old Testament is replete with symbolisms that prefigure persons, actions, and events that would come to pass in the New Testament. The Old Testament therefore is full of types of which Christ Jesus is the great antitype, i.e., the final destination to which all the signposts pointed. Even Adam himself was a type of Christ and what He was coming to do. "Nevertheless death reigned from Adam to Moses, even over those who had not sinned according to the likeness of the transgression of Adam, who is a type of Him who was to come" (Rom. 5:14). This method of seeing prefiguration and fulfillment in the Bible, i.e., type and antitype, is referred to as typology. Patrick Fairbairn popularised the science of typology in the 1800s. Speaking of the relationship between the Old and New Testaments Fairbairn says,

A mutual adaptation and internal harmony binds together the Old and New dispensations, even under the striking diversity that characterizes the two in respect to a future world. And the further the investigation is pursued, the more will such be found to be the case generally. It will be found that the connection of the Old with the New is something more than typical, in the sense of foreshadowing, or prefigurative of what was to come; it is also inward and organic. Amid the ostensible differences, there is a pervading unity and agreement – one faith, one life, one hope, one destiny. And while the Old Testament Church in its outward condition and earthly relations, typically shadowed forth the spiritual and heavenly things of the New, it was also, in so far as it realized and felt the truth of God presented to it, the living root out of which the New ultimately sprang. The rude beginnings were there, of all that exists in comparative perfection now. Another advantage resulting from a correct knowledge and appreciation of the Typology of ancient Scripture, *is the increased value and importance with which it invests the earlier portions of revelation*... For the whole of the Old Testament will be found to rise in our esteem, in proportion as we understand and enter into its typological bearing.[17]

---

[17] Patrick Fairbairn, *The Typology of Scripture: Viewed in Connection with the Whole Series of The Divine Dispensations*, Volume 1, Fourth Edition, T & T Clark, Edinburgh, Scotland, 1864, 215.

With Adam and Eve (typologically!) clothed by God in animal skin, expelled by God from the garden, with "cherubim at the east of the garden of Eden, and a flaming sword which turned every way, to guard the way to the tree of life" (Gen. 3:24b), we won't be too surprised then to see the preincarnate Christ making temporary manifestations in various forms in the Old Testament, which, along with items, objects, and practices, all typified Him and what He was coming into the world to do. In short, these among other things, were the gospel in the Old Testament.

Now, with types and theophanies in mind, let's consider a few obvious examples. We have already acknowledged that the way to receiving eternal life by way of the tree of life had been cut off by an instrument of cutting, i.e., a flaming sword. However, there was another way. The covenant of grace.

We have already mentioned too that when God cut His covenant with Abraham, He made a theophanic appearance in that "When the sun had gone down and it was dark, behold, a smoking fire pot and a flaming torch passed between these pieces" (Gen. 15:17). And, as already noted, the pillars of fire and of cloud are theophanies, which are extensions of the smoke and fire on Mount Sinai when God came down to deliver His covenant law (Exod. 19:18).

We believe that the theophany of the Angel of the LORD is the preincarnate Christ. He appeared to Hagar (Gen. 16), to Abraham (Gen. 22), and to Moses: "And the Angel of the LORD appeared to him in a flame of fire from the midst of a bush. So he looked, and behold, the bush was burning with fire, but the bush *was* not consumed" (Exod. 3:2). He also appeared to Balaam "with His drawn sword in His hand" (Num. 22:31), to Gideon (Judges 6:12), and, remembering Abraham's encounter with God, i.e., "Behold, a smoking fire pot and a flaming torch passed between these pieces" (Gen. 15:17), consider Gideon's attack on the Midianites, "Then the three companies blew the trumpets and broke the jars. They held in their left hands the torches, and in their right hands the trumpets to blow. And they cried out, "A sword for the LORD and for Gideon!" (Judges 6:18). God appeared to Samson's future parents, Manoah and his wife: "So Manoah took the young goat with the grain offering, and offered it upon the rock to the LORD. And He did a wondrous thing while Manoah and his wife looked on—it happened as the flame went up toward heaven from the altar—the Angel of the LORD ascended in the flame of the altar! When Manoah and his wife saw *this,* they fell on their faces to the ground" (Judges 13:19-20).

Sacrifice, Angel of the LORD, swords, flames, are all reminders of man's expulsion from the garden. However, they were also pointing to Christ's future baptism of fire, when He, as per the covenant promise, would crush the serpent's head by His own death, but then "ascend up toward heaven from the altar" of His sacrifice.

The list goes on and on. The Man Jacob wrestled with all night (Gen. 33), the theophany Joshua witnessed, "[A] Man stood opposite him with His sword drawn in His hand" (Josh 6:13b), to

Shadrach, Meshach, and Abed-Nego in the fiery furnace. "'Look!' [Nebuchadnezzar] answered, 'I see four men loose, walking in the midst of the fire; and they are not hurt, and the form of the fourth is like the Son of God' ... 'Blessed be the God of Shadrach, Meshach, and Abed-Nego, who sent His Angel and delivered His servants who trusted in Him'" (Dan. 3:25; 28a).

Yes, the coming of the Angel of the LORD, the Messenger of the covenant, was specifically promised through the prophet Malachi, "'Behold, I send My messenger, And he will prepare the way before Me. And the Lord, whom you seek, will suddenly come to His temple, even the Messenger of the covenant, in whom you delight. Behold, He is coming,' Says the LORD of hosts" (Mal. 3:1).

The list of Old Testament theophanies could be greatly extended. These are just a few examples. Indeed, even when we move from the Old into the New Testament, we can still see theophanies, such as the tongues of fire on people's heads on the day of Pentecost (Acts 2:3). However, all theophanies, even the tongues of fire, point to Christ, and so do all the Old Testament types, from the tree of life to the rainbow, to the Sabbath, to circumcision and Passover, to the sacrificial system, to the temple and everything in it, to the annual feasts, to the prophets, priests, and kings, all this and more, all these types pointed to the great antitype, Jesus Christ.

Thus, the saints (i.e., true believers) in both Old and New Testaments looked to the Messiah, the Christ, to the One who would be anointed covenantally in His baptism with water, and with the

Holy Spirit, (symbolised by the pouring or sprinkling of water on people's heads, Isa. 32:15; Matt. 3:13-17; Mark 1:9-11; Luke 3:21-22; John 1:29-34), the One who, at His last covenant meal transformed the Passover into the Lord's Supper (Luke 22:19-20).

Thus, God's eternal covenant of redemption was differently administered at different periods throughout the Old Testament, but all of it spoke of Christ, the promised Seed of the Woman. This is what we call the covenant of grace. It is the gracious promise of God in which He says that He shall be our God and that we shall be His people (Jer. 31:33; Heb. 8:10).

Conclusion

In our own day the shorthand way of speaking of the covenant of grace is to use the word "gospel" or "good news." The Seed of the Woman was as it were conceived in Genesis 3:15 and was born in the New Testament. However, this was no unplanned pregnancy, but had been planned from eternity as per God's eternal covenant of redemption. As Christians, He is our God, and we are His people.

COVENANT ANTICIPATED

Introduction

Having considered that a covenant in its simplest definition is a bond, we are now ready to consider how this covenant bond between God and His people had been anticipated by God in eternity past as a covenant between the Father and the Son.

In the following we shall develop, reiterate, and reinforce the covenant themes (and much more) précised above in an easy-to-read manner. Thus, having seen that the gospel is the covenant of grace by another name, and that both the covenant of grace and the covenant of works are simply different administrations of the eternal covenant of redemption in time, we are now ready to consider the covenant more deeply before time began and in time.

Covenant Eternal

The Covenant is eternal because God is eternal. God is the eternally triune God. Therefore, God, Father and Son and Holy Spirit, i.e., the three persons in the Godhead, are in an eternal bond, past, present, and future. Scripture says, "A threefold cord is not quickly broken" (Eccl. 4:12b). The Westminster Larger Catechism asks and answers,

> Q. 9. *How many persons are there in the Godhead?*
> *A.* There be three persons in the Godhead, the Father, the Son, and the Holy Ghost; and these three are one true, eternal God, the same in

substance, equal in power and glory; although distinguished in their personal properties.

The word "distinguished" in the last line of the above quote must always be borne in mind when discussing the Trinity. It is very important that we only distinguish the persons but never separate them. Each person in the Godhead owns personal or private property, by which we mean that we are able to see that each person has attributes belonging only to Himself. The Father has the attribute of Fatherhood. Fatherhood does not belong to the Son, but Sonship does. Sonship does not belong to the Father or the Holy Spirit. The Spirit has neither Fatherhood nor Sonship. Therefore, the Spirit also has a distinctive attribute. Thus, the Father is not the Son or the Spirit. The Son is not the Father or the Spirit. And the Spirit is not the Father or the Son. However, though there are distinctions, the three Persons are always one God.

If we focus on the Father, we will begin to see the Son and the Spirit. Likewise, if we know more about the Son, we will understand the Persons of the Father and the Spirit better. And, of course, the more we know the Person of the Spirit, the more we begin to know the Father and the Son. How so? It is because the three Persons are one God, as revealed in Scripture. Who is the Father the Father of? The Son. Who is the Son the Son of? The Father. Who is the Spirit the Spirit of? The Father and the Son. The Spirit reveals the Son who reveals the Father (John 14:9; 15:26).

There is a Celtic-knot that symbolizes this three and oneness of God. It is called the *triquetra*, from a Latin word meaning three-cornered. (See book's cover.) The symbol is triangular, with three loops, which, if you trace each one, appear to have no beginning and no end. Though each loop is distinct from the others, the three interconnect and interpenetrate each of the others. This is the same with the eternal covenant.

If you were to look at the covenant of redemption, as it is revealed in Scripture, long enough, the covenants of works and grace begin to appear. If you study the covenant of works, the covenants of redemption and grace will begin to appear.[18] And, of course, if you look at the covenant of grace long enough, the covenants of redemption and works will begin to appear. This is because the three distinct covenants are one eternal covenant. It is all trinitarian! Later, we shall see more of this when we consider the threefold division of Old Testament law; viz, moral law, legal law (judicial, civil), and ceremonial law.

Already the astute reader will have noticed that, just as there is an order of sequence in listing the persons of Trinity, i.e., the Father, the Son, and the Holy Spirit, so there is a covenantal order, i.e., redemption, works, and grace. Shouldn't it be grace, works, and then redemption? Or perhaps works, grace, and redemption? The point being that it doesn't matter where you begin, like the Celtic-knot, each

---

[18] We mean here, of course, the covenant of works as viewed in light of the whole of Scripture, not as the pre-fall Adam would have seen it.

interconnects and interpenetrates the others. And, as within the Godhead, each reflects certain aspects of the others. However, though, like the Godhead, the covenant is one, the sequence is, covenant of redemption, covenant of works, then covenant of grace, in that order. This is because each covenant reflects each person in the Godhead. In the covenant of redemption, the Father gives the Son His eternal moral law to keep as the covenant of works on behalf of Himself and those He represents, and the Spirit applies the benefits of the Son's covenant-keeping to those who are represented. Again, it is all trinitarian.

Yes, it is impossible for finite human beings to comprehend the eternality of the triune God. And, because His triuneness has to do with His eternality, we also, on account of our finitude, have trouble comprehending God's triuneness.

Thankfully the eternal triune God has condescended to reveal Himself to us by way of His eternal covenant as per the "Book of His Covenant". As the triune God says to Abraham, the father of all who believe, "I will establish My covenant between Me and you and your descendants after you in their generations, for an everlasting covenant, to be God to you and your descendants after you" (Gen. 17:7). Note the word "establish". God had already "cut" His covenant with Abraham (Gen. 15).

It should be kept in mind that in the beginning everything was embryonic and therefore was in need of being delivered, and then developed to maturity, i.e., perfected. Says Abraham Kuyper,

Man was not created in the fullness of his power, but in the beginning of his potential, carrying in him the prophecy of what would yet develop in all of its fullness from this foundation. And consequently in the covenant of works man was promised something greater – a richer and more potent life, provided he remained faithful to God's demand. And thus it is especially from this promise that it also follows that man initially at his creation was less than what he would be, and therefore in a certain way he stood in weakness before God. He was indeed holy, but still had not yet attained to the perseverance of the saints. He was holy and just, but in a way that he could still fall. He was on the way, but on that way he was still at its beginning, and the end of the road was yet far away.[19]

God had written His eternal covenant law (albeit in pre-fall positive terms), on the heart of humanity when He created Adam (and, in time, each one of us in Adam) in His own image (Rom. 2:14-15). Thus God, while giving His blessing, mandated Adam, our pre-fall representative (with his wife Eve and their posterity), to "Be fruitful and multiply; fill the earth and subdue it; have dominion over the fish of the sea, over the birds of the air, and over every living thing that moves on the earth" (Gen. 1:28).

Tied or bonded to the triune God by His eternal covenant, pre-fall humanity (in Adam) had

---

[19] Abraham Kuyper, *God's Angels: His Ministering Spirits*, eBook version, (Translation by Rev. Richard Stienstra)

losable eternal life (but had unlosable existence). Adam could maintain his present life and secure unlosable eternal life (with all its blessings) upon condition of perfect obedience to God in all his endeavours. However, by eating the forbidden fruit, Adam broke his covenant-probation with God, while at the same time forming a covenant with the serpent, i.e., Satan, against the eternally triune God.

Yes, Adam (and humanity in him) broke covenant with God. However, being eternally triune, God cannot deny or break covenant with Himself. Therefore, God graciously and immediately after the fall began to reveal His eternal covenant as it applies to fallen humanity. Thus, the covenant of grace or gospel covenant in which the eternal triune God says to the serpent (humanity's new covenant partner), "And I will put enmity between you and the woman, and between your seed and her Seed; He shall bruise your head, and you shall bruise His heel" (Gen. 3:15).

Jesus Christ, Son of God/Son of Man, is the promised Seed of the woman (Gen. 3:15). Thus from eternity past, as witnessed by the eternal Spirit, the eternal Father has given a conditional promise to His eternal Son (as the federal or covenant head of all who are in Him), that if He, as the new Adam, were to keep the covenant of life or works perfectly, if He were to keep the eternal covenant as it applied to pre-fall Adam, then the Father would give to the man Christ Jesus the eternal life blessings that were promised to the pre-fall Adam as humanity's representative. The man Christ Jesus perfectly kept the covenant of works, and He shares His reward with all believers. "Blessed be the God and Father of our

Lord Jesus Christ, who has blessed us with every spiritual blessing in the heavenly places in Christ" (Eph. 1:3).

The eternal life promised by the Father to pre-fall Adam (and the Son of Man in eternity past and in time as the last Adam) is summed up in the eternally triune God's gracious gift of the Holy Spirit. For, Jesus said to His Church at the time of His ascension, "Wait for the Promise of the Father" (Acts 1:4).

Christ kept every jot and tittle of God's covenant law perfectly on behalf of those He represented. And He paid the penalty of death for humanity's breaking of the eternal covenant. And being the eternal second Person in the triune Godhead means that His work on the cross is of infinite value. And because "a threefold cord is not quickly broken", God raised Him from the dead. Then after ascending bodily to the right hand of majesty, both the Father and the Son poured out the Promise (as promised throughout the Old Testament's administrations of the eternal covenant), the eternal covenant's blessings upon all humanity. "The Spirit Himself bears witness with our spirit that we are children of God" (Rom. 8:16). Thus, though the man Christ Jesus already had the Spirit without measure before His ascension (John 3:34), the Holy Spirit, referred to by Jesus as "the Promise of the Father" (Luke 24:49; Acts 1:4), is the reward He received from the Father after His ascension for fulfilling the "conditional promise" (Dan. 7:13-14; John 16:7; Acts 2:33), the difference being that the Spirit could now after "mission accomplished" be shared also without measure with His Church (Joel 2:28-29; Acts 2:18; Eph. 1:3).

Jesus Christ is our covenant keeper. Indeed, Jesus Christ is our covenant. And, about Christ our eternal covenant, "Thus says God the LORD, Who created the heavens and stretched them out, Who spread forth the earth and that which comes from it, Who gives breath to the people on it, and spirit to those who walk on it: 'I, the LORD, have called You in righteousness, and will hold Your hand; I will keep You and give You as a covenant to the people, as a light to the Gentiles, to open blind eyes, to bring out prisoners from the prison, those who sit in darkness from the prison house" (Isa. 42:5-7).

The covenant, as a *conditional* promise, as in the pre-fall covenant, i.e., the covenant of works, is best understood when the man Christ Jesus as the new Adam is viewed as ascribing perfect, personal, and perpetual obedience to God in every sphere of activity even unto death.

Covenant Creational or Cosmic

The pre-fall covenant God made with Adam (as humanity's representative) is creational or cosmic. As already noted, it is referred to as the "covenant of works". However, it also includes the "cultural mandate" (which some refer to as the "dominion mandate"), whereby man (as God's image) is to, "Be fruitful and multiply; fill the earth and subdue it; [and] have dominion over the fish of the sea, over the birds of the air, and over every living thing that moves on the earth" (Gen. 1:28). Adam was to go about this dominion duty for an unspecified period, which is to say that God had put him on probation with an outward test of obedience.

The creational or cosmic aspect of the covenant can still be seen even after the Fall by studying Genesis 9:1-19, where God reveals His covenant to Noah by saying to him, "I will establish My covenant with you." Notice that God calls it "My covenant." His covenant is with Noah and with His creation. The cultural mandate that was given to Adam is restated, and now the rainbow (instead of the previous tree of life given as a covenantal sign to Adam) is to be the sign of the everlasting covenant. God says, "While the earth remains, seedtime and harvest, cold and heat, winter and summer, and day and night shall not cease" (Gen. 8:22).

Covenant People and Covenant Place

The covenant promise of people and a dwelling place for them begins right after the Fall in the promised "Seed of the Woman" (Gen. 3:15). Jesus is Eve's ultimate Seed (Gal. 3:16). His people will rest in Him. He came through the loins of those with whom God had covenanted, such as Adam, Noah, Abraham, Isaac, and Jacob (1 Chron. 1:28; Matt. 1:1-16; Luke 3:23-38).

Mary, the mother of Jesus, was related to Elizabeth, a descendant of Aaron, Moses' brother. Levi, a son of Jacob, was the father of Aaron and Moses. Thus Jesus, as to His humanity, was part of the covenant line.

The reality of the covenant line from Adam through Abraham to Jesus is attested to by considering the fact that Satan knew that the Messiah or the Christ or the Lord's Anointed was to descend through a series of faithful Hebrew ancestors. Hence,

Cain slaying his brother Abel (Gen. 4:8), Pharaoh's having all male Hebrew babies murdered when Moses was born (Exod. 1:22), and Herod's death sentence of all male Hebrew children under the age of two in Bethlehem when Jesus was born (Matt. 2:16), not forgetting that Haman sought to annihilate every single Jew! (Esth. 3:9,13). Of the Devil Jesus says, "He was a murderer from the beginning" (John 8:44). And under inspiration of the Holy Spirit John says, "Cain ... was of the wicked one and murdered his brother" (1 John 3:12).

Covenant Bloodlines

Planned in eternity past, the covenant promise of the "Seed of the woman" was sovereignly and providentially overseen by God right down to the type of blood that was to be shed on the cross. It can be demonstrated from Scripture (particularly from Matthew and Luke's chronologies regarding Joseph and Mary) that both the legal and the royal bloodlines to the throne of David are fulfilled in Jesus. One genealogy shows that Joseph, because of a curse on his family line, could not possibly be the biological father of Jesus, while the other shows that Jesus comes from royalty.

We see Jeconiah mentioned in the Matthew genealogy (Matt. 1:11). Joseph could not be the father of Jesus because God had placed a curse on Joseph's line through his forefather Jeconiah (a.k.a. Conia and Jehoiachin, listed in the Matthew genealogy) regarding the throne of David, saying, "As I live ... though Conia the son of Jehoiakim, king of Judah, were the signet on My right hand, yet I would pluck you off … Write this man down as childless, a man who shall not prosper in his days; for none of his descendants shall prosper, sitting on the throne of David, and ruling anymore in Judah" (Jer. 22:24; 28-30). Thus, if Jesus were descended physically from Joseph, He would be disqualified from sitting on David's throne. However, it was as Joseph's legal son He was legally qualified.

The legal line so called pertains to the genealogy found in Matthew 1:1-17. However, it (as does Luke's genealogy) shows that Jesus is legally entitled to David's throne. It is because of His resurrection (meaning that He now lives and reigns forever) that no other can lay a rightful claim to His throne. Thus, both genealogies show that the kingship belongs only to Jesus. His reign upon the throne of David is forever. Speaking of the genealogy in Matthew 1:1-18 William Hendriksen says,

> Matthew, therefore, by means of this genealogy and its sequel (the narrative of the virgin birth, verses 18-25), aims to show that Jesus, according to His human nature, is indeed the legitimate seed of David, in fulfilment of prophecy. From Joseph, His legal father – and thus from Joseph's ancestor, David – He receives His right to David's throne. From Mary (verse 16) – and via Mary, also from David – He receives David's flesh and blood…
>
> The … record of ancestry of Jesus Christ … shows us that Joseph, Jesus' "father" in a legal sense only, was a descendant of David and

Abraham. Through Joseph, "son of David" (verse 20) the right to the throne of David was transmitted to Jesus, the far more glorious "son of David" (verse 1).[20]

The bloodline so called pertains to that found in Luke 3:23-38. At first blush, it looks as if it is a list of Joseph's ancestors that is traced all the way back to Adam through such well-known names as David, Jacob, Isaac, and Abraham. It starts with the following words, "Now Jesus Himself began His ministry at about thirty years of age, being (as was supposed) the son of Joseph, *the son of* Heli..." Commenting on the bloodline found in the Gospel According to Luke David Brown says,

> "Being (as was supposed) the son of Joseph." By this expression the Evangelist reminds his readers of His miraculous conception by the Virgin, and His being thus only the *legal* son of Joseph.[21]

We do not want to get bogged down here. For we only wish to demonstrate in brief the covenant line from Adam to Jesus. But Bible commentators wrestle with the two genealogies as listed by Matthew and Luke. Matthew is clearly listing Joseph's

---

[20] William Hendriksen, *New Testament Commentary Matthew*, The Banner of Truth Trust, Edinburgh, Scotland, Reprinted 1976, 111 & 145.

[21] David Brown, *Jamieson, Fausset, and Brown, A Commentary Critical, Experimental, and Practical on the Old and New Testaments, Volume Three*, Eerdmans Publishing, Grand Rapids, Michigan, Reprinted 1989, 235.

genealogy. However, because Luke has clearly shown his readers that not Joseph, but God through the Holy Spirit is Jesus's Father, the genealogy is actually that of Mary, Jesus's mother.

"Then the angel said to her, 'Do not be afraid, Mary, for you have found favour with God. And behold, you will conceive in your womb and bring forth a Son, and He shall be called JESUS. He will be great, and will be called the Son of the Highest; and the Lord God will give Him the throne of His father David'" Luke 1:30-32. Whereas Matthew listed the legal line, Luke here is listing the royal line and that line goes through Mary not Joseph to Jesus's "father David". Says Norval Geldenhuys,

> That Matthew gives the family tree of Joseph and Luke that of Mary also fits in beautifully with the contents of the first chapters of their Gospels. For Matthew throughout gives the antecedents (announcement of the birth, the birth itself, the childhood years) as seen from the standpoint of Joseph, while Luke we feel from beginning to end that we are concerned with the course of events from Mary's point of view... A conclusive proof that Mary was indeed of Davidic origin is the fact that the Jewish opponents of Christianity in the first centuries never denied the Davidic origin of Jesus. Since they knew the Christian claim that He was only the Son of Mary, they would certainly have attacked His Messiahship on that ground, if they knew or even surmised that He was not a descendant of David.[22]

Let us add in another quote from William Hendriksen to add weight to the view that Luke's genealogy is that of Mary. Says Hendriksen,

> [E]ven in the Talmud [*Haghigha* 77.4], Mary is called "the daughter of Heli," which is correct only if Luke's genealogy is interpreted as referring to Mary's – and not to Joseph's – family tree… The Sinaitic-Syriac MS. renders Luke 2:4 as follows: "They [both Joseph and Mary] were of the house and lineage of David."[23]

And let us add even more weight by quoting Martin Llyod-Jones on the same subject,

> In Matthew you have the genealogical tree of Joseph, whereas in Luke you have the tree of Mary; and in both instances, you see, the Scriptures are careful to tell us that He was not the son of Joseph; He was the son of Mary. And therefore, Luke shows us how Mary was a direct lineal descendant from the great King David. So the Lord Jesus Christ is of the seed of David through His mother Mary.[24]

---

[22] Norval Geldenhuys, *The New International Commentary of the New Testament: The Gospel of Luke*, Eerdmans Publishing, Grand Rapids, Michigan, 1979, 152.

[23] William Hendriksen, *New Testament Commentary Luke*, The Banner of Truth Trust, Edinburgh, Scotland, Reprinted 1979, 225.

[24] D. Martyn Lloyd-Jones, *Romans, Exposition of Chapter 1, The*

If we add it all together, we see that Jesus has a legitimate claim to David's throne because of Joseph's lineage. However, the claim is on account of His being the legal son of Joseph and not because He was the physical offspring. Nowhere does the Bible claim that Jesus had a physical father. And, we have seen that Jesus could not inherit David's throne if Joseph was His biological father because of the curse on his forefather, Jeconiah's, line. Like Adam, God is Jesus's Father. Thus, both are called "the Son of God" (Luke 1:35; 3:38). Says Guy Waters,

> Jesus is descended from Adam (cf, "son of Adam," Luke 3:38). But while Jesus is "of Adam," He is not "in Adam," because, Paul tells us elsewhere, Jesus is the "second" or "last Adam" (1 Cor. 15:45, 47).[25]

As to Jesus's humanity, Mary conceived Jesus by the power of the Holy Spirit (Luke 1:35), and we are told that Elizabeth, the mother of John Baptist, was Mary's cousin (Luke 1:36), and was descended from Aaron (Luke 1:5; 1 Chron. 6:3, 50-53). So, Jesus, the covenantally promised Messiah, the promised Prophet (Deut. 18:18; John 4:25-26), the promised Priest (Psa. 110:4; Heb. 5:6. 19; 7:15-24) and the promised King (Isa. 9:6-7; Jer. 23:5; Matt.

Gospel of God, The Banner of Truth Trust, Edinburgh, Scotland, 1985, 108.

[25]Guy Prentiss Waters, J. Nicholas Reid, and John R. Muether, *Covenant Theology: Biblical, Theological, and Historical Perspectives*, Crossway, Wheaton, Illinois, 2020, 86.

16:28; Acts 13:22-23; Rev. 19:16) arrived legally and regally through Joseph and Mary.

Since Jesus has been resurrected from the dead He now lives and reigns forever as Prophet, Priest, and King. And because all the Old Testament promises are fulfilled in, by, and through Him, it all ends with Him. For not only is Jesus the promised Messiah, He is also the last Prophet, the last Priest, and the last King. Indeed, He is the final word that God has spoken to humanity (Heb. 1:2).

The covenant bloodline ran from the first Adam to the last Adam. It ends with Jesus. By shedding His royal blood, He has become the legal inheritor of all the kingdom promises. His resurrection from the dead means that He is the new Adam. Whereas the old humanity ended by dying in, by, and through the first Adam, the new humanity began in, by, and through the resurrection and the life of the last Adam. "Then He who sat on the throne said, 'Behold, I make all things new'" (Rev. 21:5a).

Yes, people would call out to Jesus naming Him, "Son of David!" (Matt. 9:27; Luke 18:38), while the demons called Him, "Son of the Most High God." Jesus, being divine and human in one Person forever, is both. His throne is forever because God's covenant is eternal.

Covenant Book and Covenant Law

The Bible is "the Book of the Covenant" (Exod. 24:7). The writer to the Hebrews refers to this "Book of the Covenant" as "the Book of the Law" (Heb. 9:19). Thus, in the Bible covenant and law are often synonymous terms.

At this early point we would do well to remind ourselves of two important things when studying God's covenant: First, God revealed His covenant progressively. Second, His covenant and law always has grace attached. Says Rowland Ward,

> The Bible is a covenant book, and its two parts could be better described as the Old Covenant and the New Covenant … The unfolding of God's gracious covenant is progressive. Covenant theology at its best is keen to pay attention to this unfolding of God's purposes. The covenant of grace was given in promise to Adam immediately after he sinned (Gen. 3:15), was continued through Noah (Gen. 6:18; 9:1-17) and formalised with Abraham in the covenant of circumcision (Gen. 17). All believers are beneficiaries of the covenant with Abraham (Gal. 3:7). The special administration adopted in the covenant with Moses (Exod. 19), did not annul the Abrahamic covenant or alter its gracious character (Gal. 3:17ff). The covenant with David to establish the throne forever (2 Sam. 7:12) focused the covenant in a single person. The promise of a new covenant made in Jeremiah's time (Jer. 31 & 33) involves what is foreshadowed in the return from exile being brought to realisation. Christ came in accordance with the everlasting covenant and ratified the new covenant in His blood (Luke 22:20), the climax of God's covenant purpose.[26]

[26] Rowland S Ward, *God & Adam: Reformed Theology and the*

The revelation of the covenant, i.e., the Scriptures, was written down over a period of some fifteen hundred years involving around forty authors from Moses through Paul, overseen by the Holy Spirit, the third Person in the Godhead. The Scriptures and the Holy Spirit testify to the covenant between the Father and the Son, the Holy Spirit always working with the Word. Also, the Scriptures and the Holy Spirit are the two witnesses that condemn fallen man to death, "Whoever is deserving of death shall be put to death on the testimony of two or three witnesses; he shall not be put to death on the testimony of one witness" (Deut. 17:6 with John 8:17; cf. Rev. 11:3).

Speaking of the Word Jesus says, "You search the Scriptures ... these are they which testify of Me" (John 5:39). Speaking of the Holy Spirit Jesus says to His disciples, "But when the Helper, whom I shall send to you from the Father, the Spirit of truth who proceeds from the Father, He will testify of Me. And you will bear witness, because you have been with Me from the beginning" (John 15:26-27). He then goes on to say to them, "When He, the Spirit of truth, has come, He will guide you into all truth; for He will not speak on His own authority, but whatever He hears He will speak; and He will tell you things to come. He will glorify Me, for He will take of what is Mine and declare it to you" (John 16:14-15).

Jesus had already said the following to His Disciples, "But the Helper, the Holy Spirit, whom the

Creation Covenant, (Lansvale, NSW: Tulip Publishing, 2019), 6-8.

Father will send in My name, He will teach you all things, and bring to your remembrance all things I have said to you" (John 14:26). Jesus refers to the Spirit as another "Helper" (John 14:16). Before He ascended bodily into Heaven, and before He and His Father had sent "another Helper" (i.e., the Holy Spirit), Jesus acting as the first "Helper," gave a clear illustration of what the Holy Spirit was coming to do when, after His resurrection, He walked along the road to Emmaus with two of His disciples who had not recognized Him. They relayed to Him who Jesus was and the things that had happened to Him. Scripture records what happened next. He said to them, "'O foolish ones, and slow of heart to believe in all the prophets have spoken! Ought not the Christ to have suffered these things and to enter into His glory?' And beginning at Moses and the Prophets, He expounded to them in all the Scriptures the things concerning Himself" (Luke 24:26-27).

The Scriptures testify of Jesus, who He is, what He was going to do, and what He has done. The present Helper, i.e., the Holy Spirit, uses the Scriptures too. For Jesus says, "When He has come, He will convict the world of sin, and of righteousness, and of judgment" (John 16:7).

The law of nature was written by God on Adam and Eve's hearts. This is what we mean by "covenant law." It is the natural law of God and is an aspect of man as created in the image and likeness of God. Even after the fall, and even though humanity seeks to suppress this knowledge in unrighteousness, God the Holy Spirit still uses it for His purposes (Rom. 1:18-19, 2:15). For example, when Abraham lied to the pagan king Abimelech of Gerar, by hiding the fact that Sarah was his wife, God convicted Abimelech (who had taken Sarah into his household). Thus, God prevented Abimelech from sinning, and in particular from breaking the 7th Commandment. When Abimelech learned that Sarah was married to Abraham, he confronted him. Therefore, because of natural law he knew in his heart that adultery was wrong. "Then God said to him in the dream, "Yes, I know that you have done this in the integrity of your heart, and it was I who kept you from sinning against me. Therefore I did not let you touch her" (Gen. 20:6). Thus, God uses His covenant law to restrain evil in the world.

The Ten Commandments are God's summary of the covenant law. Therefore, the law of nature or natural law is the same as the Decalogue (meaning the ten words). Therefore, whether pre- or post-fall, God's covenant law is to be applied in accordance to whichever period of covenant administration humanity is under. In other words, the "general equity", i.e., the principles of God's covenant law, is to be applied to every facet of human life and activity in accordance with the covenant book. The psalmist has the right idea where he says, "Your word I have hidden in my heart, that I might not sin against You" (Psalm 119:11).

We will elaborate on the use of God's covenant law later. However, for now notice in the following that God's moral law, as it did before the fall, continues to be "a perfect rule of righteousness" even after the fall. The Westminster Confession of Faith 19 says,

1. God gave to Adam a law, as a covenant of works, by which he bound him and all his posterity to personal, entire, exact, and perpetual obedience; promised life upon the fulfilling, and threatened death upon the breach of it; and endued him with power and ability to keep it.

2. This law, after his Fall, continued to be a perfect rule of righteousness; and, as such, was delivered by God upon mount Sinai in ten commandments, and written in two tables; the first four commandments containing our duty toward God, and the other six our duty to man.

3. Besides this law, commonly called moral, God was pleased to give to the people of Israel, as a Church under age, ceremonial laws, containing several typical ordinances, partly of worship, prefiguring Christ, his graces, actions, sufferings, and benefits; and partly holding forth divers instructions of moral duties. All which ceremonial laws are now abrogated under the New Testament.

4. To them also, as a body politic, he gave sundry judicial laws, which expired together with the state of that people, not obliging any other, now, further than the general equity thereof may require.

The covenant book reveals how the covenant law was and is to be used as a perfect rule of righteousness during each administration of the covenant, including today. This perfect rule of righteousness is revelation of the very character of the eternal triune God. Says Kenneth Gentry,

> Structuring the God-ordained task of man in the world is a distinctive legal framework, which is abundantly exhibited in Scripture. The legal structure is known as 'covenant.' The Bible is very much a covenant document. Even a cursory reading of Scripture demonstrates the Bible has a strongly covenantal cast: the word 'covenant' occurs almost 300 times in the Old Testament and thirty times in the new.[27]

Before the fall the covenant law was the basis for the covenant of works. After the fall, because of original sin, i.e., our sinful nature, none of us (apart from Jesus) is able to keep the covenant of works, and are in need therefore of God's saving grace, as per the covenant of grace. The first covenant, i.e., the covenant of works, because of our indwelling sin, simply condemns all who are not under the covenant of grace, no matter how hard they try to keep the covenant of works as "a perfect rule of righteousness."

Scripture refers to God as "Father and Son and Holy Spirit" (Matt. 28:19b), or, as stated in a disputed verse, "the Father, the Word, and the Spirit; and these three are one" (1 John 5:7). If we keep in mind that God is triune, i.e., three Persons in one Godhead,

---

[27] Kenneth L. Gentry, *The Greatness of the Great Commission*, Institute for Christian Economics, Tyler, Texas, 1993, 15.

otherwise referred to as the Trinity, we will have little trouble understanding the nature of the everlasting and eternal covenant. Indeed, covenant theology begins with and is firmly grounded in the triune nature of God. Covenant law reveals God's character.

The following was written at the same time and by the same people who compiled the Westminster Confession and the Larger and Shorter Catechisms. It is part of what is called "The Sum of Saving Knowledge." It gives a brief description of God, His nature, what He does, and our (covenantal) relationship to Him.

Head I.
Our Woeful Condition by Nature, Through Breaking the Covenant of Works.

Hos. 13:9. "O Israel, thou hast destroyed thyself."

1. THE Almighty and eternal God, the Father, the Son, and the Holy Ghost, three distinct persons in the one and the same undivided Godhead, equally infinite in all perfections, did, before time, most wisely decree, for His own glory, whatsoever comes to pass in time: and does most holily and infallibly execute all His decrees, without being partaker of the sin of any creature.

2. This God, in six days, made all things of nothing, very good in their own kind: in special, He made all the angels holy; and He made our first parents, Adam and Eve, the root of mankind, both upright and able to keep the law written in their heart. Which law they

were naturally bound to obey under pain of death; but God was not bound to reward their service, till He entered into a covenant or contract with them, and their posterity in them, to give them eternal life, upon condition of perfect personal obedience; withal threatening death in case they should fail. This is the covenant of works.

3. Both angels and men were subject to the change of their own free will, as experience proved, (God having reserved to Himself the incommunicable property of being naturally unchangeable:) for many angels of their own accord fell by sin from their first estate, and became devils [i.e., demons]. Our first parents, being enticed by Satan, one of these devils speaking in a serpent, did break the covenant of works, in eating the forbidden fruit; whereby they, and their posterity, being in their loins, as branches in the root, and comprehended in the same covenant with them, became not only liable to eternal death, but also lost all ability to please God; yea, did become by nature enemies to God, and to all spiritual good, and inclined only to evil continually. This is our original sin, the bitter root of all our actual transgressions, in thought, word, and deed.[28]

---

[28] *The Confession of Faith, The Larger and Shorter Catechisms, with the Scripture Proofs at Large: together with The Sum of Saving Knowledge,* Free Presbyterian Publication, Glasgow, Fourth reprint 1985, 323.

The covenant is eternal and is eternally grounded in the triune Godhead, and this eternal covenant includes mankind as represented by our federal or covenant head, Adam, in the covenant of works. After entering into and upon Adam's breaking of the covenant of works the LORD God was pleased to reveal another aspect of the same eternal covenant, the covenant of grace. Says Louis Berkhof,

> The Bible teaches that there is but a single gospel by which men can be saved. And because the gospel is nothing but the revelation of the covenant of grace, it follows that there is but one covenant. The gospel was already heard in material promise, Gen. 3:15, was preached unto Abraham, Gal. 3:8, and may not be supplanted by any Judaistic gospel, Gal. 1:8, 9.[29]

So, the first covenant was the covenant of works, and the second covenant was the covenant of grace. Though the covenant of grace was differently administered at different times through history, it remains as one and the same covenant from the fall of Adam to Christ and still stands today.

In the covenant of works the focus is on the law, and in the covenant of grace the focus is on the gospel. However, all through Scripture where the law is present there also is the gospel and where the gospel is present there also is the law. Ligon Duncan

---

[29] Louis Berkhof, *Systematic Theology*, Eerdmans, Edinburgh, Reprinted June 1991, 279.

provides this note of caution regarding the use of the word "grace",

> For God to covenant is for God to lovingly and generously stoop down, to willingly associate himself with his inferior – that is, with humanity. It should be noted that the confession does not identify this "voluntary condescension" of God as "grace," nor does it speak of "grace" in the context of its presentation of the prefall covenant. While some orthodox covenant theologians have spoken of God's grace or graciousness in the covenant of works, the foregoing point should be borne in mind – it protects against a misuse and misunderstanding of "grace" in relation to the first covenant.[30]

In the covenant of works, therefore, let us not misunderstand God's grace as having anything to do with salvation as we understand it. Salvation by grace through faith has to do with the covenant of redemption. Any grace shown by God in the covenant of works has to do with His condescension, His "lovingly and generously stooping down" to enter into a covenant with Adam as representative of all humanity. Yes, grace abounds in the garden of Eden, but only as God's common grace to humanity, and not His saving grace to His elect.

---

[30] Guy Prentiss Waters, J. Nicholas Reid, and John R. Muether, *Covenant Theology: Biblical, Theological, and Historical Perspectives*, Crossway, Wheaton, Illinois, 2020, 27.

In the Old Testament we see the law emphasised, and in the New Testament we see the gospel emphasised. Though there is much of God's favour, kindness, and generosity, i.e., "grace", in the covenant of works, the law is emphasised. And though there is law in the covenant of grace, the gospel is emphasised. Therefore, the whole Bible is the Book of the Covenant. It reveals God's eternal covenant in all its aspects. (Later on we will have a deeper look as to why the Old Testament can be referred to as the Old Covenant, and the New Testament as the New Covenant, if the covenant of grace began immediately after Adam fell.) Says E.B. Hosking,

> An examination of Scripture shows that its whole structure is covenantal and cannot be adequately studied, let alone applied, without this in mind. Furthermore, it requires at least a rudimentary understanding of the nature of the covenant in the first place. It is astounding that it took to until the time of the Reformation as the starting point of the serious re-affirmation of the truth of the Word in fact. Work on covenant theology since has been deep and extensive, but despite what has been written more needs to be said for there remains a serious lack of understanding of its application. No doubt this is due to confusion that continues about the subject with little determination to come to terms with the issues it raises. This, in turn, has had serious and far-reaching effects causing confusion that

extends even towards understanding the task God has given His people, let alone towards carrying it out.[31]

[31] E.B. Hosking, *The Covenants in Creation: The History of Salvation and the Continuing Significance*, Coral Coast Printers, Bundaberg, Queensland, 2004, 16.

COVENANT COMMANDS

Introduction

Having considered that a covenant in its simplest definition is a bond, and that this covenant bond between God and His people had been anticipated by God in eternity past as a covenant between the Father and the Son, we are now ready to consider that the covenant bond came with commands summarised in the Decalogue as "a rule of righteousness".

We've been soaring in the heavens of eternity, peering into wonderful things, while having a good God's eye view of things on earth below. But let's now come in for a landing and place our feet on *terra firma* and make some practical applications. Or, to change the analogy, in the following we will, as it were, pull off the highway, turn into a rest stop, sit at a wooden picnic table full of interesting carvings, and have a bite as we continue to plot our course. Let's see if any of that covenant stuff actually works on planet earth.

We are able to drive our cars from A to B using a "satnav" (i.e., a satellite navigation system). A satnav gives verbal audible commands to the driver. If we accidently take a wrong turn, it will correct and help bring us back onto the right track.

Now, when we think of commands in the Bible, we tend to think of the Ten Commandments, the Decalogue. Before we travel there, from what we've already seen, let's keep in mind who God is. As the Trinity He is in an eternal covenant bond with Himself. Being covenantal by nature, in the "counsel of peace", God the Father has entered into a covenant with God the Son which is witnessed by the Holy Spirit. Herman Bavinck gives this reminder,

> The Father is pre-eminent in the works of creation and redemption; He represents the Trinity; hence, He is often called God, even by Christ. Nevertheless, the Son and the Holy Spirit are also God.[32]

Now, as we shall see more fully later, the Father in this covenant of redemption represents the Trinity, while the Son represents the elect, i.e., those humans who have been chosen by the Father in eternity past to give to the Son in future time. The conditions for the Son to receive the blessings promised by the Father is by, as a man, personally, perfectly, and perpetually keeping all of God's commands in all their applications. The revelation of the covenant of redemption began when God entered into a pre-fall covenant with Adam, commanding him to be fruitful, multiply, fill the earth, and subdue it, while also commanding him to refrain from eating the forbidden fruit.

At first blush, it may seem strange that the pre-fall covenant with Adam has anything to do with redemption since he hasn't even fallen yet. However, if you keep your eyes on Christ, even at this point, all will become clear. In short, we shall see that whereas Adam is the covenant-breaker, Christ is the covenant-

---

[32] Herman Bavinck, *The Doctrine of God*, Translated by William Hendriksen, Banner of Truth, Reprinted 1991, 266.

keeper. But let's not get done for speeding by getting too far ahead of ourselves! The Ten Commandments,

"And God spoke all these words, saying:
'I am the Lord your God, who brought you out of the land of Egypt, out of the house of bondage.
'You shall have no other gods before Me.
'You shall not make for yourself a carved image— any likeness of anything that is in heaven above, or that is in the earth beneath, or that is in the water under the earth; you shall not bow down to them nor serve them. For I, the Lord your God, am a jealous God, visiting the iniquity of the fathers upon the children to the third and fourth generations of those who hate Me, but showing mercy to thousands, to those who love Me and keep My commandments.
'You shall not take the name of the Lord your God in vain, for the Lord will not hold him guiltless who takes His name in vain.
'Remember the Sabbath day, to keep it holy. Six days you shall labour and do all your work, but the seventh day is the Sabbath of the Lord your God. In it you shall do no work: you, nor your son, nor your daughter, nor your male servant, nor your female servant, nor your cattle, nor your stranger who is within your gates. For in six days the Lord made the heavens and the earth, the sea, and all that is in them, and rested the seventh day. Therefore the Lord blessed the Sabbath day and hallowed it.
'Honour your father and your mother, that your days may be long upon the land which the Lord your God is giving you.

'You shall not murder.

'You shall not commit adultery.

'You shall not steal.

'You shall not bear false witness against your neighbour.

'You shall not covet your neighbour's house; you shall not covet your neighbour's wife, nor his male servant, nor his female servant, nor his ox, nor his donkey, nor anything that is your neighbour's'" (Exod. 20:1-17).

Notice that God identifies who He is. He is the Lord. He is God. He is the One set His people free from their captivity. He wants them to show their gratitude to Him for His undeserved grace to them by their wilfully being obedient to Him. Watch out for speed cameras!, but let's fast-forward 1500 years. Let's learn from Jesus,

> Hearing that Jesus had silenced the Sadducees, the Pharisees got together. One of them, an expert in the law, tested him with this question: "Teacher, which is the greatest commandment in the Law?"
> Jesus replied: "'Love the Lord your God with all your heart and with all your soul and with all your mind.' This is the first and greatest commandment. And the second is like it: 'Love your neighbour as yourself.' All the Law and the Prophets hang on these two commandments." (Matt. 22:34-40).

Jesus had been doing battle with theological legalists and theological liberals. The Pharisees, the theological legalists, had just asked Jesus back in Matthew 22:17, "Tell us then, what is Your opinion? Is it right, [some render this word as "lawful", is it lawful] to pay the imperial tax to Caesar or not?" In other words, is it in accordance with the Old Testament Scriptures to pay taxes to Caesar? To which Jesus gave His famous reply, "Give back to Caesar what is Caesar's, and to God what is God's" (Matt. 22:21.)

Then the Sadducees, the theological liberals, the ones who don't believe in the future Resurrection or in angels, also tried to trip up Jesus in His words. Matthew 22:28, "Now then, at the resurrection, whose wife will she be of the seven, since all of them were married to her?" Jesus replied telling them that at the Resurrection people will neither marry nor be given in marriage, but will be like the angels in Heaven. Yes, you Sadducees, "You are in error because you do not know the Scriptures or the power of God."

"When the crowds heard this, they were astonished at His teaching" (Matt. 22:33). Should we pay taxes? Yes! Should we believe in the Resurrection? Yes! Why? Because the Scriptures and the power of God tell you to. Verses of Scripture could be piled up about paying taxes, the Resurrection, and the power of God. And it's all about knowing the Scriptures, including the Old Testament. With that background, I'd like us to consider Matthew 22:37-40 in particular.

Jesus replied: "'Love the Lord your God with all your heart and with all your soul and with all your mind.' This is the first and greatest commandment. And the second is like it: 'Love your neighbour as yourself.' All the Law and the Prophets hang on these two commandments." (Matt. 22:37-40).

A Table for God

Jesus had been duelling with the Pharisees, then the Sadducees who were all trying to trip Him up in His words. Now it's the turn of an expert in the Law. Notice what Jesus says is the first and greatest commandment: "Love the Lord your God with all your heart and with all your soul and with all your mind." That is part of the *Shema*, named after the first Hebrew word in Deuteronomy 6:4-5, a portion of Scripture well known to the Old Testament people even as a prayer. The word itself means to give ear, pay attention, listen: "Hear, O Israel: The LORD our God is one. Love the LORD your God with all your heart and with all your soul and all your strength. These commandments that I give you today are to be on your hearts. Impress them on your children." (Deut. 6:4-6b).

What was the promise that God made in Jeremiah 31:33-34 picked up again in Hebrews 10:16? "This is the covenant I will make with them after that time says the Lord. I will put My laws in their hearts, and I will write them on their minds." "Love the Lord your God with all your heart and with all your soul and with all your mind." God has written His laws on your heart, soul, and mind as per His promise, e.g., "I will sprinkle clean water on you, and you will be clean; I will cleanse you from all your impurities and from all your idols. I will give you a new heart and put a new spirit in you; I will remove from you your heart of stone and give you a heart of flesh. And I will put my Spirit in you and move you to follow my decrees and be careful to keep my laws" (Ezek. 36:25-27).

What laws? God's laws! What are God's laws? Hint. There're ten of them. The Decalogue, God's ten words, i.e., the Ten Commandments, have been written by God the Holy Spirit on every Christian's heart. Think about that. Paul says, "For we know that the law is spiritual" (Rom. 7:14a). And we know that spiritual things are spiritually discerned (1 Cor. 2:14). Your heart, like the Ark of the Covenant of old, now contains the Ten Commandments. Wow!

God spoke ten commands, i.e., ten times we read, "and God said, 'Let there be…, Let Us…'" etc. in Genesis 1, as He spoke things into being. No doubt there is a relationship between those ten words spoken by God and the ten words, as in the Ten Commandments.

Are you able to rattle off the Ten Commandments like you can the Lord's Prayer? Anyway, loving God with all your heart, soul, strength, and mind has to do with what we call the *first* table of the Law. It's a table for God.

A table, if you don't know, is a tablet, like the two tablets of stone, upon which the finger of God had written the Ten Commandments, you know, the ones that Moses came down the mountain with.

God, the same LORD who brought Israel out of Egypt the land of slavery, has brought you the Christian out of the world, i.e., the land of slavery to self, sin, and Satan.

Pharaoh was a puppet of Satan. Pharaoh represented the Devil. All of us are in bondage to Satan till the LORD our God sets us free from our captivity to sin. Once He sets you free, then He gives you a new heart, a new nature, and a new record.[33] He writes His laws on your heart and mind.

Now, firstly, you are to have no other gods but God. Secondly, you are not to form any false images of God in your mind or physically with your hands. And you have certainly not to bow down, i.e., submit to any of them. Thirdly, you are not to take the LORD's name in vain. You are not to misuse His name. And fourthly, you are to work diligently six days a week. But you are to set aside one day out of every seven to Sabbath, i.e., is to rest. Sabbath means rest, i.e., rest in God.

Put God first in everything. Form no idols. Always honour His name. And whether you're a butcher, baker, candlestick maker, or even retired, honour God by doing stuff for six days, but mind and rest one day in every seven, together with other members of God's family. Go to church on Sunday and rest in the Lord, i.e., rest in the finished work of Christ.

The Lord's Day, i.e., the Christian Sabbath, is a window through which we glimpse Heaven. Take

---

[33] All credit to Dr Henry Krabbendam (professor in the theological department of Covenant College) for alerting me in a lecture to the new heart, new record, and new nature motif.

away the Sabbath and you take away a picture of Heaven, i.e., Christians at rest with the Lord in their midst. Says Rudi Schwartz,

> On the Lord's Day, Christians approach God in Christ's name and thank him for Christ's redemption. Their day of worship is in itself a proclamation of God's greatness and grace to an unbelieving world.[34]

His covenant promise to us, as stated in Jeremiah 30:32 for example, is, "So you will be My people, and I will be your God". This is God's covenant promise, and is a refrain repeated throughout the Scriptures. And what is God's covenant law? The Ten Commandments including the preamble, "I am the LORD your God, who brought you out of Egypt, out of the land of slavery" (Exod. 20:1b). Therefore, "You shall have no other gods before Me" etc.

God uses covenant language as He covenants with you, His people. In any covenant, generally, there is a preamble stating who the covenanting party is with a bit of history, then the covenant stipulations, which, of course, have certain penalties attached or implied for breaking any of them. Kenneth Gentry summarizes the usual covenant structure,

> 1. *Transcendence*: Usually a preamble offering an introductory statement

---

[34] D. Rudi Schwartz's *The Lord's Day: Does it Really Still Matter?*, Ark House Press, Australia, 2021, 56.

identifying the sovereignty of the covenant-making king.

2. *Hierarchy*: An historical prologue summarizing the king's authority and the mediation of his rule, by reminding of the historical circumstances of it.

3. *Ethics*: A detail of the legal stipulations defining the ethics of faithful living under the covenant bond.

4. *Oath*: The setting forth of the sanctions of the covenant, specifying the promises and the warnings of the covenant by the taking of a formal oath.

5. *Succession*: An explanation of the arrangement transferring the covenant to future generations.[35]

Therefore, when Jesus says that the first and greatest commandment is, "Love the Lord your God with all your heart and with all your soul and with all your mind", He is simply summarizing the first table of the Law. And, in accordance with the 1st Commandment, He is putting God first.

Then He goes on to talk about the second table. Before we look at the second table, i.e., the table for your neighbour, let us summarize. The first four Commandments teach us our duty towards God.

---

[35] Kenneth L. Gentry, *The Greatness of the Great Commission*, Institute for Christian Economics, Tyler, Texas, 1993, 18. See also Ray R, Sutton's, *That You May Prosper* for more detailed information on the covenant structure.

1. No god but God. 2. No images of God. 3. No misusing His name. And 4. No forgetting to honour Him by taking one day's rest every week.

How do you keep the first table? You've to do so by using the new spirit that God has given you along with your new heart, i.e., the spirit of love. You keep the first table of the law by loving "the Lord your God with all your heart and with all your soul and with all your mind" out of gratitude for what He has done for you in Jesus Christ.

A Table for Your Neighbour

The second table of God's law teaches us our duty towards our fellow human beings. Now, if you're anything like me, and I know you are, because we're all fallen human beings, you'll find some people harder to love than others.

Though not always true because we're fallen, but it's usually easiest to love mum, dad, i.e., parents, then sisters, brothers, i.e., siblings, cousins, then friends. However, you'll find as you go through life that there're some people who bring out the worst in you, maybe the playground bully, some religious nutcase, or some politician, just fill in the blanks.

Anyway, some people seem to have a gift of showing you that, like chips and bashes, and old beer and wine stains on a wooden table, there still remain sin-stains on your heart. There is a residue of sin that can spoil the beauty of the new heart that God has given you, the new fleshly table or tablet with the law written on it by His finger, i.e., your heart.

However, if you find yourself detesting, i.e., hating another human being, the good news is that, for the Christian, the Holy Spirit will convict your spirit of this wrongdoing, i.e., this breaking of God's law. Which of the Ten Commandments specifically teaches us not to hate? Yes, the "You shall not murder" Commandment, i.e., the 6th Commandment.

Jesus summarizes the last six Commandments, i.e., the second table of the law by saying, "Love your neighbour as yourself." Where did He get that idea from? Yes, Leviticus 19:18, "You shall not take vengeance, nor bear any grudge against the children of your people, but you shall love your neighbour as yourself: I am the Lord" (Lev. 19:18).

How do you love your neighbour as yourself? By honouring fathers and mothers, i.e., all those in lawful authority, by not murdering other human beings either physically or spiritually, i.e., by hating them in your heart. By being sexually pure before marriage and during marriage, by not stealing possessions from others, including their good name, by not telling lies, i.e., distorting the truth, and by not sinfully desiring or coveting or lusting after things. Dead easy! Not!

Some people think those signs you see on approaches to motorways are funny, the ones that say, "Wrong Way. Go Back". The two tables of the law, or, as summarized by Jesus in these two commandments about loving God and your neighbour as yourself, are a signpost. The Commandments point you to Jesus.

Of the two commandments, i.e., the summary of the two tables of the law, Jesus says, "All the Law and the Prophets hang on these two commandments." Jesus is speaking of the Old Testament when He says, "the Law and the Prophets". Another way of saying Old Testament is Old Covenant. The Old Testament or Covenant shows us our need for a new covenant. In Acts 15:10 Peter calls the old covenant with all its stipulations, "a yoke that neither we nor our ancestors have been able to bear." The Apostle Paul puts it like this in Galatians 3,

> "Why, then, was the law given at all? It was added because of transgressions until the Seed to whom the promise referred had come. The law was given through angels and entrusted to a mediator. A mediator, however, implies more than one party; but God is one.
> Is the law, therefore, opposed to the promises of God? Absolutely not! For if a law had been given that could impart life, then righteousness would certainly have come by the law. But Scripture has locked up everything under the control of sin, so that what was promised, being given through faith in Jesus Christ, might be given to those who believe." Before the coming of this faith, we were held in custody under the law, locked up until the faith that was to come would be revealed. So the law was our guardian until Christ came that we might be justified by faith. Now that this faith has come, we are no longer under a guardian. (Gal. 3:19-22).

The administration of the covenant of grace under Moses was very strict. There was the *Moral* Law, i.e., the Ten Commandments, there was the *Judicial* or *Civil* Law that applied to Israel as a corporate body. And then there was the *Ceremonial* Law. The Ceremonial Law essentially was the Gospel in the Old Testament, wherein everything, from Circumcision to Passover, Tabernacle to Temple, animal sacrifices to High Priests were all signposts pointing to Jesus.

But now that the reality to which the signposts were pointing has come, the Ceremonial Law has been done away with. We can study, gather, and apply general principles from Old Testament Judicial or Civil Law, but it has gone with the dissolution of Israel as a Theocratic state with the coming of Christ, and especially at the demolition of the Temple. However, the moral law, i.e., the Ten Commandments, remains.

The Presbyterian Church of Babinda up in Far North Queensland had a huge block of wood with the Ten Commandments written on it standing behind the pulpit, forcing the congregation to view them every Sunday. The church building was demolished in a cyclone during the 1980s. The only thing left standing was the huge block of wood bearing the Ten Commandments!

It's interesting to note the word "hang" in, "All the Law and the Prophets *hang* on these two commandments." These two commandments summarizing the Ten Commandments are the two well-driven nails upon which the whole of the Bible, Old and New Testaments, like a picture hangs.

The Ten Commandments, and as summarized by Jesus in the two commandments, love God and neighbour, are revelation of the character of God, in whose image and likeness we have been made. Christians are being remade into that perfect image.

A Table for Two

Jesus brings the two tables of the Law together. The writer to the Hebrews says,

> "In the past God spoke to our ancestors through the prophets at many times and in various ways, but in these last days he has spoken to us by his Son, whom he appointed heir of all things, and through whom also he made the universe. The Son is the radiance of God's glory and the exact representation of his being, sustaining all things by his powerful word. After he had provided purification for sins, he sat down at the right hand of the Majesty in heaven" (Heb. 1:1-3).

Jesus, the Son, is the "exact representation" of God's being. Who is Jesus? Jesus is God and man in one Divine Person forever. Jesus is the One who is answering the question that the lawyer put to Him to test Him, "Teacher, which is the greatest commandment in the Law?" Then Jesus summarizes the two tables of the Law. "Love the Lord your God with all your heart and with all your soul and with all your mind.' This is the first and greatest commandment. And the second is like it: 'Love your neighbour as yourself.'"

If Jesus is truly God, then you are to love Him as God. Jesus first in all things. No false images of Him. No using His name as a swear word. Remembering Him at work, rest, and play, and that we rest in Him.

And if Jesus is truly man, then we are to love Him as we love ourselves. Honour Him as you would your parents, look out for His wellbeing as in not murdering Him in any way shape, or form. Be faithful to Him as a bride to her Husband, His church being His bride. Not stealing from Him, including not stealing any of His glory. Not denying or lying about Him. And not coveting anything but Him.

Jesus is the incarnation of God. Isaiah says that He is our covenant. Of Jesus, God says, "I will keep You and give You as a covenant to the people, as a light to the Gentiles" (Isa. 42:6b, cf. Isa. 49:8). Jesus is God's covenant promise, and He is His covenant law. Everyone on Judgment Day will be judged by and against Jesus. As Peter says in Acts 10:42, "And He commanded us to preach to the people, and to testify that it is He who was ordained by God to be Judge of the living and the dead" (Acts 10:42).

Jesus is God clothed in the garments of human flesh. He is the Middle Person in the Godhead, the Father, the Son, and the Holy Spirit. Three Persons, but one God.

Where does the love come from with which you are to love God with all your heart, soul, and mind, and love your neighbour as yourself? Love comes from God. God is love. Love is eternal because God is eternal. The eternal Father eternally loves the eternal Son and the eternal Spirit, just as the Son eternally loves the Father and the Spirit, and as the Spirit eternally loves the Father and the Son. Says J.V. Fesko,

> The covenant of redemption… is a manifestation of the intra-trinitarian love that exists among Father, Son, and Holy Spirit, a love that the triune God decreed to bestow upon sinful and fallen creatures in spite of their rebellion. The *pactum salutis* is the eternal love of the triune God for the elect, the Son's bride.[36]

So, we see then that each Person in the Godhead loves the Other Persons. Each Person, therefore, loves God and He loves His Neighbour as Himself. Each Person is looking out for the wellbeing of each of the other Persons, and for the Godhead as a whole. Thus, God loves God and His Neighbour as Himself.

When God said, "Let Us make man in Our image, according to Our likeness" He did so by writing His covenant law, albeit in positive terms, upon man's heart. Paul in Romans 2:15 alludes to this when he says that the Gentiles, "have the requirements of the law written on their hearts" and talks about their consciences either accusing them or excusing them.

---

[36] J.V. Fesko, *The Trinity and the Covenant of Redemption*, Mentor Imprint by Christian Focus Publications Ltd., Geanies House, Fearn, Ross-shire, 2016, 141.

So, to be made in the image and likeness of God, whatever else it means, means that we were designed by God to reflect Him by loving God and our neighbour as ourselves. But we don't! How do we know we don't? God's law shows us that we don't. And the Holy Spirit convicts us, saying as it were, "Wrong Way. Go Back". And so we are to look away from ourselves to the Saviour of sinners, i.e., Jesus, for forgiveness.

Jesus is God's Law as it were with arms and legs. He loved God with all His heart, soul, and mind, and He loved His neighbour as Himself. Indeed, He kept God's law in its entirety perfectly! And He did it for love. "For God so loved the world that He gave us His only begotten Son, that whoever believes in Him should not perish but have eternal life" (John 3:16).

The Son honoured His Father by being obedient to Him even unto death. And, by dying on the cross to pay for our sins He has reconciled us to God. Jesus Christ is the two tables of the Law in the flesh.

The gospel is the spirit of the law. The spirit of the law is about loving God and your neighbour as yourself. Therefore, not only is Jesus the law of God with arms and legs, but He also is the gospel of God. The law convicts us of our sins and the gospel shows us how to have our sins forgiven.

Conclusion

Jesus is the perfect picture of God and man reconciled. He has two natures. He is God and He is Man in perfect harmony. And He is the table for two so to speak. He is where humans can meet with God, just you and Jesus.

Because of Him you now can sit down with God and sup with Him. Because of Him, you the Christian, are no longer at war with God and with your neighbour. Because of Him you are now, albeit imperfectly, but, unlike before you were converted, able to love God with all your heart, all your soul, and all your mind, and love your neighbour, including even the unlovable, as yourself.

COVENANT FORMED

Introduction

Having considered that a covenant in its simplest definition is a bond, and that this covenant bond between God and His people had been anticipated by God in eternity past as a covenant between the Father and the Son. And having seen that the covenant bond came with commands summarised in the Decalogue as "a rule of righteousness", we are now ready to consider that the covenant was formed with a view to Christ redeeming (fallen) creation and the people chosen by His Father to be His bride.

Keeping in mind that the perfect rule of righteousness is to love God and to love your neighbour as yourself, and that God wrote that rule on the table of humanity's heart when He created us, we are now ready to focus our attention on the only man who kept this rule perfectly in all aspects of His life from birth to death.

From this we already know, therefore, that none of us is born with a clean slate (*tabula rasa*). John Calvin used the term *sensus divinitatis* (sense of divinity) to describe our innate knowledge of God. It is also called *sensus deitatis* (sense of deity), and *semen religionis* (seed of religion). This is what we mean by use of the term "a perfect rule of righteousness." It is simply to image the God who made us, i.e., the Godhead who in Himself loves God and His Neighbour as Himself. Of course, when Adam rebelled against God, our imaging of God became distorted but not completely obliterated. However, the new and replacement Adam is the only perfect likeness of God. For He is "the express image of His person" (Heb. 1:3).

In the following we shall consider what Christ was coming into the world to do in terms of the covenant of redemption.

Covenant Promise

The Apostle Paul says to the Corinthians, "I determined not to know anything among you except Christ and Him crucified" (1 Cor. 2:2). To know anything about Christ and His crucifixion is to learn who Christ is and what His crucifixion means.

Is Christ just some man, perhaps even a good man, who was nailed to a tree over two thousand years ago? Who is Christ and why did He die the way He did? The short answer to this and such like questions is that Christ is God and Man in one divine Person forever, and His human death on the cross was to reconcile His people to God. Put simply, Christ and His crucifixion is all about God's everlasting covenant, His bond of reconciliation, i.e., the covenant of redemption.

Nigel Lee says, "A covenant is an oath between two or more persons promising blessing for obedience and threatening a curse for disobedience."[37] O Palmer Robertson likes to define the Biblical covenant thus, "A covenant is a bond in blood sovereignly administered."[38] However, I prefer Robert Rollock's (1555-98) less complicated definition, "The covenant of God generally is a

---

[37] Francis Nigel Lee, *Creation, Flood, and Conquest*, E-book, 2.
[38] O Palmer Robertson, *The Christ of the Covenants*, Presbyterian and Reformed Publishing, New Jersey, 1980, 4.

promise under some one certain condition."[39] Charles Hodge elaborates on this preferred definition,

> A covenant is a promise suspended upon a condition. It is beyond controversy that God did make such a promise to Adam, to Abraham, and to the Hebrew nation through Moses; and these transactions are in Scripture constantly called covenants. It does not, therefore, seem very reverent to speak of God as belittling His truth by the form in which He presents it.[40]

Let us as we proceed settle then for the simple definition that a covenant is *a conditional promise*.

Covenant Bond

As "the Lamb slain from the foundation of the world" (Rev. 13:8b), Christ and the blood He poured out on the cross is His people's bond with God, their everlasting covenant bond. As a king's letter of old bears the stamp of the king's seal in wax, so Christ's blood seals the everlasting covenant everlastingly.

Christ's crucifixion seals space, time, and matter forever. Thus, Christ envelops all creation. Or, to put it another way, all creation is inside the envelope that is Christ. "In Him all things consist" (Col. 1:20). Therefore, Christ is His people's

---

[39] Robert Rollock, *A Treatise of God's Effectual Calling*, 1603, 6.

[40] Charles Hodge, *Systematic Theology*, Eerdmans, Grand Rapids, Michigan, (1871-73), Reprinted 1981, Vol. 3, 549.

covenant (Isa. 42:6; 49:8), because He is *the* covenant.

If we keep Christ, the Middle Person in the Trinity, as our focus then we shall see that all of God's covenants in the Bible are really just different administrations in time of the one covenant or *conditional* promise. "For all the promises of God in Him are Yes, and in Him Amen, to the glory of God through us" (2 Cor. 1:20). Thus, Christ our covenant also is our hermeneutic, our method of interpretation, which is to say that Christ, as revealed in Scripture, interprets the covenant in "covenant theology" for us. Says Palmer Robertson,

> All God's promises have conditions and promises. At the same time, the various covenants of redemption have the absolute certainty that all the conditions will be met. They will be met by the Lord Jesus Christ, who has come to save his people from their sins by fulfilling in himself the conditions of the covenant.[41]

Covenant Work

In covenant theology the Father promised the Son certain things upon *condition* that the Son fulfils every condition of the covenant perfectly. Thus, the Father gave the Son "work" to do for which the Son, upon completion, would be fully rewarded as

---

[41] O Palmer Robertson, *Israel and the Nations in God's Covenants, Covenant Theology: Biblical, Theological, and Historical Perspectives*, Edited by Waters, Reid, and Muether, Crossway, Wheaton, Illinois, 2020, 520.

promised in the agreement. In His great High Priestly prayer Jesus says to His Father, "I have glorified You on earth. I have finished the work which You have given Me to do" (John 17:4). While shedding His blood on the cross He said, "It is finished" (John 19:30).

What "work" had the Father given Jesus to do?

HEAD II.

The Remedy Provided in Jesus Christ for the Elect by the Covenant of Grace. *Hos. 13:9.*

"O Israel, thou hast destroyed thyself; but in me is thine help."

1. ALBEIT man, having brought himself into this woeful condition, be neither able to help himself, nor willing to be helped by God out of it, but rather inclined to lie still, insensible of it, till he perish; yet God, for the glory of His rich grace, has revealed in His word a way to save sinners, viz. by faith in Jesus Christ, the eternal Son of God, by virtue of, and according to the tenor of the Covenant of Redemption, made and agreed upon between God the Father and God the Son, in the council of the Trinity, before the world began.

2. The sum of the Covenant of Redemption is this: God having freely chosen unto life a certain number of lost mankind, for the glory of His rich grace, did give them, before the world began, unto God the Son, appointed Redeemer, that, upon condition He would

humble himself so far as to assume the human nature, of a soul and a body, unto personal union with His divine nature, and submit Himself to the Law, as surety for them, and satisfy justice for them, by giving obedience in their name, even unto the suffering of the cursed death of the cross, He should ransom and redeem them all from sin and death, and purchase unto them righteousness and eternal life, with all saving graces leading thereunto, to be effectually, by means of His own appointment, applied in due time to every one of them. This condition the Son of God (who is Jesus Christ our Lord) did accept before the world began, and in the fulness of time came into the world, was born of the Virgin Mary, subjected Himself to the Law, and completely paid the ransom on the cross: But by virtue of the foresaid bargain, made before the world began, He is in all ages, since the fall of Adam, still upon the work of applying actually the purchased benefits unto the elect; and that He doth by way of entertaining a covenant of free grace and reconciliation with them, through faith in Himself; by which covenant, He makes over to every believer a right and interest to Himself, and to all His blessings.

3. For the accomplishment of this Covenant of Redemption, and making the elect partakers of the benefits thereof in the Covenant of Grace, Christ Jesus was clad with the threefold office of Prophet, Priest, and King: made a Prophet, to reveal all saving knowledge to His people,

and to persuade them to believe and obey the same; made a Priest, to offer up Himself a sacrifice once for them all, and to intercede continually with the Father, for making their persons and services acceptable to Him; and made a King, to subdue them to Himself, to feed and rule them by His own appointed ordinances, and to defend them from their enemies.[42]

Jesus Christ has perfectly fulfilled all the conditions of the everlasting covenant to date. Therefore, to be enveloped by Christ (i.e., clothed in His righteousness) is to be inside the King's blood-sealed letter delivered to the household of God. Says Charles Hodge,

> It was in Christ, as their head and representative, they were chosen to holiness and eternal life, and, therefore, in virtue of what he was to do in their behalf. There is a federal union with Christ, which is antecedent to all actual union, and is the source of it. God gave a people to his Son in the covenant of redemption. Those included in that covenant, and because they are included in it, – in other words, because they are in Christ as their head and representative, – receive in time the gift of the Holy Spirit, and all other benefits of

---

[42] *The Confession of Faith, The Larger and Shorter Catechisms, with the Scripture Proofs at Large: together with The Sum of saving Knowledge*, Free Presbyterian Publication, Glasgow, Fourth reprint 1985, p. 324.

redemption. Their voluntary union with Christ by faith is not the ground of their federal union, but, on the contrary, their federal union is the ground of their voluntary union. It is, therefore, in Christ, i.e., as united to him in the covenant of redemption, that the people of God are elected to eternal life, and to all the blessings therewith connected. Much in the same sense the Israelites are said to have been chosen in Abraham. Their relation to Abraham and God's covenant with him, were the ground and reason of all the peculiar blessings they enjoyed. So our covenant union with Christ is the ground of all benefits which we, as the people of God, possess or hope for.[43]

To really know Christ and Him crucified, one has to understand the everlasting covenant, the covenant of redemption, as revealed in Scripture. Christ is the middle Person in the Father, the Word, and the Spirit triunity of the Godhead. It wasn't the Father or the Spirit who became flesh. It was the Word or Son of God who, while ever retaining His divinity, became a man.

God, who is a plurality of Persons, is one, and as such, is in covenant within and with Himself. God's everlasting covenant (or conditional promise) is that should any Person in the Godhead stop loving God and His Neighbour as Himself within the ontological Trinity, God should no longer be God – for then He would have broken the everlasting

---

[43] Charles Hodge, *Ephesians*, (1856. Banner of Truth, Edinburgh, 1991), 9.

covenant, the very expression of His character and being.

Conclusion

God is eternal, having no beginning or end. Therefore, perhaps it is a bit of a misnomer to speak of the everlasting covenant being *formed* in the Godhead. To form something suggests that the thing formed had a beginning. But God is eternal, i.e., without beginning or end. Therefore, the everlasting covenant includes everything that the eternal God has in mind, such as creation, its planned execution to bring it into existence, its upkeep and redemption in relation to the elect of God, and its final consummation.

God's promise to us is through Christ. Our bond with God is in Christ. We are saved by the work of Christ. Christ is all and in all (Col. 3:11).

It is the everlasting covenant of redemption within the Godhead that God extends in Christ to include all of His creation while incorporating all of His people.

COVENANT & THE TRINITY

Introduction

Having considered that a covenant in its simplest definition is a bond, and that this covenant bond between God and His people had been anticipated by God in eternity past as a covenant between the Father and the Son. And having seen that the covenant bond came with commands summarised in the Decalogue as "a rule of righteousness", and that the covenant was formed with a view to Christ redeeming creation and the people chosen by His Father to be His bride, we are now ready to tackle the covenant and the Trinity.

Whereas the temptation is to begin theology at Christ on the cross and work your way back to eternity, the Calvinist system of theology, to which this author subscribes, begins with God, the triune God, the Trinity, and works its way from eternity through time. That is why our main focus has been on the covenant of redemption in eternity, before we turn to the covenants of works and grace in time.

Covenant Preamble

Theologians speak of the ontological Trinity and the economic Trinity. These technical terms should not be seen as any sort of hurdles. For these two terms help us to understand who and what God is. First, God is Father and Son (or Word) and Holy Spirit (or Ghost). Thus, the Father, the Son, and the Holy Spirit are three distinct Persons. However, these three identified Persons are one God – the Trinity.

To speak of the ontological Trinity is to speak

of the God who was able to have formulated in eternity the covenant of redemption in the counsel of peace. The following is a brief description of the ontological Trinity. Says Westminster Confession of Faith chapter 2, paragraph 3,

> In the unity of the Godhead there be three Persons of one substance, power, and eternity: God the Father, God the Son, and God the Holy Ghost. The Father is of none, neither begotten nor proceeding; the Son is eternally begotten of the Father; the Holy Ghost eternally proceeding from the Father and the Son.

If God were not triune, there would have been no covenant of redemption. However, we notice the three Persons in the Godhead are of the same substance and equal in power. Each Person is eternal, i.e., with no beginning or end. No Person or Persons lords it over the other Person or Persons. However, there is an order of being.

The eternal Father is generated by none, but He eternally generates the eternal Son. And the eternal Spirit eternally proceeds from both the Father and the Son. Thus, the Father has never been without the Son or the Son the Father. Nor have the Father and the Son been without the Spirit or the Spirit without the Father and the Son. They are in an eternal covenant bond of love, always have been, always are, and always will be. Thus, the ontological Trinity.

Whereas the ontological Trinity refers to who God is, the economic Trinity refers to what God does.

The covenant of redemption is an outworking of the very nature of God, i.e., of who God is. The Father loves the Son and the Spirit. The Son loves the Father and the Spirit. And the Spirit loves the Father and the Son. Each person in the Godhead loves God, and each person loves His Neighbour as Himself.

Of the Ten Commandments, the first four show us our duty to God, and the last six our duty to our neighbour. Thus, the Decalogue reveals in time the eternal character of God. What does God do? He eternally loves God and His Neighbour as Himself. God created man in His own image and likeness to likewise keep the Ten Commandments in His creation. The economic Trinity pertains to God and His relation to His creation, and to man as His representative in creation. J.V. Fesko says,

> God is love and thus love characterizes the intra-trinitarian relationships as well as His decreed and executed redemption. The Father predestines the elect in love (Eph. 1:4-5); He sent His Son in love (John 3:16; Rom. 5:8). And Christ's outpouring of the Spirit at Pentecost was equally an outpouring of love: 'God's love has been poured into our hearts through the Holy Spirit who has been given to us' (Rom. 5:5; cf. Titus 3:5-6; Acts 2:17). It stands to reason, then, that the Father's promise to give His Son the Spirit to carry out His mission as covenant surety was a promise to anoint Him with love. The Father poured out the Spirit and anointed Him in love that Christ might render His obedience in love, and

this loving obedience gave Him the right to unleash the outpouring of the Spirit, another manifestation of trinitarian love.[44]

Although all three persons in the Godhead are involved in each of the following, the Father is usually referred to as the Creator, the Son as the Redeemer, and the Spirit as the Consummator. However, as we look at the role of each of the three Person in the covenant of redemption, to help us understand, let us here refer to the Father as the Proposer in the covenant and its details, the Son as the Procurer, and the Spirit as the covenant's Perfector.

Covenant Proposer

To make a proposal is to put forth a plan to another party or parties. For instance, a marriage proposal is a plan to get married till death do you part (Rom. 7:2; 1 Cor. 7:39). In the counsel of the eternal Godhead the Father proposed to the Son that He would give the Son a people as numerous as the stars in the yet to be created sky (Gen. 15:5 with Gal. 3:16). The Father has chosen (elected) this people (the church) from the mass of the yet to be created humanity viewed in their fallen state (Rom. 11:32; Gal. 3:22).[45]

---

[44] J.V. Fesko, *The Trinity and the Covenant of Redemption*, Mentor Imprint by Christian Focus Publications Ltd., Geanies House, Fearn, Ross-shire, 2016, 349-50.

[45] For discussion on the issue of *Supralapsarianism* and *Infralapsarianism* see, e.g., Louis Berkhof's *Systematic Theology*, pp. 118-125; Charles Hodge's *Systematic Theology Vol 2*, pp. 316-320; RL Dabney's *Systematic Theology*, pp. 232-

The Father purposed to grant the Son a kingdom of these redeemed sinners, even whole nations of subjects loyal to His Son, tried, true, and tested. In short, the Father says to the Son, "Ask of Me, and I will give You the nations *for* Your inheritance, and the ends of the earth *for* Your possession" (Psa. 2:8). Therefore, the Father has promised the Son a bride (i.e., *the nations*) and a home (i.e., *the ends of the earth*) in which they both should dwell forever.

Indeed, the Father promised the Son, and has since given Him, rulership over the whole of the then yet to be created creation. We see evidence the Father kept His promise where Jesus says, "All authority has been given to Me in heaven and on earth" (Matt. 28:18; 1 Cor. 15:24). However, just as there are certain conditions in a marriage contract, so there were certain strings attached to the covenant between the Father and the Son of eternity past.

The Age of Chivalry is the time when knights wore shining armour. Sir Walter Scott romanticised this era with his novel "Ivanhoe". The legends of King Arthur and the Knights of the Round Table helped too. If you know anything about the Age of Chivalry, you will know something about kings granting loyal subjects huge tracts of land and such like. (A "Royal Grant Covenant.") Well, God the Father (before the foundation of the earth) is

---

234; Herman Bavinck's *The Doctrine Of God*, pp. 359-365; AA Hodge's *Outlines of Theology,* pp. 231-234; WGT Shedd's *Dogmatic Theology 3rd Edition*, pp. 30; 340; 361 and Glossary 1; Robert L Reymond A *New Systematic Theology of the Christian Faith 2nd Edition*, pp. 480; 479-88.

proposing something like this, only on a grander scale, to God the Son. However, as with kings and knights of old, certain conditions of obedience are involved, including much more than rescuing a beautiful damsel in distress from an evil fiend!

One major *condition* was that the Son would represent to the death those whom the Father *promised* to give Him. Scripture reveals that God the Father "chose us in Him before the foundation of the world ... having predestined us to adoption as sons by Jesus Christ to Himself, according to the good pleasure of His will" (Eph. 1:4-5). However, something was wrong with every one of these people: all were fallen in Adam. Adam represented the entire human race in the covenant of works; which covenant he broke (Hos. 6:7), bringing God's death penalty upon himself and all his posterity in him (Rom. 5:12-21). Therefore, all are in rebellion against God and His authority over them. "For all have sinned and fall short of the glory of God" (Rom. 3:23). Yet the Father has chosen a bride for His Son from this fallen mass of sinful and depraved humanity. However, our sin and guilt must be dealt with (Rom. 3:23; 5:12).

Who would like to represent, for instance, Adolf Hitler in a court of law? Who could get him off with his crimes against God and his neighbour (i.e., humanity)? In this, you can see a little of what it must have been like for the Son to stand as our Advocate (1 John 2:1).

The cost of sinning against God is death (Gen. 2:17; Rom. 6:23). His justice demands it. The Father is proposing that the Son assume responsibility for His bride and become her legal representative. And remember, this people are hell-bent on destroying God. But, in order to receive the royal inheritance, i.e., a *bride* and a place for *her* to live (John 14:2-3; Rev. 2:12), the Son must first fulfil every jot and tittle of His Father's proposal (John 19:30; Heb. 9:12). He must rescue His bride, the damsel in distress, from the clutches of that evil fiend, the Devil (Matt. 12:29; Mark 3:27; Luke 13:16; John 12:31; Acts 26:18; Eph. 2:2; 1 John 3:8).

Covenant Procurer

The Son acted as *Mediator* and *Surety* of the covenant on behalf of the people chosen by the Father. He procured from the Father all that the Father had promised Him by fulfilling the conditions of the contract or covenant with the Father. He kept His end of the agreement even unto death. Therefore, the Father is awarding Him His promised inheritance. The Son kept His end of the bargain and so did the Father (Psa. 2:8; Matt. 28:18; John 19:30).

Having already acknowledged the Trinity and the covenant of redemption in eternity past, let us now begin at the cross and work our way back to the beginning. Christ died on the cross to save a people from its sins (Matt. 1:21; Rom. 5:8). Acts 20:28 speaks of the church which "He purchased with His own blood." From whom did Jesus Christ purchase His Church? The devil? No! He purchased this people from God the Father. Christ died to satisfy God's divine justice. By this we mean that because God is a just God, He cannot let sin go unpunished. Therefore, Christ received God's just punishment on behalf of those whom the Father promised (Isa. 53:4-12).

All sin must be punished, and damages paid for. Hence one of the main conditions of the covenant was that the Son represent a sinful people, chosen by the Father before the foundation of the world (Eph. 1:3-12), and in time, to be purchased or redeemed by the Son from the mass of condemned humanity (John 17:12; 20). "Through one man sin entered the world, and death through sin, and thus death spread to all men, <u>because all sinned</u>" (Rom. 5:12). Scripture tells us then that *all* are sinners in Adam because *all* sinned in Adam. Adam represented us in the Garden of Eden. Christ represented *only* His people (Matt. 1:21; Rom. 5:12; 1 Cor. 15:22; 49).

"The wages of sin is death" (Rom. 6:23). Hence the everlasting covenant has to do with redeeming people condemned to everlasting death, which means everlasting conscious torment (Isa. 66:24; Matt. 25:46; Mark 9:43-48; Rev. 20:10; 21:18). Hence the reason why some refer to the covenant as the covenant of redemption. Christ procured the redemption of His people on Calvary's cross (1 Cor. 15:3-4).

In order to pay the price demanded by the Father for sin, the eternal Son of God had to become the Son of Man and lay down His human life. A life for a life (Gen. 9:5-6; Lev. 24:17), i.e., a *perfect* life in exchange for a huge portion of a condemned and *imperfect* humanity (Isa. 53:12; 2 Cor. 5:21; Rev. 7:9).

Can you imagine the President of the USA leaving the comfort of the White House and going to the electric chair so that a bunch of murderers on death row should be spared? Yet God the Son agreed to do this and a whole lot more. And He willingly agreed to it before the foundation of the world, i.e., to become a man, placing Himself under God's law and vowing to keep it perfectly as a *covenant of works* (Gen. 1:27; 2:16-17; Lev. 18:5b; Neh. 9:29; Matt. 19:16-27; Rom. 10:5; Gal. 3:12). "But when the fullness of the time had come, God sent forth His Son, born of a woman, born under the law, to redeem those who were under the law, that we might receive the adoption as sons" (Gal. 4:4-5). Therefore, in accordance to the covenant with His Father, the eternal Second Person of the Trinity humbled Himself by assuming a human body and a reasoning soul, and came and dwelt among fallen humanity (Matt. 26:38; John 1:14; Heb. 2:14).

CS Lewis likens this great act of condescension to that of you or me becoming a slimy snail or a cockroach to live among them! The picture then is one of the Son of God waiting for that precise moment when the Father would send Him to procure the redemption of fallen creation.

Jesus, then, came to do everything the Father proposed in eternity past. The following are a couple of verses of Scripture which illustrate this: "For I have come down from heaven, not to do My own will, but the will of Him who sent Me. This is the will of the Father who sent Me, that of all He has given Me I should lose nothing, but should raise it up on the last day". "Then Jesus said to them, 'When you lift up the Son of Man, then you will know that I am He, and that I do nothing of Myself; but as My Father taught Me, I speak these things. And He who sent Me is with Me. The Father has not left Me alone, for I always do those things that please Him'" (John 6:38-39; 8:28-29; John 17:1-11).

The Son did on earth everything He had covenanted with the Father. He fulfilled everything the Father had proposed, keeping to the minutest detail all the stipulations of the everlasting covenant (John 17:4).

The Father also upheld the covenant, providing the Son everything needed to fulfil the rescue mission. For example, Christ says of God, "A body You have prepared for Me" (Heb. 10:5b). The Father also promised the Son the Spirit without measure so that as the Son of Man He could perform His mission on earth. "For He [Christ] whom God has sent speaks the words of God, for God does not give the Spirit by measure. The Father loves the Son, and has given all things into His hand" (John 3:34-35).

Revelation 13:8b speaks of "the Lamb slain from the foundation of the world." This reinforces the fact that the Son knew exactly what He had come to do, the plan being "decided" in the counsel of the Trinity in eternity past. There the covenant of redemption was formulated and the terms agreed upon. The Father made this promise to the Son, "I will keep You and give You as a covenant to the people, as a light to the Gentiles" (Isa. 42:6).

The everlasting covenant was *solemnised* at Jesus' baptism (Matt. 3:15). Here Jesus identified Himself with sinful humanity, in particular, those chosen by His Father from the fallen mass of humanity, i.e., His bride. When Jesus was baptised by John, He was not only anointed with water, but also with the Holy Spirit (Isa. 44:3; 61:1; Luke 4:18; John

1:33; Acts 10:38,44-45,47; 11:16). Christ's baptism was also a sign that Jesus was indeed the Christ (Matt, 3:11,15,17; Luke 3:16; John 1:29-34). He was *anointed* as Prophet, Priest, and King of His people, as were prophets, priests, and kings in the Old Testament (Lev. 8:12; 1 Kings 19:16; 2 Kings 9:3; Matt. 2:2; John 6:14; Heb. 8:1). (Anointed = *Christ* in New Testament Greek, and *Messiah* in Old Testament Hebrew). In a word, the man Jesus, as Prophet, Priest, and King, is Mediator of the covenant of grace (1 Tim. 2:5; Heb. 8:6; 9:15; 12:24).

However, Jesus was not baptised to have His own sins washed away, for He had no sin of His own. (2 Cor. 5:21). Rather, like the flood in Noah's day, Christ's baptism was to wash away the sin of the world (Isa. 52:15a; Ezek, 36:25-27; Joel 2:28-29; Acts 2:17-18; 38-39). For, did not John the Baptiser say, as Jesus approached him to be baptised, "Behold! The Lamb of God who takes away the sin of the world"? (John 4:29).

We'll pick up on this later when we look at covenant baptism, but at this point don't miss the connection between water baptism and the outpouring of the Holy Spirit. John Macleod comments:

> Neil Macmichael...may not have been perhaps a great theologian; but he had a tart way of putting things that made them stick in the memory. Here is an illustration: He was applying what the Apostle says of the fathers who were all baptised unto Moses in the cloud and in the sea [i.e., 1 Cor. 10:1-2] and he said: '1. The Israelites were baptised, both adults

and infants; for the Apostle declares it. 2. They were not immersed, a fact which Moses and other inspired writers testify. 3. The Egyptians who pursued them were immersed. 4. The Israelites had baptism without immersion, and the Egyptians immersion without baptism. 5. The baptism of the Israelites was salvation, and the immersion of the Egyptians drowning'.[46]

The three Persons of the Trinity were involved in the baptism of Christ, as with our baptism (Matt. 28:19). Christ's water baptism was the *sign* and *seal* of the *reality* of His virtually simultaneous Spirit baptism. At His water/Spirit baptism, the voice of the Father boomed from heaven, "You are My beloved Son in whom I am well pleased" (Mark 1:11). The Spirit, like water poured from heaven, came upon the Son like a dove (Mark 1:10-11). Here was the beginning of Christ's ministry. Afterwards, Jesus, in a synagogue, would read from the Scriptures, applying it to Himself: "The Spirit of the Lord is upon Me, because He has anointed Me to preach the gospel" (Isa. 61:1-2b; Luke 4:18).

There is an old wedding tradition in which the groom carries his new bride over the threshold into the safety of their new home. At His baptism Christ betrothed Himself to His bride, i.e., His church (Eph. 5:2; 30 NKJV). The water is a picture of His poured-out blood, which cleanses (Ex. 24:6-8; Num. 8:7; 19:13, 18, 21; Heb. 10:29; 12:24;), and His poured-out Spirit

[46] John MacLeod, *Scottish Theology*, Knox Press & Banner of Truth Trust, 1974, p. 253-4

who sanctifies (1 Pet. 1:2). Christ, as it were, smeared His own blood, even the blood of the everlasting covenant on the lintel and the two doorposts (Exod. 12:13, 22-23) of His heavenly kingdom as He crossed the threshold of death with His bride safely in His arms (Exod. 12:7,13; 1 Cor. 3:9b; 5:7b; Acts 20:28). All true members of Christ's household are therefore safe from the destroying angel, i.e., the wrath of God.

The Father promised to give the Son everything required to procure what He had proposed. Says J.V. Fesko,

> Although the Son is the covenant surety, He is not alone in His work. Redemption is an act of the triune God – the Father sends the Son, the Son executes His mission as covenant surety, and the Father and the Son send the Spirit to apply the Son's work of Christ to the elect. The Son's work as surety, however, is pneumatically charged – Christ executes His mission in the power of the Holy Spirit. The Spirit is integral to the Son's work as covenant surety.[47]

When as a man He fulfilled all the conditions of the Father's proposal, the Son was then in a position to receive all the promises of the Father, in particular the Holy Spirit, whom He would pour out from Heaven on His church (Ezek. 39:29; Joel 2:28; Zech. 12:10; Acts 2:16:18; 10:45). "For all the

---

[47] J.V. Fesko, *The Trinity and the Covenant of Redemption*, Mentor Imprint by Christian Focus Publications Ltd., Geanies House, Fearn, Ross-shire, 2016, 318.

promises of God in Him are Yes, and in Him Amen, to the glory of God through us" (2 Cor. 1:20). "And being assembled together with them, He commanded them not to depart from Jerusalem, but to wait for the Promise of the Father, "which," He said, "you have heard from Me; for John truly baptized with water, but you shall be baptized with the Holy Spirit not many days from now" (Acts 1:4-5). Keep in mind what John had said about Jesus, "I indeed baptize you with water; but One mightier than I is coming, whose sandal strap I am not worthy to loose. He will baptise you with the Holy Spirit" (Luke 3:16b).

So, after He ascended to heaven, just as John the Baptizer had signified by pouring water upon the heads the repentant believers, and upon Jesus's head to fulfill all righteousness (Matt. 3:15), and just as the Father had sent the Spirit upon His Son at His water baptism, so the Father and the Son were going to pour out the Spirit to baptize the Son's bride.

Notice the order and sequence. The Father sends the Son, and the Father and the Son send the Spirit. Thus, the economic Trinity in time operates in the same manner as the ontological Trinity in eternity where "the Father is of none, neither begotten nor proceeding; the Son is eternally begotten of the Father; the Holy Ghost eternally proceeding from the Father and the Son."

Covenant Perfector

The two covenanting parties in the covenant of redemption are God the Father (representing the Trinity), and God the Son (representing those chosen in eternity by the Father, i.e., the elect). To make any agreement legal, even an everlasting covenant, there must needs be two or more witnesses (Deut. 19:15). While on earth Jesus bore witness of Himself in what He said and did, saying, "The Father who sent Me bears witness to Me" (John 8:18). However, the Holy Spirit has always borne witness to the everlasting covenant to the redeemed (Neh. 9:20, 30; 1 Pet. 1:10-11). Hence the covenant of grace is an in time legal and binding agreement of the covenant of redemption in eternity past between the Father and the Son as witnessed by the Holy Spirit. Says J.V. Fesko,

> [A] seemingly forgotten concept that theologians should reconsider and employ is that the Spirit is the bond of love between the Father and the Son.[48]

Gretna Green in Scotland is famous for marriages. Many a young couple has eloped to tie the knot there over the blacksmith's anvil all in the name of romance! A couple from Australia married in Gretna Green. However, the wedding was not without a hitch. They overlooked the *legal* need for willing witnesses to bear testimony to the signing of the marriage covenant (Matt. 18:16). Eventually in the street outside they found a couple of willing candidates!

The eternal Spirit has testified to the everlasting covenant between the Father and the Son from eternity (John 15:26; Heb. 9:14). In time and

---

[48] J.V. Fesko, *The Trinity and the Covenant of Redemption*, Mentor Imprint by Christian Focus Publications Ltd., Geanies House, Fearn, Ross-shire, 2016, 349.

space, He is the most willing and chief Witness to the "signing of the covenant" between the Father and the Son which was ratified and signed in Christ's blood at Calvary's cross (1 Pet. 1:2).

The role of the Holy Spirit was to move men chosen by the Father to write the Bible (2 Pet. 1:22). Hence the Book of the Covenant, the infallible and inerrant document which records the history, and reveals the plan, of redemption (2 Tim. 3:16). Jesus says of the Holy Spirit, "He will glorify Me, for He will take what is Mine and declare it to you. All things that the Father has are Mine. Therefore I said that He will take of Mine and declare it to you" (John 16:14-15).

Since all creation belongs to God, it stands to reason that He would have put in place many general tokens and signs as witness to His everlasting covenant, e.g., the rainbow, day and night, the sun and the moon (Gen. 9:16; Jer. 33:20; Psa. 89:34-37). Then there were the particular signs of Circumcision and Passover, which were superseded by Baptism and the Lord's Supper (Col. 2:11-12; 1 Cor. 5:7).

It is the role of the Spirit, therefore, to record the revelation of the covenant, i.e., the Bible. He testifies to the covenant by, and in, the Scriptures. He bears testimony by His two sacraments, and in particular through the proclamation of the gospel. Says Charles Hodge,

> The blessing promised, therefore, was the blessing of redemption through Christ. His promise to Abraham was a repetition of the promise made to our first parents after the fall,

this promise was the Gospel. The Gospel or *euaggelion* has a definite meaning in the Scriptures. It means the announcement of the plan of salvation through Christ, and the offer of that salvation to everyone that believes.[49]

The everlasting covenant of redemption in the form of the covenant of grace was consummated by the outpouring of the Holy Spirit on the Day of Pentecost (Acts 2:1-47). The gospel (i.e., the covenant of grace) is to go out to all nations (Matt. 28:18-20; Mark 16:15; Luke 24:46-47; Acts 1:8). The Triune God, by the proclamation and spread of His gospel, calls His elect, and by His Spirit regenerates those for whom Christ died, and (re)writes His moral law upon their hearts (Jer. 31:33; Heb. 8:8, 10:16).

The Holy Spirit through the "Great Commission" (Matt. 28:16-20) consummates and re-establishes also the "Cultural Mandate" (Gen. 1:26-28, 9:1-7). Thus, for those who believe in Christ and His righteous works for salvation, the covenant of grace becomes again the *unbroken* covenant of works, which is kept by the believer only in the power of the Spirit (Rom. 8:1-5; Gal. 5:16). Nigel Lee says,

> And God the Holy Spirit writes that Decalogical Law once again in their hearts. The Spirit Himself wrote His Law in the heart of man before the fall. He Himself is the very own indwelling Engine and Engineer, Who now gives His adopted children the desire and

---

[49] Charles Hodge, *Systematic Theology*, Eerdmans, Grand Rapids, Michigan, Reprint 1981, Vol. 3, 550.

ability to walk in that Law – as their very own way of expressing their gratitude to the Triune God for so great a salvation freely given them by the Father through the Lord Jesus.[50]

Hence, the Holy Spirit in due time, as the Perfector, presents and applies to every believer the redemption promised by the Father and procured and purchased by the Son (John 1:11,12; Titus 3:5,6; Eph. 1:13,14; 2:8).

---

[50] Francis Nigel Lee, *God Triune In The Beginning* – And For the 21st Century, www.dr-fnlee.org

PART TWO
The Covenant of Works

"Like Adam, they have broken the covenant" (Hos. 6:7).

INTRODUCTION

Having considered the covenant of redemption, and having seen that because it is trinitarian, it is impossible to study the covenant of redemption without also considering its relationship to the covenants of works and of grace. Like the Father and the Son and the Holy Spirit, you can't have one without the others. Therefore, because we have already studied the covenant of redemption, we already know something of the covenant of works, which of course is our main focus in the following.

In Part One, when considering the covenant of redemption, we mentioned that even some Christians switch off to the teachings of covenant theology because of preconceived negative notions. Their various biases preclude them from gaining a fuller and deeper understanding of God and what He is doing with and in the world He created. We said,

> Covenant theology is about the gospel. But, unlike Jonah's gourd (Jon. 4:6-9), covenant theology did not spring up overnight and wither as quickly. It has always been the teaching of the Bible. Yes, like the gospel itself, it is sometimes popular, and sometimes less popular. This book seeks to make it popular again.

As we attempt to make covenant theology popular again, one of the main sticking points for those who shun covenant theology has been the covenant of works. Perhaps it is simply because of the word "works" in the title. Evangelicals, fixated on justification by faith, have an aversion to anything that has to do with works in the Bible, smelling the dead rat of legalism. This is perhaps why some may even shun the Old Testament, styling themselves as "New Testament" Christians. Martyn Lloyd-Jones pulled no punches when he said,

> A Christian who does not know his Old Testament is – forgive the expression – just a fool. You need your Old Testament; you cannot understand the New without it.[51]

Saying much the same thing centuries before, Saint Augustine made famous the statement usually rendered, "The new is in the old concealed; the old is in the new revealed." Another version is, "The New Testament is latent in the Old; the Old Testament becomes patent in the New." If we cannot understand the New without the Old Testament, then I would add that you cannot understand the gospel without the law, which in turn is to say that you cannot fully understand what Christ was doing on the cross without first having understood the covenant of works. The Westminster Larger Catechism provides a useful summary that will help us to plot our course for what is to follow:

Q. 20. *What was the providence of God toward man in the estate in which he was*

---

[51] D. Martyn Lloyd-Jones, *Romans, Exposition of Chapter 9, God's Sovereign Purpose*, The Banner of Truth Trust, Edinburgh, Scotland, 1991, 60.

created?

A. The providence of God toward man in the estate in which he was created, was the placing him in paradise, appointing him to dress it, giving him liberty to eat of the fruit of the earth; putting the creatures under his dominion, and ordaining marriage for his help; affording him communion with Himself; instituting the Sabbath; entering into a covenant of life with him, upon condition of personal, perfect, and perpetual obedience, of which the tree of life was a pledge; and forbidding to eat of the tree of knowledge of good and evil, upon the pain of death.

The covenant of life is simply another name for the covenant of works where the focus is on the eternal life promised upon the completion of the works required. This is the same eternal life promised to those who repent and believe in the gospel (John 3:16). The obvious difference being that Adam, in the former, did not need the redemption planned in the covenant of redemption. It was only after he had fallen that Adam (and the rest of humanity) needed salvation. Westminster Larger Catechism,

Q. 21. *Did man continue in that estate wherein God at first created him?*
A. Our first parents being left to the freedom of their own will, through the temptation of Satan, transgressed the commandment of God, in eating the

forbidden fruit, and thereby fell from the estate of innocency wherein they were created.

In the following we shall be looking in more detail how the covenant of works was broken, the affect it had on humanity, and the penalties incurred for this covenant breach. But don't panic, it won't be all doom and gloom, for we shall see the hope that our gracious God provided for us in our self-inflicted state of sin and misery, i.e., Christ.

Building on what has already been established in Part One, and not forgetting Old Testament prefigurations, types, and theophanies, we shall now focus our attention on the pre-fall "Adam, who is a type of Him who was to come" (Rom. 5:14b). Says J.V. Fesko,

> When Paul identifies Adam as a 'type' [τύπος] of the one to come (Rom. 5:14), he has in mind a comparison between historical, not mythical, realities. Such is the nature of biblical typology – it places Old Testament historical events, places, and people in an analogous relationship to New Testament historical events, places, and people.[52]

---

[52] J.V. Fesko, *Adam and the Covenant of Works*, Mentor Imprint by Christian Focus Publications Ltd., Geanies House, Fearn, Ross-shire, 2021, 297.

COVENANT BROKEN

Introduction

When Adam fell, he not only transgressed the outward command to not eat the forbidden fruit, but also the inner commands God had written on his heart. When Adam transgressed the covenant of works his conscience kicked in. It was like a law-enforcement officer banging on his door in the middle of the night. "Police! Open up in the name of the law." As effective as hiding under the bedcovers, Adam's first thought was to hide his shame behind some sewn-together fig leaves, then among some trees, as he tried to escape from the law (Gen. 3:7-8). Clearly Adam was afraid of the Lord (Gen. 3:10).

The apostle Paul calls this confrontation, "the terror of the Lord", which for the rest of us, unlike for Adam, will take place on judgment day when it is too late to be reconciled to God. "For we must all appear before the judgment seat of Christ, that each one may receive the things *done* in the body, according to what he has done, whether good or bad. Knowing, therefore, the terror of the Lord, we persuade men; but we are well known to God, and I also trust are well known in your consciences" (2 Cor. 5:10-11).

To be reconciled to God through belief in the gospel is to escape "the terror of the Lord" on judgment day. The apostle Peter reminds us of the salvation of those inside the ark at the judgment of God during the great flood in Noah's day, "There is also an antitype which now saves us—baptism (not the removal of the filth of the flesh, but the answer of a good conscience toward God), through the resurrection of Jesus Christ" (1Pet. 3:21). And notice that Paul says to Timothy that it is all about love, "The aim of our charge is love that issues from a pure heart and a good conscience and a sincere faith" (1 Tim. 1:5).

Covenant Conscience

Actively loving God and ones' neighbour as oneself is the outward expression of the character of God and is the summary of the moral aspect of the everlasting covenant. As such, God's covenant is morally binding upon all moral beings. Though God covenanted only with His own likeness and image, i.e., with Adam as humanity's representative in the covenant of works, moral beings include humanity and angels, both of which God created as very good (Gen. 1:31).

The first table of the law, i.e., the first four of the Ten Commandments, show humanity's duty toward God, and the second table, i.e., the last six, express one's duty toward one's neighbour. It was this love for God and love for neighbour that God wrote on humanity's heart upon our creation. Thus, the covenant law (also known as the Ten Commandments or Decalogue) was stamped, albeit in positive terms, upon our innermost being (Rom. 2:14-15). Calvin alludes to the essential sameness of the inward law and that of the two tables that comprise the Ten Commandments,

> Now that inward law, which we have … described as written, even engraved, upon the hearts of all, in a sense asserts the very same

things that are to be learned from the Two Tables. For our conscience does not allow us to sleep a perpetual insensible sleep without being an inner witness and monitor for what we owe God, without holding before us the difference between good and evil and thus accusing us when we fail in our duty. But man is so shrouded in the darkness of errors that he hardly begins to grasp through this natural law what worship is acceptable to God . . . Accordingly (because it is necessary both for our dullness and for our arrogance), the Lord has provided us with a written law to give us a clearer witness of what was too obscure in the natural law, shake off our listlessness, and strike more vigorously our mind and memory.[53]

The Apostle Paul speaks of the sameness of God's law as it is written inwardly on the hearts of all human beings and that which is written outwardly in the Ten Commandments where he says, "When Gentiles, who do not have the law, by nature do the things in the law, these, although not having the law, are a law to themselves, who show the work of the law written in their hearts, their conscience also bearing witness, and between themselves *their* thoughts accusing or else excusing *them*" (Rom. 2:14-15).

The interaction of the individual with his/her own conscience is the law of God confronting each fallen human being personally. However, it was on

[53] John Calvin, *The Institutes of the Christian Religion*, Battles Edition, Book 2:8:1.

account of our fallen nature, like grime on a tombstone obscuring what is written thereon, that God first wrote His decalogue on two stone tablets. Thus, there are now two copies of God's Law available to man, the first comprising of the outward or objective written law, and second comprising of the inward or subjective law written on the conscience, which, as the apostle Paul describes, can become "seared with a hot iron" (1 Tim. 4:2).

Like two copies of the Ten Commandments, the outward and the inward law mirror each other as a clear and ever-present reminder of the two parties in the pre-fall covenant, i.e., God and Adam. Again, Calvin helps us to underline the testimony of the law,

> It is a fact that the law of God which we call the moral law is nothing else than a testimony of natural law and of that conscience which God has engraved upon the minds of men.[54]

Covenant Condition

Upon his creation God entered into a covenant with Adam as the head of humanity's household with the following outward test being given to Adam, "Then the LORD God took the man and put him in the garden to tend and keep it. And the LORD God commanded the man, saying, 'Of every tree in the garden you may freely eat; but of the tree of the knowledge of good and evil you may not eat, for in the day that you eat of it, you will surely die'" (Gen. 2:15-17). Says Robert Rollock,

---

[54] Ibid., Book 4:20:16.

The Covenant of Works, which may be called a legal or natural covenant, is founded in nature, which is pure and holy, and in the Law of God, which was in the first creation engraved in man's heart. For after God had created man after His own image, pure and holy, and had written His Law in his mind, He made a covenant with man. In it He promised him eternal life upon the condition of good and holy works which should correspond to the holiness and goodness of their creation and conform to His Law.[55]

Thus, when the LORD God said to Adam, "Of every tree in the garden you may freely eat; but of the tree of the knowledge of good and evil you may not eat, for in the day that you eat of it, you will surely die" He was simply entering into a *conditional promise* or covenant with Adam which was to last for an unspecified time. We don't know exactly how long Adam's probation was supposed to last simply because Adam broke the covenant before his probation had ended. Abraham Kuyper's comments on how quickly this may have happened,

[A]s soon as Adam receives the probationary command, Satan approaches Eve, and through her, Adam, seeking by deception to have her contravene that commandment.[56]

[55] Robert Rollock as quoted by Rowland S Ward, *God & Adam, Reformed Theology and The Creation Covenant*, New Melbourne Press, Wantirna, 2003, 95-6 (see also 100-1).
[56] Abraham Kuyper, *God's Angels: His Ministering Spirits*,

At this point it will be useful to know how God's law is understood covenantally. It will help us to understand the conditional nature of God's pre-fall covenant of works and how this covenant includes the inward law of God written on Adam's heart. In other words, the outward command for Adam not to eat the forbidden fruit incorporates with it the whole law of God. Paying particular attention to number 4 in the following we see that the Westminster Larger Catechism Q&A 99 states our understanding of God's law and how it applied to Adam pre-fall and to all humanity thereafter, thus,

> For the right understanding of the Ten Commandments, these rules are to be observed:
> 1. That the Law is perfect, and binds everyone to full conformity in the whole man unto righteousness thereof, and unto entire obedience forever; so as to require the utmost perfection of every duty, and to forbid the least degree of every sin.
> 2. That it is spiritual, and so reaches the understanding, will, affections, and all other powers of the soul; as well as words, works, and gestures.
> 3. That one in the same thing, in divers respects, is required or forbidden in several commandments.
> 4. That as, where a duty is commanded, the contrary sin is forbidden; and where a sin is

(Translation by Rev. Richard Stienstra), Kindle Edition.

forbidden, the contrary duty is commanded: so, where a promise is annexed, the contrary threatening is included; and, where a threatening is annexed, the contrary promise is included...[57]

Therefore, it is our understanding that when God threatened Adam with death on pain of eating the forbidden fruit in disobedience, He was at the same time promising him life upon obedience, (for Adam was permitted to eat of every other tree, including the Tree of Life). However, because God's law by its very nature penetrates and permeates the whole of man's being (on account of who man is, i.e., the image of God whose character is expressed in His law), when Adam ate of the forbidden fruit, he broke God's Ten Commandments. Says Robert Lewis Dabney,

> Every one is familiar with the Bible account of the condition of this covenant: the eating or not eating of the fruit of a tree called the "tree of the knowledge of good and evil." This prohibition was, obviously, a 'positive' command ... [Was] this single, positive precept substituted, during Adam's probation, [for] all the moral law[?] In other words: Was this the only command Adam now had to observe: the only one by the breach of which

[57] *The Confession of Faith, The Larger and Shorter Catechisms, with the Scripture Proofs at Large: together with The Sum of Saving Knowledge*, Free Presbyterian Publication, Glasgow, Fourth reprint 1985, 182-183.

he could fall? Presbyterians answer this in the negative. We regard all the moral law known to Adam is represented in this command, as the crucial test of his obedience to all. The condition of his covenant was perfect compliance, in heart and act, with all God's revealed law. This is manifest from the unreasonableness of any moral creature's exemption from the law of God, which is immutable. It appears also, from all the representations of the Covenant of Works, where the obedience required is to the whole law. It appears, finally, from this obvious view: that a consistent sense of moral obligation was the only thing which could have given to Adam's compliance with the positive prohibition, any moral significance or worth.[58]

Lest we miss the obvious, while under the covenant of works, had Adam, for instance, murdered Eve but had not eaten the forbidden fruit, he would have broken the conditional promise.

It was God's everlasting covenant that was revealed to Adam when God entered into this pre-fall covenant with him, which is to say that God graciously promised Adam (on behalf of humanity as its federal or covenant head) the yet to be consummated creation and all the benefits of everlasting life in it – upon condition of Adam's perfect covenantal obedience to God.

---

[58] Robert Lewis Dabney, *Systematic Theology*, first published 1872, Banner of Truth, Edinburgh, Reprinted 1996, 304-5.

With our definition of a covenant being a *conditional promise* in mind, it is easy to see how the pre-fall Adam, as humanity's federal head, i.e., covenant representative, was bound by the conditional promise (or threat) of what we have been thus far referring to as the covenant of works. It is succinctly stated in the Westminster Confession of Faith 19:1-2 thus,

1. God gave to Adam a law, as a covenant of works, by which He bound him, and all his posterity, to personal, entire, exact, and perpetual obedience; promised life upon the fulfilling, and threatened death upon the breach of it; and endued him with power and ability to keep it.

2. This law, after his fall, continued to be a perfect rule of righteousness; and, as such, was delivered by God upon mount Sinai in Ten Commandments, and written in two tables; the first four commandments containing our duty towards God, and the other six our duty to man.[59]

Covenant Cultural

Adam (with the help of his wife) was to obey God's cultural mandate, which means that he was to keep on loving God and his neighbour as himself, i.e., he was to keep God's law for an unspecified period in

---

[59] *The Confession of Faith, The Larger and Shorter Catechisms, with the Scripture Proofs at Large: together with The Sum of Saving Knowledge*, Free Presbyterian Publication, Glasgow, Fourth reprint 1985, 79-81.

all his daily activities. Thus, the pre-fall Adam was on probation. Again, in his usual lucid way, Robert Dabney seeks to answer a question regarding the pre-fall covenant transaction,

> Why is it supposed that an obedience for a limited time would have concluded the Covenant transaction? The answer is, that such a covenant, with an indefinite probation, would have been no covenant of life at all. The creature's estate would have been still forever mutable, and in no respect different from that in which creation itself placed him, under the first natural obligation to his Maker. Nay, in that case man's estate would be rightly called desperate; because, he being mutable and finite, and still held forever under the curse of the law, which he was, any day, liable to break, the probability that he would some day break it would in the infinite future mount up to moral certainty. The Redeemer clearly implies that the probation was to be temporary, in saying to the young ruler: 'If thou wilt enter into life, keep the commandments.' If probation had no limits, his keeping them could never make him enter in. Here again, Adam's representative character unavoidably implies that the probation was temporary. His personal action under the trial was to decide whether his posterity were to be born heirs of wrath, or adopted sons of God. Had his probation been endless, their state would have been wholly

unsettled. Only a moment's reflection is needed, to show the preposterous confusion which would arise from that state of facts. Adam's trial still continuing thousands of years after Seth's birth, for instance, and after his glorification, if the father then fell, the son's glorification must have been revoked.[60]

The cultural or dominion mandate is included in the following, "Then God said, 'Let Us make man in Our image, according to Our likeness; let them have dominion over the fish of the sea, over the birds of the air, and over the cattle, over all the earth and over every creeping thing that creeps on the earth.' So God created man in His own image; in the image of God He created him; male and female He created them. Then God blessed them, and God said to them, 'Be fruitful and multiply; fill the earth and subdue it; have dominion over the fish of the sea, over the birds of the air, and over every living thing that moves on the earth'" (Gen. 1:26-28).

Again, this pre-fall administration of God's everlasting covenant is commonly referred to by theologians as the covenant of works[61] (or sometimes the covenant of life[62]), whereby God by His grace enters into a covenant with Adam (against the devil),

---

[60] Robert Lewis Dabney, *Systematic Theology*, first published 1872, Banner of Truth, Edinburgh, Scotland, Reprinted 1996, 305.

[61] See e.g., Westminster Confession of Faith 7:2; 19:1, 6; The Sum of Saving Knowledge, Head 1:2; The Practical use of Saving Knowledge, Introduction; 2, 3.

[62] See e.g., Westminster Larger Catechism 20, Westminster Shorter Catechism 12.

threatening death to Adam for disobedience to its conditions and, conversely, life should Adam fulfil the conditions. It was this aspect of the everlasting covenant that Christ came to fulfil after Adam failed to keep the covenant law. Says William Ames (1576-1633),

> Because man in this animal life understands by the senses and is led by the hand, as it were, from sensible to intelligible and spiritual things, outward symbols and sacraments were added to the spiritual law to illustrate and confirm it. These symbols contained a special and positive law, a profession of general obedience to the law of nature put in man before, and a solemn confirmation of promises and threats as sanctions.
>
> Because Adam was the first of mankind, from whom all men come, a law was given to him not only as a private person, as among the angels, but as a public person or the head of the family of man. His posterity were to derive all good and evil from him, Acts 17:26; Romans 5:18-19; 1 Corinthians 15:21-22 … In the sanction of this law there was a promise of continuing animal [i.e., earthly] life, a later exaltation to spiritual [i.e., heavenly eternal] life, and a threat of bodily death, which had no place among the angels. Given this interpretation, the Law of God or His Covenant with man in the creation was, *Do this and you will live; if you do it not you shall die.* In these words there is, first, a command

and then a promise – you do it and you shall live – and last a threat – if you do it not, you shall die.

In this covenant there were two symbols or sacraments. The reward for obedience was marked by a tree, namely, that of life, and the punishment for disobedience was marked by a tree, namely that of the knowledge of good and evil. The one was the sacrament of life and the other the sacrament of death.[63]

Though we don't know the exact moment, we shouldn't overlook the fact that the angel who was to become Satan had already fallen before Adam's fall. Thus, evil was already present in God's creation. The Serpent/Satan used the woman to help convince Adam that he should break his covenant with God against Satan and instead bond with him in his rebellion against God (2 Cor. 11:3; 1 Tim. 2:14). It was when Adam deserted God and joined himself to the Serpent/Satan in a covenant against God, that "The LORD God said to the serpent, 'Because you have done this, you are cursed more than all cattle, and more than every beast of the field; on your belly you shall go, and you shall eat dust all the days of your life. And I will put enmity between you and the woman, and between your seed and her Seed; He shall bruise your head, and you shall bruise His heel'" (Gen. 3:14-15).

---

[63] William Ames, *The Marrow of Theology*, Translated from the third Latin edition 1629 by John Dykstra Eusden, Baker Books, Grand Rapids, 1997, 113.

Christ is the Seed of the woman (Gen. 3:15; Gal. 3:16). He is the same Seed promised to Abraham (Gen. 22:18). He crushed the serpent's head at the Place of the Skull (i.e., Calvary) when He was crucified and subsequently resurrected. Thus, Christ as the new or replacement Adam kept the covenant the old Adam failed to keep, and He also paid the price of death that humanity owed God for breaking the everlasting covenant. "The earth is also defiled under its inhabitants, because they have transgressed the laws, changed the ordinance, broken the everlasting covenant" (Isa. 24:5). "Like Adam, they have broken the covenant" (Hos. 6:7).

Covenant Cleaving

The institution of marriage is a vivid expression of God's everlasting covenant. Marriage between a man and a woman is morally binding. Fidelity is expected in the marriage covenant. In other words, moral obedience to the covenant's conditions is expected. Should either party cease to actively love the other party, the covenant bond is broken. However, "a threefold cord is not quickly broken" (Eccl. 4:12b), by which we here mean that there are three parties in any marriage-covenant: a husband, a wife, and God.

The first marriage on earth took place when God married Adam and Eve in the beautiful Garden of Eden (Gen. 2:22-24). Trouble began in the marriage-covenant when Adam (and Eve) sought to exclude God by instead bonding with Satan. Adam, as covenant representative, subsequently broke the everlasting covenant by eating the forbidden fruit.

Therefore, God ejected them from His house (i.e., the Garden of Eden). Adam and Eve, by leaving the garden, entered a hostile environment – the world that had now come under the sway of the devil.

On account of Adam being the head of the household of humanity meant that, when he sinned, his whole household became morally corrupted in and with him. "Therefore, just as through one man sin entered the world, and death through sin, and thus death spread to all men, because all sinned" (Rom. 5:12). "All have sinned and fall short of the glory of God" (Rom. 3:23).

The Apostle Paul is referring to Christ and His bride and to the time when God married Adam and Eve where he says, "For we are members of His body, of His flesh and of His bones. *'For this reason a man shall leave his father and mother and be joined to his wife, and the two shall become one flesh.'* This is a great mystery, but I speak concerning Christ and the church" (Eph. 5:30-32). God formed Eve from one of Adam's ribs. She was part of him. She was one with him, as in the covenant of marriage. Thus, Adam was to love God and Eve as he loved himself.

Christ became betrothed or engaged to be married to His bride when "The Word became flesh and dwelt among us" (John 1:14). "But when the fullness of the time had come, God sent forth His Son, born [or made] of a woman" (Gal. 4:4). Thus, though He continued to be the middle Person in the Trinity, Christ as it were left His Father and joined Himself to His church, (leaving and cleaving), and, upon His death and resurrection, the two would become one flesh, i.e., members of His body, of His flesh, and of His bones.

Christ shares our humanity while sharing God's divinity. Therefore, Christ is God and man in one divine Person forever. He shares His divinity equally with the Father and the Spirit. And He shares His humanness with all humanity. However, just as the old Adam was married to one bride only (Eve), so the new Adam Jesus Christ is married to one bride only, His church, or more properly, those chosen by His Father, "For he chose us in him before the creation of the world to be holy and blameless in his sight" (Eph. 1:4).

What is the church? In its simplest definition the church is the covenant community of God. To be sure there are visible and invisible aspects of the same church (Church Militant and Church Triumphant). However, the church is one. Heaven and earth are united in the church. But, unlike the heavenly aspect of the church which comprises only of the truly redeemed, the institutional or visible church on earth is made up of regenerate and unregenerate individuals, which is to say that on earth there is an admixture of those who are truly in Christ and those who are outside.

Conclusion

When Adam broke the everlasting covenant, he divorced himself and Eve (and all their posterity) from God to bond with the devil against God. By eating the forbidden fruit, Adam thus formed another covenant, i.e., with the Serpent and death. This covenant with death was expressed by rebellious

Israel, to whom the Lord said in judgment, "Your covenant with death will be annulled; your agreement with the realm of the dead will not stand. When the overwhelming scourge sweeps by, you will be beaten down by it" (Isa. 28:18). And it still stands today for all who remain rebellious, "But even if our gospel is veiled, it is veiled to those who are perishing, whose minds the god of this age has blinded, who do not believe, lest the light of the gospel of the glory of Christ, who is the image of God, should shine on them" (2 Cor. 4:3-4).

There is however good news for all who trust in the last Adam for salvation. "Although he was a son, he learned obedience through what he suffered. And being made perfect, he became the source of eternal salvation to all who obey him" (Heb. 5:8-9).

COVENANT & ADAM *(Adam Wakes)*

Introduction

Having seen that the covenant of works included an outward command, plus the Decalogue written on humanity's heart, plus the cultural mandate, i.e., to be fruitful, multiply (in marriage), fill the earth and subdue it, and have dominion over all of earth's creatures, we are now ready to focus our attention on the first man, our covenant head, our federal representative, in the covenant of works.

"Then the LORD God formed a man from the dust of the ground and breathed into his nostrils the breath of life, and the man became a living being" (Gen. 2:7).

Have you ever heard the phrase, "I don't know him from Adam"? Some people substitute "a bar of soap" for Adam. However, the phrase was used way back in 1840/41 by Charles Dickens in his book, *The Old Curiosity Shop.*

The line, "I don't know him from Adam" suggests that we don't know a person. Do you know that bloke over there? No. I don't know him from Adam. Therefore, both that person over there and Adam are strangers to you.

Who was Adam and what was he like? Well, for a start, Adam is called "the son of God" (Luke 3:38). Why would he be called the son of God? Well, Adam didn't have a human father. He was the very first man. He was the original, as in the first, human being.

In the following we'll try to build a bit of a picture of Adam. Then instead of saying, "I don't know that person from Adam", we'll be able to say, "I may not know that person, but I know Adam.

Mud Man

So, what do we know about Adam from that verse above? God crafted Adam, gave him the breath of life, and Adam became alive. Therefore, we know that Adam wasn't some sort of primate. He didn't evolve over millions of years from pond-scum or slime. Adam wasn't the descendant of some hairy gorilla, or a cheeky chimpanzee, or a relation to either. Adam was no monkey's uncle. He was, as Luke the physician says, "the son of God." Therefore, as "the son of God" Adam before the fall could say, "Abba, Father" to God!

Adam was the son of God because the LORD God, (i.e., *Jehovah-Elohim* which technically refers to the middle Person in the Godhead),[64] "formed a man from the dust of the ground" on the sixth day of creation.

I don't want us chasing after a red herring here. But the name Adam, the Hebrew word for man, sounds like "adamah". And because that word "adamah" as used for "ground" can sometimes mean red or ruddy, some believe that Adam was formed from red earth. Well, maybe. But notice what the text actually says, "So, the LORD God formed Adam's body from the dust of the ground." It wasn't the ground per se. It was the dust of the ground. The Hebrew word for dust means grey, as in powdered. Hence clay, earth, and when wet or moist, mud.

---

[64] Dr Francis Nigel Lee, *Jahweh – Jehovah* Dr F N Lee - Sermon Jahweh – Jehovah (dr-fnlee.org)

So, what colour was Adam's skin? It was the colour of the dust that God had created beforehand. Grey. Grey, as you know, is the colour that has no colour. Grey is neither black nor white. It is intermediate. However, the word Adam has tied up with it red, ruddy, rosy, flush, you know, like good Australian red ochre. Therefore, the grey clay, i.e., the moist dust, the mud if you will, that God used to form him, only took on a ruddy pigmentation after God had breathed into Adam's nostrils and the blood started coursing through his veins. We don't like to think about it, but we return to grey when God takes our breath away. "For dust you are and to dust you will return" (Gen. 3:19b).

The Hebrew word "formed" (Hebrew יָצַר, *yâtsar*), in "the LORD God formed a man from the dust of the ground", gives the idea of the mud being pressed, squeezed into shape. Maybe not quite like a cookie-cutter forming the shape of a gingerbread man from the doughy mixture, but perhaps more of a potter fashioning, sculpting, forming the moist clay or mud as we're calling it.

There's an old toast where the toaster raises his glass and says, "Here's mud in your eye!" I don't think anyone really knows where that toast came from. Some say it refers to the soldiers in WWI having to dig, live, fight, and perhaps die in muddy trenches. However, I like the idea that the toast "Here's mud in your eye" refers to Jesus spitting on the ground and making mud with His saliva and placing that mud on the eyes of a man who had been born blind (John 9:6). As when *Jehovah-Elohim* enabled Adam, the original mud-man, to open his

129

eyes, so *Jehovah-Jesus* enabled the blind man to see! "Here's mud in your eye!" means here's to your health!

So, once formed, the LORD God then did something really special. He raised the man out of the dust of the earth. He brought Adam to life. Does this remind you of anything? Resurrection perhaps? Anyway, we're told that "Now the LORD God had planted a garden in the east, in Eden; and there He put the man He had formed" (Gen. 2:8). Therefore, Adam was placed in the Garden, i.e., Paradise.

So, this man of dust, this dustman, if you will, received the breath of life from God. God exhaled His breath and the man inhaled it and became a living being, i.e., a living soul, an animated creature. Elihu in Job 33:4 knows what's going on here where he says, "The Spirit of God has made me; the breath of the Almighty gives me life." Says J.V. Fesko,

> Echoing Genesis 2:7 and Job 33:4, Jesus performed a living parable when He breathed upon His disciples: "Peace be with you. As the Father has sent me, even so I am sending you. And when he had said this, breathed on them and said to them, 'Receive the Holy Spirit'" (John 20:21-22). God was creating the new heavens and earth through the Spirit and the last Adam, but this creative activity has its precedence in the Son's and the Spirit's work of creation both in the cosmos at large and in its microcosmic creation of Adam.[65]

---

[65] J.V. Fesko, *Adam and the Covenant of Works*, Mentor Imprint by Christian Focus Publications Ltd., Geanies House, Fearn,

The Spirit of God, as you know, hovered or brooded or fluttered over the face of the deep when God brought the earth into being (Gen. 1:2). And here He is bringing the first man, "the son of God" into being from the earth that arose out of that deep. By this we are reminded of what the angel said to Mary, "The Holy Spirit will come on you, and the power of the Most High will overshadow you. So, the holy One to be born will be called the Son of God." (Luke 1:35). But let's not get ahead of ourselves.

Though speaking of Jacob, a.k.a. Israel, Deuteronomy 32:11-12 may as well be speaking of Adam, "Like an eagle that stirs up its nest and hovers over its young, that spreads its wings to catch them and carries them aloft. The Lord alone led him; no foreign god was with him." Says Meredith Kline,

> The verb used in [Genesis 1] verse 2b (*m ̔raḥepēt*) occurs again in the Pentateuch only in Deuteronomy 32:11. There, by the use of this verb, the divine activity in leading Israel through 'the waste howling wilderness' (v. 10) on the way to Canaan is likened to that of an eagle hovering protectively over its young, spreading out its wings to support them, and so guiding them on to maturity. In Exodus 19:4 God similarly describes himself as bearing Israel on eagles' wings.
> It was actually by means of his Glory-Presence that God thus led his people at the time of the exodus. It was in the pillar of

Ross-shire, 2021, 404.

cloud and fire that he went before them in the way and afforded them overshadowing protection. To describe the action of the Glory-cloud by the figure of outspread wings was natural, not simply because of the overshadowing function it performed, but because of the composition of this theophanic cloud.[66]

So, the Holy Spirit, the Breath of God, hovers over Adam and breathes the breath of life into him. And, as Adam wakes, the blood flows through his veins. Capillaries and arteries are crimson-rich, oxygenated by the breath of God. He becomes a living being. "The life of a creature is in his blood" (Lev. 17:11).

Adam breathes his first breath, but God still holds his breath in His hand. For, "In His hand is the life of every creature and the breath of all mankind" (Job 12:10).

This is astonishing! RNA, DNA, red corpuscles, cells at the molecular level, hair follicles, sinews, muscles, skin, eyes that adjust to light etc. Adam can see. He can hear. He can smell. He can taste. He can touch. Yes, Adam wakes!

David, the sweet psalmist, captures the picture well where he says, "I praise You because I am fearfully and wonderfully made; Your works are wonderful, I know that full well." (Psa. 139:14). Isn't our God awesome? A human being is an incredible

---

[66] Meredith G. Kline, *Images of the Spirit*, Eugene, OR, Wipf and Stock Publishers, 1999, 14.

design. A magnificent piece of crafted machinery. Built by God to worship and to serve God.

Moral Man

We know from other places in the Bible that Adam had "true righteousness and holiness" (Eph. 4:24). And he had "knowledge according to the image of Him who created him" (Col. 3:10). Adam wakes and has righteousness, holiness, and a knowledge of God. He is a moral being.

What did Adam know about God? He knew that God was righteous, holy, and full of knowledge. How so? Because the LORD God had created Adam in His own image and likeness (Gen. 1:26). Thus, when the LORD God formed man, He imprinted His own character on man. Like an image and inscription is pressed into a coin, so God pressed His image into man and wrote the eternal expression of His character on man's heart.

What is the eternal expression of God's character, and where do we find it? As Paul says to the Romans, "Indeed, when Gentiles, who do not have the law, do by nature things required by the law, they are a law for themselves, even though they do not have the law. They show that the requirements of the law are written on their hearts, their consciences also bearing witness, and their thoughts sometimes accusing them and at other times even defending them" (Rom. 2:14-15).

Adam wakes with righteousness, holiness, a knowledge of God, and the requirements of God's law written by the finger of God already on his heart. He is fearfully and wonderfully made indeed!

And what are the requirements of God's law? Are they the multiple ceremonial requirements that Israel under Moses had to perform? No! Are they the abundance of judicial or civil laws Israel had to keep? No! By God's law written on the heart we mean those Ten Commandments that were written on the clay tablets by the finger of God. These same Ten Commandments are written by the finger of God on the heart of every human being God by His grace is pleased to convert His elect, as per the Jeremiah 31:33 and Hebrews 8:10.

To be sure, the Ten Commandments that God wrote on Adam's heart were in a positive form, not in the negative post-fall form. However, the summary of the Decalogue pre-fall or post-fall remains the same. It is as Christ, the last Adam, the "express image" of God (Heb. 1:3), summarized it, i.e., to love God and your neighbour as yourself (Matt. 22:37-40).

We noted above that the eternal Father eternally loves the eternal Son and the eternal Spirit, just as the Son eternally loves the Father and the Spirit, and as the Spirit eternally loves the Father and the Son. And we saw, therefore, that each Person in the Godhead loves the other Persons. Each Person, therefore, loves God and He loves His Neighbour as Himself. Each Person is looking out for the wellbeing of each of the other Persons, and for the Godhead as a whole. Thus, God loves God and His Neighbour as Himself. This is the character of God.

Adam, the image and likeness of God, was created to expressly image the character of God in creation. In short, he too was to love God and His neighbour as himself. The Ten Commandments add more detail to the summary, the first four of which express how we are to love God, and the last six how we are to love our neighbour as ourselves.

What are Ten Commandments in positive form?

1. Worship God exclusively.
2. Worship God spiritually.
3. Worship God sincerely.
4. Worship God as He will be worshipped.
5. Respect authority.
6. Respect the life and rights of others.
7. Be pure and loyal.
8. Be honest.
9. Be truthful.
10. Be happy and content.[67]

These are the Ten Commandments before the fall that were written on Adam's moist 'clay' heart. After the fall, God wrote the same Commandments in negative form on tablets of hardened clay, (i.e., stone, metaphorically like Adam's heart after he had fallen).

Then after Christ's resurrection, ascension and pouring out of His Spirit, regenerated Christians have the same Commandments written on their renewed hearts, as per God's promise, "'This is the covenant I will make with the people of Israel after that time,' declares the LORD. 'I will put my law in their minds and write it on their hearts. I will be their God, and they will be my people'" (Jer. 31:33). "The people of Israel" is the church, made up of believing Jews along

---

[67] Francis Nigel Lee, (quoting Yost), *The Covenantal Sabbath*, The Lord's Day Observance Society, London, 1966, 24.

with believing Gentiles who have been engrafted into the same olive tree (Rom. 11:17).

The Commandments were first written on soft and fleshy 'clay'. Then, secondly, after the fall of man they were written on hard clay. Then, lastly, after conversion, the stony heart is removed and replaced with a fleshy tablet with the Commandments written on them (2 Cor. 3:3). Adam is special. None of the animals have God's law written on their hearts. Only man is a free moral agent. Animals just do whatever animals do, neither moral nor immoral.

The Ten Commandments on the hearts of human beings before God converts them are like the writing on old gravestones, hard to read. On Loch Lomondside where I grew up, I visited a church graveyard where some of the gravestones had inscriptions from around 1745 and shortly after, when Bonnie Prince Charlie and his men fought at Culloden.[68] Across the other side of the loch at Luss, there're graves belonging to Vikings!

Anyway, let's fix our eyes back upon God. In the Godhead the Father loves the Son and the Spirit, the Son the Father and the Spirit, and the Spirit loves the Father and the Son. Thus, each Person in the Godhead loves God, and He loves His neighbour as Himself. Man was made in the image God, i.e., to love God and his neighbour as himself. The Ten Commandments teach us how to do this.

---

[68] "An ancient graveyard, in the Scottish tradition, is sited to the south of the Church and contains headstones recording burials from the 17th century to the 1890's." Drymen Parish Church : Our History (drymenchurch.org)

Messiah Man

It is far better to know Jesus than Adam! But knowing Adam helps us to know Jesus better. Jesus, as you know, is the Messiah, the Christ, i.e., the Anointed. What does the Messiah-Man have to do with the Moral-Man, the Mud-Man Adam? Well, like love and marriage and the horse and carriage, you can't have one without the other.

In fact, the apostle Paul calls Jesus "the last Adam". In 1 Corinthians 15:45 he says, "So it is written: 'The first man Adam became a living being'; the last Adam, a life-giving spirit.'" Paul wrote, "So it is written." Written where? He's referring to the verse we're looking at in particular, i.e., Genesis 2:7, "Then the LORD God formed a man from the dust of the ground and breathed into his nostrils the breath of life, and the man became a living being."

So, here's the thing. What was Adam and his posterity supposed to be like? What were they supposed to do? The Westminster Confession of Faith in chapter 4 paragraph 2 provides a helpful summary:

> After God had made all other creatures, He created man, male and female, with reasonable and immortal souls, endued with knowledge, righteousness, and true holiness after his own image, having the law of God written in their hearts, and power to fulfill it; and yet under a possibility of transgressing, being left to the liberty of their own will, which was subject unto change. Besides this law written in their hearts, they received a command not to eat of the tree of the

knowledge of good and evil; which while they kept were happy in their communion with God, and had dominion over the creatures.

As you know, because it's ancient history, Adam used the liberty of his own free will and transgressed. By sinning against God, for Adam, and for the rest of humanity in him, sin obscured his knowledge of God, and he lost his righteousness and holiness. Adam lost his happy communion with God. Therefore, enter Jesus, the "second man". "The first man was of the dust of the earth; the second Man is of heaven" (1 Cor. 15:47).

Jesus is the replacement Adam. He came to do what the first man Adam failed to do, i.e., be obedient to God in the covenant of works. He was conceived by the power of the Holy Spirit in the womb of Mary (Matthew 1:20 & Luke 1:35). And just as the LORD God used the dust of the ground to form the first man, so He used Mary's substance to form the last Man. "But when the set time had fully come, God sent His Son, born of a woman, born under the law" (Gal. 4:4).

And, just as Adam the son of God was made in the image and likeness of God, so "The Son is the radiance of God's glory and the exact representation of His being" (Heb. 1:3a). Jesus had God's law written on His heart and had the power to fulfill it. He came to do what Adam didn't do. "Then I said, 'Here I am – it is written about Me in the scroll – I have come to do Your will, My God'" (Heb. 10:7). Thus Jesus.

Here's the other thing. God is the Creator. Adam is a creature. We must always maintain the

Creator/creature distinction. Christ as God took upon Himself a human nature. Jesus was like us in every way apart from sin (Heb. 4:15). Jesus, like Adam, had a body, a soul, and a human spirit. In the Garden of Gethsemane He said, "My soul is overwhelmed with sorrow to the point of death" (Matt. 26:38). On the cross, "Father, into Your hands I commit My spirit" (Luke 23:46). His body was laid in a tomb (Matt. 27:59). Like Adam, like Jesus, every human being is a soul-spirit with a body.

We must maintain the Creator/creature distinction with the two natures of Christ. Jesus has the Creator or Divine nature, and He has a human nature. Don't confuse His two natures. He is one Divine Person with two natures forever. Being the God-Man, the Messiah-Man had a great knowledge of God. And He was holy and righteous. What do we mean by knowledge of God, holiness, and righteousness? It has to do with the Creator/creature distinction.

Only man is the image of God, not angels or birds or fish or animals. Knowledge of God is inherent in man, for only man has God's law written on his heart. Holiness has to do with being set apart. The Creator transcends the creature. Man transcends, i.e., is set apart from, all other creatures. And righteousness has to do with being moral, i.e., keeping God's law written on your heart.

And, unlike Adam, Jesus was obedient to God's law. "For just as through the disobedience of the one man the many were made sinners, so also through the obedience of the one man the many will be made righteous" (Rom. 5:19). "And being found in appearance as a man, He humbled Himself by becoming obedient to death—even death on a cross!" (Phil. 2:8).

We mentioned the following verse in reference to the first Adam taking his first breath. Now we mention it in reference to the second Adam taking His last breath, "In His hand is the life of every creature and the breath of all mankind" (Job 12:10). While on the cross, and just after saying to the repentant thief, "Today you shall be with Me in Paradise", "Jesus called out with a loud voice, 'Father, into Your hands I commit My spirit.' When He had said this, He breathed His last" (Luke 23:46).

And what about His resurrection? "At the place where Jesus was crucified, there was a garden, and in the garden a new tomb, in which no one had ever been laid" (John 19:41). Adam was placed in a garden. And here's the body of the last Adam being placed (in a tomb) in a garden but needing the Breath of God to breathe on Him, into His nostrils to bring Him to life. The LORD God, i.e., *Jehovah-Elohim*, the middle Person in the Godhead, wanted His uncorrupted body back.

What was Adam when God formed Him? Adam was a gardener. And the second Adam after He was resurrected? Mary Magdalene saw Him standing there. "He asked her, 'Woman, why are you crying? Who is it you are looking for?' Thinking He was the gardener, she said, 'Sir, if You have carried Him away, tell me where You have put Him, and I will get Him" (John 20:15).

Jesus was in a garden, and He was thought to be the gardener. The first man Adam and the second Adam have a lot in common.

Conclusion

When we read the words, "Then the LORD God formed a man from the dust of the ground and breathed into his nostrils the breath of life, and the man became a living being" (Gen. 2:7), we should think of Jesus. Why? Because we've seen that Jesus is the new man. When the LORD God formed Adam, He had the Man Jesus in mind. That's why you see all the connecting parallels between the two.

If you want to know what Adam, the son of God, was like before he fell, then look to Jesus. Adam wakes anew in Jesus.

COVENANT & ADAM *(Adam Works)*

Introduction

Having seen that the covenant of works included an outward command, plus the Decalogue written on humanity's heart, plus the cultural mandate, and that the first man, was our covenant head in the covenant of works, and that the first Adam was a type of the last Adam, we are now ready to focus our attention what on what Adam was commissioned by God to do.

"The LORD God took the man and put him in the Garden of Eden to work it and take care of it" (Gen. 2:15).

Do you remember your very first job? Your first paying job? I used to deliver newspapers. And I used to deliver milk to doorsteps. However, I did these things when I was still at school. What was your first real job? Mine was when I began an apprenticeship in a Glasgow shipyard. That was my first real job. I had to agree to certain conditions before I could serve that four-year apprenticeship. If I broke any of those conditions of employment, my career was over. Therefore, essentially, I was on probation until I passed the final exam.

What we're looking at in the following is Adam's first job. And it was a real job with wages and everything.

Working Conditions

Adam was to work and take care of God's Garden of Eden. Or as the ye olde KJV puts it, Adam was to dress it and keep it. Or, as the ESV puts it,

Adam was to work it and keep it. And, just for good measure, the NKJV says that Adam was to tend it and keep it. When you look up the words in the original Hebrew here (הָרְמָשֹׁלוּ דְבָעֹל), you could also say it like this: God gave Adam the job of cultivating and guarding His garden. And isn't that what gardeners do? They foster, nourish, and encourage things to grow while they guard, protect, and police the garden against all kinds of marauders, be they fungal mildew blight, devouring insects, birds, animals, reptiles, yeah, including talking snakes!

God gave Adam one job. He had one job to do. He was to take care of God's special garden. And how hard would that be? God had already created everything and had declared it all to be "very good" in Genesis 1:31.

It's not like Adam had to work hard clearing thorns and thistles from fields so that he could plant and grow some potatoes or corn or wheat or whatever. No! God had taken him and had placed him in the beautiful garden that God had planted eastward in a place called Eden. This garden is also called Paradise. So, how hard would this job be, the first job, the first real job, the first paying job in the entire universe since God has created it?

You'd have to agree that the working conditions were like the garden itself, very good. And a little later God even gave Adam a helper, a suitable or comparable helper (Gen. 2:18).

Adam could have tea or coffee breaks, "smoko", whenever he wanted. He wouldn't even have to pack a lunch and commute by train to work like I had to do as a sixteen-year-old. Actually, it was my mum, bless her, that made my lunch for me. Scrambled egg on bread that I used to toast in the shipyard's canteen. But I digress!

Adam was right at his place of employment. He didn't need to walk, drive, or ride his bicycle in the rain or take a train. He didn't have to worry about forgetting his lunch or leaving it on the train. For he was working for a great boss – God Himself!

Did the LORD God give Adam any time off? Which of the Ten Commandments gives instruction about work? The 4th Commandment?

> Remember the Sabbath day by keeping it holy. Six days you shall labour and do all your work, but the seventh day is a sabbath to the LORD your God. On it you shall not do any work, neither you, nor your son or daughter, nor your male or female servant, nor your animals, nor any foreigner residing in your towns. For in six days the LORD made the heavens and the earth, the sea, and all that is in them, but he rested on the seventh day. Therefore the LORD blessed the Sabbath day and made it holy" (Exod. 20:8-11).

Of course, before the fall of humanity in Adam, the 4th Commandment as written by God on Adam's heart would have read something like, "Worship God as He will be worshipped." But the principle remains the same.

We see at the beginning of Genesis 2 the words, "Thus the heavens and the earth were completed in all their vast array. By the seventh day

God had finished the work he had been doing; so on the seventh day he rested from all his work. Then God blessed the seventh day and made it holy, because on it he rested from all the work of creating that he had done."

Thus, though it's harder to see after and because of the fall, we see that the 4th Commandment is creational. It is embedded in creation. And, Adam, being part of God's creation, and having been made in God's image and likeness, would have known that he was to work six days for God and rest with God one day out of every seven.

On what day was Adam created? The sixth? And at what time on the sixth day? It was after God had made all the livestock, the creatures that move along the ground, and the wild animals. Therefore, though Adam was created on the sixth day, what was he to do when he got out of bed the next morning? Was he to work or was he to rest? Well, it was God's Sabbath. Therefore, Adam began his employment, his first job, by having the day off.

Could it get any easier for the very first man? God gives him a cushy job looking after His perfect garden, and He gives him a day of rest beforehand!

So, Adam was to rest one day in every seven. And on the day of rest, he was to worship God as He will be worshipped. Adam was to break up each week into six days working for God and one day resting with God. Those were the conditions of employment, and the working conditions were great too.

Adam knew how to operate in God's garden because God had already written His Ten Commandments, including the fourth, inwardly on

Adam's heart when He had created him in His image. But there was an outward condition, or test. "And the LORD God commanded the man, 'You are free to eat from any tree in the garden; but you must not eat from the tree of the knowledge of good and evil, for when you eat from it you will certainly die'" (Gen. 2:16-17).

So, there you have it. Adam could pick and eat the fruit of every tree in the garden and have it for lunch. The only exception was the fruit of one tree, a tree called the knowledge of good and evil. Excellent working conditions!

And, you know what it's like sometimes when you're planning on doing work in your garden at home if you've got one. Sometimes you can't work in the garden because it's pouring rain. Mind you, it always seemed to be pouring of rain in Scotland where I grew up. Outside-workers, such as bricklayers, would be, what they called, "rained off".

However, Adam would never get "rained off" where he worked. For it says in Genesis 2:5 that the LORD God had "not sent rain on the earth", but that "streams came up from the earth and watered the whole surface of the ground" (Gen. 2:6).

Other versions refer to the streams as a mist, vapour, a fog. Isn't that what happens some mornings? The grass is wet even though it hasn't rained. How is that? Well, we say that the grass is wet due to dew, wet with dew.

But, whether it's springs of water bubbling up from the ground or a good scotch mist, Adam would never get "rained off" and sent home. His home was in the garden, and his working conditions were perfect. No sweat! He was to work it and take care of it. One job! That's all Adam was asked to do: one job!

Wage Conditions

Adam was to labour in the garden. God had laid everything on for him. He had graciously given Adam an apprenticeship by graciously entering into a reciprocal agreement with him. Adam did not disagree or complain to God when God gave him the gardener's job.

And what does the Bible say about the labourer? "The worker deserves his wages" (Luke 10:7 NIV). And what were the wage conditions? "You are free to eat from any tree in the garden; but you must not eat from the tree of the knowledge of good and evil, for when you eat from it you will certainly die."

So, Adam would continue to live, as in not die, and he could continue to work in the garden for as long as he was obedient to God. But if he disobeyed God, i.e., if he sinned against God, what would happen? What does the Bible say? "The wages of sin is death" (Rom. 6:23a).

When Adam, was working in the garden by taking care of it for God, when he was cultivating and guarding it, as per the agreement, he was on probation. Wait! I hear you say, What agreement? And what's this probation he keeps on talking about? Well, I'm glad you asked!

When God made Adam from the dust of the ground He created him with a knowledge of God, he was created as holy and righteous. The knowledge of

God that Adam had upon his creation was summarised in the moral law that God had already written on his heart. i.e., the Ten Commandments, albeit in positive form.

God created man upright (Eccl. 7:29) and with a conscience that would either accuse or excuse him for his thoughts, words, and actions (Rom. 2:15). Therefore, God created Adam as His own image and likeness. God has knowledge of God, is holy and is righteous. Same for Adam. Therefore, when God commanded Adam that he was free to eat of every tree in the garden bar one, He was entering into a contract, a conditional agreement, with Adam. We'll call this conditional agreement a covenant, a covenant in this case (as we have already established) being a conditional promise.

Now, you should know that some Christians don't like to call the pre-fall arrangement between God and Adam a covenant. Their reasoning is usually because the word covenant is not used in the Bible until Genesis 6:18 where God said to Noah, "But I will establish My covenant with you…" But denying the covenant between God and Adam because the word is not used is like denying that Noah was married to his wife because the word marry is not used until Genesis 19:14! But we're told in Matthew by Jesus that, "As it was in the days of Noah, so it will be at the coming of the Son of Man. For in the days before the flood, people were eating and drinking, marrying and giving in marriage, up to the day Noah entered the ark."

And where would we be with the triune God if we had to find a verse that calls God the Trinity?

There is no specific verse, but we can see clearly from the whole of Scripture that the Godhead is Father, Son, and Holy Spirit, the Trinity. But there is a verse specifically referring to Adam and God's covenant with him in Hosea 6:7. Most Bible versions (e.g., NLT, ESV, Berean Study Bible, NASB, CSB, Holman, ASV, Douay Rheims Bible, ERV, ISV, Literal Standard Version, New Heart English Bible, World English Bible, Young's Literal Translation, Amplified Bible, etc.), say, "Like Adam they have transgressed the covenant." But some versions say, "at Adam" instead of "like Adam".

The well-known Bible commentator Matthew Henry (1662-1714), commenting on Hosea 6:7 says,

> As Adam broke the covenant of God in paradise, so Israel had broken his national covenant, notwithstanding all the favours they received.[69]

That a pre-fall covenant between God and Adam is no novel or minority theological view, Roland S. Ward points us to John Owen,

> The master English theologian John Owen (1616-83) notes in the first of his volumes on Hebrews published in 1668: "That God created man in and under the terms and law of a covenant, with a prescription of duties and promise of reward, is by all acknowledged."[70]

---

[69] Matthew Henry, *Matthew Henry's Commentary on the Whole Bible: Complete and Unabridged in One Volume*, Peabody, Hendrickson, 1994, 1477.

Anyway, God's pre-fall agreement with Adam is what many theologians, including the Westminster Confession of Faith, call the covenant of works. And that is why we are looking at Adam's working, wage, and warranty conditions.

So, what have we got? If Adam would keep the conditions of this agreement that God had so graciously condescended to enter into with him, then he at the end of an unspecified period of time, i.e., after he has completed his probation, his apprenticeship, God would award him with his promised, as part of the agreement, "journeyman's papers". When Adam had finished serving his apprenticeship God would have declared that Adam was a fully-fledged tradesman.

My family and I moved to Australia from Canada in 1990. Australia was looking for plumbers. Beginning as a sixteen-year-old, I had served a four-year plumbing apprenticeship in Scotland. When I had finished that, I decided to move back to Canada, the place of my birth, to work as a journeyman plumber.

The Australian government accepted my application. So, it was to Australia's sunny shores that I was inclined to roam. I had a UK and a Canadian plumbing licence. But the Australian government required me to do three-months on probation by working for a plumbing company before they would issue me with a plumbing licence. I couldn't get a job

---

[70] Roland S, Ward, *God and Adam Reformed Theology and the Creation Covenant*, Tulip Publishing, Lansvale, NSW, 2019, 105.

because I didn't have a licence and I couldn't get a licence because I didn't have a job! So I became a Presbyterian minister instead!

So, Adam is on probation. Yes! But where's the promise of this gracious award of God to Adam, you know, his journeyman's papers, his tradesman licence, upon completion of his apprenticeship? Well, it's in the words "for when you eat from it you will certainly die" (Gen. 2:17b). It's the promise that runs all through the Bible: Do this and live! Do that and die! Adam, obey God and you'll live. Disobey God and you'll die.

Adam was threatened with death for disobedience to the conditions of his probationary employment in the garden. And, conversely, on the flipside, he had been promised life, even everlasting life. Yes, Adam was someone who had an inbuilt knowledge of God, and he was holy and was righteous.

And importantly, had he successfully completed his apprenticeship as we're calling it by passing the final exam, i.e., not eating of the forbidden fruit of the tree of the knowledge of good and evil for an unspecified time period, then God would have showered him with blessings. Unlosable everlasting life! Bliss! Heaven on earth! Wonderful wages (as symbolized by the promissory token of the Tree of Life).

How easy would it have been for Adam before the fall simply to delight himself in God and God's creation in God's beautiful garden? Adam, putter around in the garden, cultivate it and keep an eye out for anything that might damage any of it. Rake a few leaves. Easy! One job!

Excellent working conditions and excellent wage conditions. But enter, the dragon. Adam decided that he had a better offer. That he himself and not God could be the judge of right and wrong. That he could be his own boss. That no one could boss him around and tell him what to do.

Warranty Conditions

If you're well off enough to buy a new car or a TV or a toaster or whatever, you'll be familiar with what a warranty is. A warranty basically is a guarantee given by the manufacturer to the purchaser of an article, that promises to repair, replace, or refund, if necessary, but only within a specified period of time.

Here's Adam, the father of humanity. And who was Adam's manufacturer? God. And had God manufactured a product with a defect in it? No! God had created all things "very good", including Adam. Was God anywhere obliged in the pre-fall contract that He had entered into with Adam to fix him or even replace him should anything go wrong with him? No!

Did Adam even know there was a warranty? No! Did he know any of the conditions of the warranty? Again, no! So, when did Adam discover that God had guaranteed to repair and replace the defective and damaged Adam? It was only after Adam sinned.

Isn't God gracious? He was going to repair Adam even though Adam had completely gone against the Manufacturer's conditions of use. Like someone test-driving a new car by doing doughnuts and revving the living daylights out of the engine and driving it through flooded creeks and all the rest, so Adam had not followed the Manufacturer's clear instructions.

But God is gracious. He showed Adam (and Eve) the warranty that He had prepared before they sinned. When? When He covered their nakedness with animal skin before expelling them from the garden of Eden (Gen. 3:21.) Jesus is "the Lamb slain from the foundation of the world" (Rev. 13:8.) Yes, Jesus is "the Lamb of God who takes away the sin of the world" (John 1:29). Jesus is the replacement Adam, the "second man" (1 Cor.15:47).

To be repaired, Adam and Eve and every other human being will need to be covered by and cleansed with His shed blood (1 John 1:7.) God clothing Adam and Eve with skin points directly to Christ's sacrifice on the cross. So, enter, the dragon-slayer, Jesus, the replacement Adam. Says Herman Bavinck,

> The difference between the covenant of works and grace is that God now approaches us not in Adam but in Christ, who fulfilled all the obedience required of Adam. Christ is the second and last Adam who restores what the first Adam had corrupted; he is the head of the new humanity.[71]

---

[71] Herman Bavinck, *Reformed Dogmatics: Sin and Salvation in Christ*, Vol. 3, Baker Academic, Grand Rapids, Michigan, 2006, 195.

Jesus was an apprentice. Then He became a tradesman, a qualified carpenter even. As an apprentice learning the trade from Joseph, His (supposed) father, Jesus was on probation. But He was also on probation as Adam's replacement. For, like Adam, He was also under the covenant of works. But, because the work He had to do was far greater than Adam's, He was promised a far greater reward for its completion. Says Thomas Watson, "How soon are we broken upon the soft pillow of ease? ... Adam in paradise was overcome, when Job on the dung-hill was a conqueror."[72]

How long was Jesus's probation? Well, we know it must have ended when He died on the cross aged thirty-three. And we know that His probation began when His ministry began, "Now Jesus himself was about thirty years old when he began his ministry" (Luke 3:23). Therefore, although Jesus had lived a sinless life up till then, His probation as the covenant representative or federal head of His people officially began when He was baptised by John to fulfill all righteousness, i.e., to keep the covenant of works. "Then Jesus came from Galilee to the Jordan to John, to be baptized by him. John would have prevented him, saying, 'I need to be baptized by you, and do you come to me?' But Jesus answered him, 'Let it be so now, for thus it is fitting for us to

---

72 Thomas Watson, *The Art of Divine Contentment: An Exposition of Philippians 4:11*, Free Presbyterian Publications, Glasgow, Scotland, (First published 1855, republished no date), 49-50. The Art of Divine Contentment: An Exposition of Philippians 4:11 (grace-ebooks.com)

fulfill all righteousness.' Then he consented" (Matt. 2:13-15).

So, the question that has been left dangling throughout the book so far is: How long would Adam have had to have kept the covenant of works before God would have granted him all the benefits that went with the unlosable everlasting life God had graciously promised him when He entered into the covenant of works with him? Would three years have covered it for the first Adam as it did for the last?

We would not wish to be guilty of speculating where Scripture seems to be silent. However, think of Adam in the garden. Think of Old Testament Israel after having crossed the River Jordan into the promised land whose very waters Jesus had been baptised with. Now consider the following. God told Israel, "When you come into the land and plant any kind of tree for food, then you shall regard its fruit as forbidden [Heb. *uncircumcised*]. Three years it shall be forbidden to you; it must not be eaten. And in the fourth year all its fruit shall be holy, an offering of praise to the Lord. But in the fifth year you may eat of its fruit, to increase its yield for you: I am the Lord your God" (Lev. 19:23-25).

Right, let's bring it all together. Don't say this out loud, but what happens when you're hammering in a nail, and you smack your thumb with the hammer instead? What would have happened if Jesus had cursed or blasphemed or physically sinned in any way? He would have, like Adam, transgressed the covenant.

And when did the last Adam Jesus's probation end? It ended on the cross when He said, "It is finished" (John 19:30).

Conclusion

We have seen that God graciously laid on everything for Adam when He entered into the covenant of works with him in the garden. Great working conditions, wages, and a hidden warranty. But what was it like for Adam's replacement? Nowhere to lay His head, being challenged and mocked at every turn by every liar, cheat, and even the devil himself. Then He was nailed to a cross and horribly crucified to death.

But what was the promised reward to Jesus for His perfect keeping of the covenant of works till the end of His probation? A bride and a beautiful place where He can live with her, i.e., an uncountable amount of people and Heaven on earth. (Psa. 2:8 and Rev. 7:9 with 21:2; Heb. 12:2-3).

So what does all of this mean for you and for me? Well, if you are one of those Christians that beat themselves for never being good enough, then remember that there were only two people that could ever have been good enough, that could have done enough good works to receive the gracious reward God promised, viz., Adam pre-fall and Jesus post-Fall. The rest of us are disqualified.

Remember that you are not the one on probation. You have already received everlasting life. You are a fully-fledged "tradey" or craftsman or craftswoman in Jesus. Your licence is the resurrected Jesus.

So, when we read the words of Genesis 2:15, "The LORD God took the man and put him in the Garden of Eden to work it and take care of it" we should think of Jesus. Why? Because we've seen that Jesus is the new Adam. When the LORD God put Adam in the garden to work it and take care of it, He had the Man Christ Jesus in mind.

Where was Jesus when He finished all His probationary work? "At the place where Jesus was crucified, there was a garden, and in the garden a new tomb, in which no one had ever been laid" (John 19:41). He went from probation to Paradise to receive from God the promised reward!

COVENANT & ADAM *(Adam Weds)*

Introduction

Having seen that the covenant of works included an outward command, the Decalogue, the cultural mandate, and that Adam was our covenant head, a type of the last Adam, and that Adam was on probation while he worked for God, we are now ready to look at marriage.

"Then the LORD God made a woman from the rib he had taken out of the man, and he brought her to the man" (Gen. 2:22).

Getting married is one of life's major events. For those of you who are or have been or want to get married, you'll know that it's important to find the right match. Me? I've been punching way above my weight for well over forty years now! Dorothy may or may not agree, but our marriage was, as they say, "a match made in heaven". Basically, my mother chose my wife for me. And how right she was!

Well, in the following we're going to look at a match made in Heaven.

The Match

So, the LORD God made a woman and brought her to the man. Where did He find this woman? Well, we're told that, just as the LORD God had made the man, then He also made the woman. However, things were a little different for the manufacture of the woman. The man had been made from the dust of ground (Gen. 2:7), and the woman from one of Adam's ribs (Gen. 2:21-22).

Do you remember Dolly the Scottish sheep? Actually, Dolly was a Finn-Dorset sheep, but it took place in Scotland back on 5th July 1996. Dolly was the first mammal ever to be cloned. She grew up and even had given birth to six lambs before dying on 14 February 2003. Why am I telling you this? Well, it's so you won't think it strange that God can take one of Adam's ribs and make a woman out of it.

So, this is a significant, intricate, and delicate piece of surgery that the LORD God performed on the man. God didn't just reach His hand into Adam's side and grab hold of one of his ribs. No! It says in Genesis 2:21-22a, "So the Lord God caused the man to fall into a deep sleep; and while he was sleeping, he took one of the man's ribs and then closed up the place with flesh. Then the Lord God made a woman from the rib he had taken out of the man."

If you've ever had major surgery, you'll know that there is an anaesthetist who puts you under before the surgeon operates on you. The LORD God put Adam under, and by "under" we mean something that more resembles death than ordinary sleep. But while Adam was under, He reached into his side and removed one of his ribs and stitched Adam up again. Therefore, the first man had a wound in his side.

We're not told what God did with Adam's rib, other than making the woman from it. Did God take the rib, replicate, and multiply its DNA and cells so that it became a clone of the first man? Well, there were certain differences between Adam and Eve. He was male and she was female. Or, to say it another way, he was a man, and she was a woman, i.e., a man with a womb, if you will, a womb-man.

The word for rib here is for a curved thing, a plank or a beam, something from a person's or animal's side. The same word is used in Daniel 7:5 and other places where it clearly means rib or ribs. The Hebrew word for womb is a different word. So, like my mother's lentil soup, we'll stick to ribs.

Now, unlike Adam who was formed from the dust of the ground, Eve was made into a woman. (The word here is more like "built", which is the same word for building the Temple). Can there be anything more beautiful to a Christian man than a woman built by God, made in Heaven?

"The Lord God said, 'It is not good for the man to be alone. I will make a helper suitable for him'" (Gen. 2:18). Other versions say comparable rather than suitable. Adam got to name all the livestock, birds, and wild animals, and not one was suitable for him, not even a chimpanzee. He didn't name a cayote Wily E. or call a parrot Polly or a sheep Dolly. By naming the animals is meant studying their essence and defining and cataloguing them.

So, how would it have looked to Adam when God brought to him the woman that He had specially built for him? "The man said, 'This is now bone of my bones and flesh of my flesh; she shall be called 'woman,' for she was taken out of man'" (Gen. 2:23). Adam knew exactly what the woman was. Not only did Adam get to name all the animals but he called his bride 'woman', and "He named his wife Eve, because she would become the mother of all the living" (Gen. 3:20). But, like the angels desiring to look into the things of God, so the man would want to explore the deep mysteries of his bride.

Theologians say that God is inscrutable, beyond "scrute", you know, enigmatic. Married men have been known to say the same thing about their own wives! In all seriousness, in any pre-marriage counselling I did, I would usually mention the title of a book I've never read and don't particularly recommend. Just to get the meaning of inscrutability across, I would say that men are from Mars and women are from Venus. That, of course, is not true, but it illustrates the fact that men and women are anatomically different, that they are constructed differently. In the beginning, one was formed from dust and the other built from a rib. This also leaves open all the other possible design differences between males and females that God intentionally built into men and women.

Now, just before we move on, let me mention what God commissioned Adam and Eve to do. Some call this commissioning the Creation Mandate or Dominion Mandate. Others, like me, prefer to call it the Cultural Mandate. It's found in Genesis 1:26-28,

> Then God said, "Let us make mankind in our image, in our likeness, so that they may rule over the fish in the sea and the birds in the sky, over the livestock and all the wild animals, and over all the creatures that move along the ground." So God created mankind in his own image, in the image of God he created them; male and female he created them. God blessed them and said to them, "Be fruitful

and increase in number; fill the earth and subdue it. Rule over the fish in the sea and the birds in the sky and over every living creature that moves on the ground.

Simply put, the cultural mandate means that Adam and Eve and posterity were to expand the borders of the garden of Eden throughout the whole world to the glory of God.

Let's sum up and move on by just saying that Adam met his true and perfect match when the LORD God brought the woman to the man. And let's note that Adam paid a price for his wife. It cost him a rib and he had the scar to prove it!

The Marriage

"Who gives this woman?" Again, "Then the LORD God made a woman from the rib he had taken out of the man, and he brought her to the man" (Gen. 2:22). So, the LORD God Himself brought the woman to the man. Therefore, Adam didn't meet Eve on some dating app or site or in a pub or out walking with the dog or in the frozen food section of the supermarket. No! The LORD God walked Eve down the aisle and gave her to the man to be his lawfully wedded wife, for him to keep, love, and cherish, to have and to hold from that day forward, for better, for worse, for richer, for poorer, in health and in sickness, for as long as they both shall live.

Who doesn't love a good wedding? I had the pleasure of walking my daughters down the aisle and giving them away, and then also conducting the wedding ceremony. And we see here, that not only was He the Father of the bride and gave her away, but the Lord was also the celebrant who conducted the marriage ceremony. The term "leave and cleave" comes from the marriage between Adam and Eve: "Therefore shall a man leave his father and his mother, and shall cleave unto his wife: and they shall be one flesh" (Gen. 2:24 KJV).

One time some Pharisees were harassing Jesus, asking dumb questions. "Haven't you read," he replied, "that at the beginning the Creator 'made them male and female,' and said, 'For this reason a man will leave his father and mother and be united to his wife, and the two will become one flesh'? So, they are no longer two, but one flesh. Therefore, what God has joined together, let no one separate" (Matt. 19:4-6).

To enter into marriage is to enter into a covenant. I like the way Charles Hodge describes a covenant as a promise suspended upon a condition.[73] Thus, a covenant is a conditional promise. The Reformed theologian O Palmer Robertson adds a bit more detail when he says that a covenant is a bond in blood sovereignly administered.[74]

Well, where's the bond in blood with Adam and Eve? Could it be when the LORD God pierced Adam's side? You would think that there would have to have been some blood involved in that. "Bone of my bone, flesh of my flesh." Perhaps, but what about the rest of us? Well, like Adam and Eve, when we get

[73] Charles Hodge, *Systematic Theology*, Eerdmans, Grand Rapids, Michigan, (1871-73), Reprinted 1981, Vol. 3, 549.
[74] O Palmer Robertson, *The Christ of the Covenants*, Presbyterian and Reformed Publishing, New Jersey, 1980, 4.

married, ordinarily we have what is called a honeymoon, you know, a trip to Niagara Falls, Las Vegas, "Bris Vegas" or wherever?

Now, there's a peculiar verse in Deuteronomy that illustrates what we're talking about here. "Her father will say to the elders, "I gave my daughter in marriage to this man, but he dislikes her. Now he has slandered her and said, 'I did not find your daughter to be a virgin.' But here is the proof of my daughter's virginity." Then her parents shall display the cloth before the elders of the town" (Deut. 22:17).

A bond in blood sovereignly administered, i.e., a covenant. Marriage, including the very first marriage, i.e., of Adam and Eve, testifies to this. It is sovereignly administered by swearing an oath to God, and a vow to each other that they are now one flesh.

Now, that is marriage. It is a covenant. And the condition of the promise is till death do us part. But what about divorce? Did Adam have any grounds to divorce his wife?

God's Ten Commandments are in the heart of humanity, i.e., on the heart of every individual including Adam and Eve (albeit in positive terms). What is the Commandment that specifically deals with marriage? The 7th Commandment? "You shall not commit adultery" (Exod. 20:14). In pre-fall positive terms the 7th Commandment would be something like, "Be pure and loyal."

Anyway, we should notice the word "adult" in adultery. Though it takes two adults to commit adultery, the word "adult" in adultery is actually from the French "ad", as "to", and "alterare", as in alter.

So, the English word "adultery" means "to alter", as in to adulterate, or apostatise. It is to break covenant.

So, what we have in the garden of Eden is Adam and Eve in the covenant of marriage. And prior to that, we have Adam as the representative or federal head of humanity in the covenant of works with God. Both covenants, i.e., marriage and works, are conditional promises. However, they are also bonds in blood sovereignly administered.

What should Adam have done when he discovered that Eve had been talking with the subtle serpent? What should he have done when she offered him the forbidden fruit to eat? Divorce is no small thing. But the Westminster Confession of Faith in 24:6 says that "Nothing but adultery, or such wilful desertion as can no way be remedied by the church or civil magistrate, is cause sufficient of dissolving the bond of marriage…"

Did Adam have grounds to divorce Eve when the Devil deceived her, and she began to alter her covenant of marriage by listening to the Devil and then encouraging Adam to eat the fruit of the tree of the knowledge of good and evil by handing it to him?

Adam could've called on the Lord. "Lord! The woman that You gave to be with me has been obeying someone other than You through me as her husband, and now she wants me to eat the forbidden fruit! Help! Please fix her or let me divorce her and get a new wife!"

But no! Adam went along with Eve and the serpent Satan against God. So, Adam, as the head of humanity, broke the covenant with God. Adam was on probation, remember? He, and mankind, was engaged, betrothed to God, and upon completion of his probation, humanity would have been fully wed to Him. Do you remember when Joseph wanted to divorce Mary when they were engaged, i.e., before they were formally married? (Matt. 1:19).

Does this give God grounds for divorcing humanity? Well, that's what the gospel, the Good News, is all about. It is about reconciliation. Humanity is separated from God because of our adultery or apostasy to the covenant. Thus, all human beings are what the KJV in Romans 1:31 calls "covenantbreakers", having "no fidelity" NIV or "faithless" ESV or "untrustworthy" NKJV. But "covenantbreakers" is the word of the day, as it sums up why the world is in the mess it's in. (Gr. ἀσύνθετος, asunthetos, covenantbreakers, 'treacherous to compacts').[75]

Adam and Eve, and humanity in them, are guilty of committing spiritual adultery. Spiritual adultery is the breaking of the 1st and 2nd Commandments by rejecting God and thus forming other gods in His stead (Exod. 20:3-4). Therefore, spiritual adultery is idolatry. God's Old Covenant or Old Testament people, i.e., the Israelites, illustrate this: "For your Maker is your husband, The Lord of hosts is His name; And your Redeemer is the Holy One of Israel; He is called the God of the whole earth" (Isa. 54:5). "'Surely, as a wife treacherously departs from her husband, So have you dealt treacherously with Me, O house of Israel,' says

---

[75] James Strong, *The New Strong's Exhaustive Concordance of the Bible*, Thomas Nelson Publishers, Nashville, Tennessee, 1984.

the Lord" (Jer. 3:20). "You also took the fine jewelry I gave you, the jewelry made of My gold and silver, and you made for yourself male idols and engaged in prostitution with them" (Ezek. 16:17).

So, just before we move on, again, Westminster Confession of Faith in 24:6 says that "Nothing but adultery, or such wilful desertion as can no way be remedied by the church or civil magistrate, is cause sufficient of dissolving the bond of marriage…"

Now, as you know, church officers and civil or governing officers are ordained by God (1 Cor. 12:28; Rom. 13:1). They are God's ministers on earth. However, for humanity as a whole and as represented by Adam, God Himself is the "Officer" who can be called upon to help to remedy the problem in the relationship between the two parties, i.e., God and all humanity.

Enter Jesus, God's Anointed, the Christ, God's chosen Messiah.

The Messiah

Adam and Eve, indeed every man and woman getting married, are a signpost that points to Jesus and the bride His Father promised Him in eternity past. As we've seen in Part 1 of this book, we call this eternal covenant promise the covenant of redemption. Thus the "bond in blood sovereignly administered" applies to the Messiah, i.e., the new Adam and His bride. For He is "the Lamb slain from the foundation of the world" (Rev. 13:8). (There's the bond in blood in the covenant of redemption!) Therefore, the outworking of the covenant of redemption in time was, first, the covenant of works before the fall, and then, the covenant of grace after the fall. The gospel is simply another name for the covenant of grace. Jesus, the new Adam, kept the covenant of works for all who believe – as the covenant of grace for all who believe.

Have you ever considered the fact that the gospel is about reconciling two warring parties? Sometimes when a husband and wife are having problems in their marriage, they seek marriage counselling. That's what we mean when we're talking about these things being "remedied by the church or civil magistrate". The church officer and civil magistrate are simply counsellors, in this particular case, marriage counsellors.

Isn't Handel's Messiah something totally brilliant? One of my favourites is "For Unto us a Child is Born" where Handel takes the words of Isaiah 9:6 and spectacularly sets them to music. "For unto us a child is born, unto us a son is given: and the government shall be upon his shoulder: and his name shall be called Wonderful, Counsellor, The mighty God, The everlasting Father, The Prince of Peace."

Counsellor? It means to advise, to deliberate, to resolve. Jesus is the Mediator, the go-between between God and humanity. He says, "No one comes to the Father except through Me" (John 14:6b.) Job says of God, "For He is not a man, as I am, that I may answer Him, and that we should go to court together. Nor is there any mediator between us, who may lay his hand on us both" (Job 9:32-33). Jesus Christ is that Mediator sent into the world by God to bring about the reconciliation. Jesus is the Arbitrator, the

Counsellor, appointed by God to settle the dispute. And Jesus being both God and man in one divine person forever, He is able lay one hand on God and the other on man.

The gospel is sometimes called the Gospel of Reconciliation, and for good reason. Listen to what the Lord's Apostle Paul says about Jesus and His gospel (underlining mine),

> For God was pleased to have all his fullness dwell in him, and through him to <u>reconcile</u> to himself all things, whether things on earth or things in heaven, by making peace through his blood, shed on the cross. Once you were alienated from God and were enemies in your minds because of your evil behaviour. But now he has <u>reconciled</u> you by Christ's physical body through death to present you holy in his sight, without blemish and free from accusation- if you continue in your faith, established and firm, and do not move from the hope held out in the gospel. This is the gospel that you heard and that has been proclaimed to every creature under heaven, and of which I, Paul, have become a servant (Col. 1:19-23).

What do we know so far? We know that the LORD God matched and married Adam and Eve and commissioned them to subdue the earth. We know that God entered into an agreement with Adam, what we call the covenant of works. And that God married Adam and Eve in the covenant of marriage.

We know that Adam broke God's works covenant. And we know that Adam and Eve broke their marriage covenant, breaking their oath to God and their vows to each other. Where does Jesus fit into all of this? Well, as the middle Person in the Trinity the pre-incarnate Christ, i.e., Christ before He became flesh in the womb of Mary, was the mediator between God and man. Therefore, it was He who walked in the garden in the cool of the day after Adam and Eve had sinned. Therefore, it was He who gave the first promise of the gospel by saying to the serpent, "I will put enmity between you and the woman, and between your offspring and hers; he will crush your head, and you will strike his heel" (Gen. 3:15). This is Messianic!

So, there is enmity between humanity and God. And there is also enmity, i.e., a war, between the serpent, his offspring and the woman, and her offspring. The woman is Eve. Her offspring is Jesus Christ, "But when the set time had fully come, God sent his Son, born of a woman, born under the law" (Gal. 4:4).

And the enmity between the seed of the serpent and the Seed of the woman would be what Jesus was talking about when He said to the Scribes and Pharisees, "You snakes! You brood of vipers! How will you escape being condemned to hell?" (Matt. 23:33).

We live in the period of reconciliation. "For God so loved the world that he gave his one and only Son, that whoever believes in him shall not perish but have eternal life" (John 3:16). Those who will not believe in Jesus to salvage their marriage contract with God are not the Son's bride, i.e., the church, and will be divorced from Him and will perish in Hell forever with the Serpent and his seed.

You need a wedding garment to attend Christ's wedding feast. You need to be clothed in His righteousness, cleansed by His blood. God clothing Adam and Eve with skin is a picture of this. Anyone without a wedding garment will be thrown "outside, into the darkness, where there will be weeping and gnashing of teeth" (Matt. 23:13). Divorced from God forever.

Conclusion

So, when we read the words, "Then the LORD God made a woman from the rib he had taken out of the man, and he brought her to the man" (Gen. 2:22), we should think of Jesus. Why? Because we've seen that Jesus is the new Adam. When the LORD God married Adam and Eve in the garden, He had the Man Christ Jesus and His bride in mind.

Do you remember the "leave and cleave" aspect of Adam and Eve's marriage in the garden? With that in mind, it is common to hear the following words of Jesus quoted at funerals, "Let not your heart be troubled: ye believe in God, believe also in me. In my Father's house are many mansions: if it were not so, I would have told you. I go to prepare a place for you. And if I go and prepare a place for you, I will come again, and receive you unto myself; that where I am, there ye may be also" (John 14:1-3 KJV). The Husband was going to prepare a home for His bride, then He will return for her.

Assuming that Joseph, Christ's adoptive father, had already died, the following verses spoken by Jesus while on the cross adds weight to this "leave and cleave" assumption, "Now there stood by the cross of Jesus His mother, and His mother's sister, Mary the wife of Clopas, and Mary Magdalene. When Jesus therefore saw His mother, and the disciple whom He loved standing by, He said to His mother, 'Woman, behold your son!' Then He said to the disciple, 'Behold your mother!' And from that hour that disciple took her to his own home" (John 19:25-27). Add it all together and we get, "Therefore shall a man leave his father and his mother, and shall cleave unto his wife: and they shall be one flesh" (Gen. 2:24 KJV). Thus, Jesus was leaving and cleaving.

How did Adam get his bride? From a wound in his side. Adam had a rib removed from his side while fully unconscious. Jesus had His side pierced on the cross while fully dead. The wound in His side was still open after He was resurrected from the dead. Therefore, the Lord God isn't finished building, i.e., preparing, Christ's bride. Jesus will return for His bride when He is finished preparing a place for her.

Jesus paid a price for His wife. It cost Him His life, and He has the scars to prove it!

COVENANT & ADULTERY

Introduction

Having seen that the covenant of works included an outward command, the Decalogue, the cultural mandate, Adam as our covenant head, a type of the last Adam, probation, and that God married Adam and Eve, we are now ready to look at adultery and divorce.

We've already asked the question: What should Adam have done when he discovered Eve wilfully neglecting him as her husband (and covenant head) by conspiring with the serpent? Did Adam have grounds for divorce when she offered him the forbidden fruit to eat? How ought Eve to have been punished? We'll speed ahead from the garden through time to see what the last Adam has to say about the subject of adultery and divorce.

We have already noted that Adam and Eve, and every man and woman getting married, are a signpost that points to Jesus and the bride His Father covenantally promised Him in eternity past. Just as earthly (Christian) marriage makes visible Christ's heavenly marriage, so divorce (with its ultimate penalty) visibilizes heavenly divorce and its consequences.

Did Jesus authoritatively proscribe the Bible's prescribed punishment for adultery (Lev. 20:10; Deut. 22:22) in the *Woman Caught in Adultery* passage (John 8:1-11) and thus effectively declare adultery, i.e., the breaking of the 7th Commandment, no longer to be a serious sin and crime? Let us consider the passage so that we may properly evaluate if this is indeed the case.

The Details

At the time of Jesus, Israel was under Roman rule. Rome permitted Israel much freedom to practice her religion. However, there was a great deal of corruption among the different religious factions such as that between the Pharisees and the Sadducees. Both these factions, with the help of the Herodians, were out to destroy Jesus. Their method was to try to destroy Jesus by getting Him offside either with the Romans or the Israelites, or preferably both! One such incident where they tried to trick Jesus is usually referred to as *The Woman Caught in Adultery.*

If one keeps in mind what Jesus has already said to the people in His Sermon of the Mount, one will have a great deal of insight into what these men were up to. Jesus has already stated in His Sermon on the Mount,

> Do not think that I came to destroy the Law or the Prophets. I did not come to destroy but to fulfil. For assuredly, I say to you, till heaven and earth pass away, one jot or one tittle will by no means pass from the law till all is fulfilled. Whoever therefore breaks one of the least of these commandments, and teaches men so, shall be called least in the kingdom of heaven; but whoever does and teaches them, he shall be called great in the kingdom. For I say to you, that unless your righteousness exceeds the righteousness of the scribes and

Pharisees, you will by no means enter the kingdom of heaven (Matt. 5:17-20).

The Dilemma

John 8:2f. records the following about the woman caught in adultery, "Now early in the morning He came to the temple, and all the people came to Him; and He sat down and taught them. Then the scribes and the Pharisees brought to Him a woman caught in adultery."

The question was this: What would Jesus teach them about adultery? Would He teach in accordance with God's own Law-Word and get the Romans offside (perhaps by becoming an opposing authority to Caesar)? Or would He teach against His own Law-Word and thus contradict His Sermon on the Mount teaching about not coming to destroy the Law and the Prophets (i.e., Old Testament teaching)? His enemies thought that one way or the other He was sure to get either the Romans or the people, or both offside!

The scribes and Pharisees said to Him, "'Teacher, this woman was caught in adultery, in the very act. Now Moses, in the law, commanded us that such should be stoned. But what do You say?' This they said, testing Him, that they might have something of which to accuse Him. But Jesus stooped down and wrote on the ground with His finger, as though He did not hear" (John 8:4-6). Here John Calvin comments thus,

> For Christ rather intended, by doing nothing, to show how unworthy they were of being

175

heard; just as if any person, while another was speaking to him, were to draw lines on the wall, or to turn his back, or to show, by any other sign, that he was not attending to what was said.[76]

Now, much has been suggested as to what Jesus wrote on the ground, but we do not know because we are not told. However, one does not need to speculate. It is a fact that the One writing on the ground is the same One who delivered His Law-Word on Mount Sinai some 1500 years earlier, "And when He had made an end of speaking with him on Mount Sinai, He gave Moses two tablets of the Testimony, tablets of stone, written with the finger of God" (Exod. 31:18).

The allusion of Jehovah-Jesus's writing on the Temple's paving stones must not be overlooked. (And remember that Jesus cast out demons with the finger of God in Luke 11:20). Jim Dodson makes an interesting observation,

> Notice where Jesus was when they brought the woman caught. He was in the Temple. When He stooped down to write, it was not in dirt. It was in stone. The first time, they do not hear; the second time they do. In Adam we don't hear; in Christ we do. The second time, He is writing it upon their hearts and they get it and disperse. He is claiming His Divinity. He gave the law and He has the right to

---

[76] Calvin's Commentaries, John-Acts, Associated Publishers and Authors, Wilmington, Delaware, (no date), 734.

interpret it. And He does so according to its Spirit. That is why the second time it convicts them. He was writing the Ten Words.[77]

The 7th Commandment is, "You shall not commit adultery" (Exod. 20:14). Leviticus deals also with sins related to *this* commandment. It should be noted that sexual sins are there referred to as sins of "uncovering". E.g., "Also, you shall not approach a woman to uncover her nakedness as long as she is in her customary impurity. Moreover, you shall not lie carnally with your neighbour's wife, to defile yourself with her" (Lev. 18:19-20). Adultery is a sin against God's institution of marriage and therefore destroys the fundamental order of society. Therefore, adultery is a *criminal* act. It is a sin that is also a crime (regardless of whether civil law ignores such).

In Old Testament times the wife was "covered" by her husband's covenantal circumcision. She was in covenant with God through her husband. Hence adulterers, and adulteresses, because of the nature of the act, were left in no doubt whatsoever that they were breaking God's *covenantal* law. Therefore, there is a sense in which adultery is an "uncovering" of the grace of God's covenant and therefore needs to be properly repented of.

The Death-penalty
The death penalty for adultery is specified in Leviticus 20:10, "The man who commits adultery with another man's wife, he who commits adultery with his neighbour's wife, the adulterer and the

---

[77] James A Dodson in a private message to the author.

adulteress, shall surely be put to death." The penalty of stoning to death for sexual sins such as adultery is found in Deuteronomy 22:13ff. The death penalty was not to be inflicted if there was only one witness (Num. 35:30; Deut. 17:6). "The hands of the witnesses [plural] shall be the first against him to put him to death, and afterward the hand of all the people. So you shall put away the evil from among you" (Deut. 17:7).

Why did the scribes and the Pharisees bring *only* the woman to Jesus and not the man too? For Deuteronomy 22:22 says, "If a man is found lying with a woman married to a husband, then <u>both of them shall die</u> – the man that lay with the woman, and the woman; so shall you put away the evil from Israel." Clearly, the Pharisees were guilty of breaking their own law on this point. Thus, they were not fit or competent witnesses. Jesus had them on this. They did not have Jesus!

"So they continued asking Him, He raised Himself up and said to them, 'He who is without sin among you, let him throw a stone at her first.' And again, He stooped down and wrote on the ground" (John 8:7-8). Jesus refused to involve Himself in their evil.

Notice what happened next, keeping in mind what the Holy Spirit would soon thereafter be coming to do in the world, i.e., He was coming to convict the world of "sin," "righteousness," and "judgment" (John 16:8-11 cited in full above). "Then those who heard it, being convicted in their conscience, went out one by one, beginning with the oldest even to the last. And Jesus was left alone, and the woman standing in the midst" (John 8:9). Christ had summoned these accusers to the judgment-seat of God, just as His Spirit, even the Holy Spirit was coming to do in the world at large.

Remember what has been said about the scribes and the Pharisees in John 8:6, "This they said, testing Him, that they might have something of which to accuse Him." To them, the woman caught in adultery was only the means towards an end. It was Jesus they wanted to be put to death, not the woman. Hypocrites! Indeed, at the end of this same chapter, it says, "Then they took up stones to throw at Him; but Jesus hid Himself and went out of the Temple, going through the midst of them" (John 8:59). On John 8:11, Calvin comments,

> They who infer from this that adultery ought not to be punished with death, must, for the same reason, admit that inheritances ought not to be divided, because Christ refused to arbitrate in that matter between two brothers, (Luke 12:13). Indeed, there will be no crime whatever that shall not be exempted from the penalties of the law, if adultery be not punished; for then the door will be thrown open for any kind of treachery, and for poisoning, and murder, and robbery. Besides, the adulteress, when she bears an unlawful child, not only robs the name of the family, but violently takes away the right of inheritance from the lawful offspring, and conveys it to strangers. But what is worst of all, the wife not only dishonours the husband

to whom she had been united, but prostitutes herself to shameful wickedness, and likewise violates the sacred covenant of God, without which no holiness can continue to exist in the world.

Yet the Popish theology is, that in this passage Christ has brought to us the Law of grace, by which adulterers are freed from punishment. And though they endeavour, by every method, to efface from the minds of men the grace of God, such grace as is every where declared to us by the doctrine of the Gospel, yet in this passage alone they preach aloud the Law of grace. Why is this, but that they may pollute, with unbridled lust, almost every marriage-bed, and may escape unpunished? Truly, this is the fine fruit which we have reaped from the diabolical system of celibacy, that they who are not permitted to marry a lawful wife can commit fornication without restraint. But let us remember that, while Christ forgives the sins of men, he does not overturn political order, or reverse the sentences and punishments appointed by the laws.[78]

At the conclusion of the *Woman Caught in Adultery* incident, Jesus said, "'Woman, where are those accusers of yours? Has no one condemned you?' She said, 'No one, Lord.' And Jesus said to her, 'Neither do I condemn you; go and sin no more'" (John 8:10b-11). Not even one accuser remained.

---

[78] Calvin's Commentaries, John-Acts, Associated Publishers and Authors, Wilmington, Delaware, (no date), 735-736.

Yes, we see grace here. Of course, we do! But there already was grace even in the Old Testament when David was not stoned for his adulterous affair with Bathsheba or the murder of her husband, Uriah. Therefore, keep in mind that, though the death penalty is the *maximum* penalty on the books, there may at times be mitigating circumstances as to why the full penalty of the law ought not to be administered. Rowland Ward provides a cautious reminder where he says,

> It should be noted that the Noahic provisions of Genesis 9:6, which include the death penalty for murder, belong to the race as a whole and predate the existence of Israel. It is here and not in the Mosaic legislation that the foundation for capital punishment should be founded, and the tendency to extend such a punishment to a multitude of lesser crimes should be resisted.[79]

Again, keep in mind that the death penalty was not to be inflicted if there was *only one* witness (Num. 35:30; Deut. 17:6).

The Determination
What can we learn from the *Woman Caught in Adultery* passage?

---

[79] Rowland S. Ward, *The Westminster Confession of Faith for the Church Today*, Presbyterian Church of Eastern Australia in Melbourne, 1992, 131.

1. That Jesus in this passage did not change one jot or tittle of the Law and the Prophets (Matt. 5:17-18). There was no charge made against the adulterous woman in Civil or Judicial Law for which she needs to defend herself. There was no one accusing her of any crime (i.e., criminal act). Therefore, she was free from any civil judgment or condemnation. Neither did Jesus condemn her, "For God did not send His Son into the world to condemn the world, but that the world through Him might be saved" (John 3:17).
2. That Jesus left open the door for God's forgiveness upon the condition of the woman's repentance when He said to her, "go and sin no more." Therefore, even those deserving of the death penalty (such as murderers and adulterers) shall receive forgiveness upon repentance from their sins. King David committed adultery with Bathsheba and murdered her husband by a fiendish plan, but truly repented.
3. That by His Spirit God judges the heart. "Marriage is honourable among all, and the bed undefiled; but fornicators and adulterers God will judge" (Heb. 14:4). The consciences of the accusers of the woman caught in adultery were convicted. Therefore, whether written on tablets of stone or written on a man's heart, God's Moral Law is the rule and therefore the authority to judge.
4. That the Judicial or Civil Law of God actually saved this woman's life! Jesus exposed the sin

of the woman's accusers by reminding them of the proper procedure for prosecution. "He who is without sin among you, let him throw a stone at her first" (John 8:11b).

5. That there could be no Judicial Law if everyone had to be sinless *by nature.* Therefore, criminal accusers must not be guilty of the same crime as the accused or guilty of falsifying or giving misleading evidence anywhere along the judicial process.

6. That accusers are to be involved in the accused's execution ("let him throw a stone at her first"). Therefore, accusers themselves must not be guilty of murdering the innocent through false and/or malevolent accusation, lest they themselves face the death-penalty.

7. That ulterior motives (i.e., sins of the heart) are judged by God.

The Declaration

It cannot be demonstrated from *The Woman Caught in Adultery* passage that Jesus forbids the death penalty for those lawfully convicted of adultery. However, it does demonstrate that due process and natural justice must prevail.

It is interesting to note what the Westminster Confession of Faith chapter 24:5 says on Marriage and Divorce, though not directly stating it, it does seem to leave the death penalty for adultery intact,

Adultery and fornication committed after a contract, being detected before marriage, giveth just occasion to the innocent party to sue out a divorce, and, after the divorce, to marry another, as if the offending party were dead.

However, with that being said, on the difficult and emotive subject of Capital Punishment, we believe RC Sproul is on the right track where he writes,

> The only sin in the New Testament requiring the death penalty is arguably first-degree murder, whereas the capital offenses in the Old Testament – children being unruly and disobedient to parents, homosexual activity, adultery, and public blasphemy – do not seem to be capital offenses any longer.[80]

The difference between the Old Testament and the New Testament is that the Israel as a body politic as established by God no longer exists. The Westminster Confession of Faith 19:4 states,

> To them also, as a body politic, He gave sundry judicial laws, which expired together with the State of that people, not obliging any other, now, further than the general equity thereof may require.

Israel's capital offenses were related to the Mosaic administration of the covenant of grace,

---

[80] RC Sproul, *Truths We Confess: A Layman's Guide to the Westminster Confession of Faith*, Volume 1, P&R Publishing, Phillipsburgh, New Jersey, 2006, 215.

which ended with the death and resurrection of Christ and the demolition of the Temple in 70 AD. However, the death penalty for murder predates the Mosaic period, (see Genesis 9). D. James Kennedy and Jerry Newcombe in *How Would Jesus Vote? A Christian Perspective on the Issues,* wrote,

> How would Jesus want us to vote on the matter of capital punishment? Opponents of capital punishment want us to believe that He would have us oppose the death penalty under any circumstances. And sometimes they aim their arguments at our emotions rather than our minds. However, I believe the Bible teaches us that that there is a place for capital punishment. Of course, there should be every possible safeguard in the exercise of capital punishment in order to protect the falsely accused from being put to death. Rather than the death penalty denying man's dignity, it upholds it.[81]

Conclusion

The authority of Jesus in *The Woman Caught in Adultery* passage is not in question. Rather, it is whether civil authorities today have Biblical authority to inflict capital punishment on adulterers that is in question. This remains open for robust discussion among Christians.

---

[81] Ron Gleason, *The Death Penalty on Trial, Taking a Life for a Life Taken,* Nordskog Publishing Inc., Ventura, California, Appendix, *A Christian Perspective on the Issues,* 2008, 112.

COVENANT CURSE

Introduction

Having seen that the covenant of works included an outward command, the Decalogue, the cultural mandate, Adam as covenant head, a type of Christ, and probation. And having considered Adam and Eve's marriage, and the temporal penalties for adultery, i.e., and divorce and even death, we are now ready to consider the penalty of death in terms of a covenant curse. What we're looking at in the following is what it means to be cursed by God in view of the covenant of works.

The Situation

Then the Lord God called to Adam and said to him, 'Where are you?' So he said, 'I heard Your voice in the garden, and I was afraid because I was naked; and I hid myself.' And He said, 'Who told you that you were naked? Have you eaten from the tree of which I commanded you that you should not eat?' Then the man said, 'The woman whom You gave to be with me, she gave me of the tree, and I ate.' And the Lord God said to the woman, 'What is this you have done?' The woman said, 'The serpent deceived me, and I ate' (Gen. 3:9-13).

We notice three obvious things that immediately happened after Adam had broken the covenant of works:

1. Adam had become self-conscious of his nakedness, even ashamed of it (Gen. 3:10).
2. Adam played the blame game, imputing his guilt to God and to the woman (Gen. 3:12).
3. Eve blamed the serpent for deceiving her into eating the forbidden fruit (Gen. 3:13).

Next, notice also that Adam had heard the Lord God's voice calling to him *before* he had run and hid from Him. The word "voice" here is the same Hebrew word as used a little later when the Lord God said to Adam, "Because you have heeded the voice of your wife, and have eaten from the tree..." (Gen. 3:17). Therefore, it was the voice of God that Adam had heard calling out to him. God had not forsaken him. However, God, before passing judgment on them, required an account from Adam for what he had done, and from Eve. However, unlike with Adam and Eve, God passed judgment on the serpent with no questions asked.

This being the penultimate chapter in our section as we work towards a climax on the covenant of works, it will be helpful for us to read the following chapter of the Confession as a brief general summary, but paying close attention to the final paragraph. Westminster Confession of Faith, chapter 6, Sections 1-6. *Of the Fall of Man, of Sin, and of the Punishment thereof*:

1. Our first parents, being seduced by the subtilty and temptations of Satan, sinned in eating the forbidden fruit. This their sin God was pleased, according to his wise and holy

counsel, to permit, having purposed to order it to his own glory.

2. By this sin they fell from their original righteousness and communion with God, and so became dead in sin, and wholly defiled in all the faculties and parts of soul and body.

3. They being the root of mankind, the guilt of this sin was imputed, and the same death in sin and corrupted nature conveyed to all their posterity, descending from them by original generation.

4. From this original corruption, whereby we are utterly indisposed, disabled, and made opposite to all good, and wholly inclined to all evil, do proceed all actual transgressions.

5. This corruption of nature, during this life, doth remain in those that are regenerated; and although it be through Christ pardoned and mortified, yet both itself, and all the motions thereof, are truly and properly sin.

6. Every sin, both original and actual, being a transgression of the righteous law of God, and contrary thereunto, doth, in its own nature, bring guilt upon the sinner, whereby he is bound over to the wrath of God, and curse of the law, and so made subject to death, with all miseries spiritual, temporal, and eternal.

Adam was promised eternal life pre-fall. Had he kept the covenant, God's justice would have obligated Him to give Adam his earned wages. However, Adam chose eternal death instead, through which all humanity became sinners, i.e., under God's curse. "For the wages of sin is death…" (Rom. 6:23a). Therefore, post-fall God's justice obligates Him to give all humanity the threatened eternal death. However, God is gracious as well as just. "But the gift of God is eternal life in Christ Jesus our Lord" (Rom. 6:23b). Whereas the first Adam earned us eternal death by failing to keep the covenant of works, the last Adam by perfectly keeping the covenant of works earned eternal life for those chosen by the Father and redeemed them by buying them back from God's justice.

If grace is the underserved blessing of God, then justice is His deserved curse. After the fall, covenant blessings and curses are grace and justice by other names. Whereas redemption is grace, condemnation is curse.

The Sinner

The tree of life and the tree of the knowledge of good and evil were in the midst of the garden (Gen. 2:9). As we already know, Adam could eat from any tree in the garden, including the tree of life, but chose death over life by eating the fruit of the tree God had forbidden him to eat. Thus, Adam and all humanity became sinners when Adam disobeyed God and ate. "Therefore, just as sin entered the world through one man, and death through sin, and in this way death came to all people, because all sinned" (Rom. 5:12). If all sinned when Adam sinned, then Adam was the covenant head of all.

It is important that we understand what sin is, and something of the depth of the sinfulness of sin. "Everyone who sins breaks the law; in fact, sin is lawlessness" (1 John 3:4). Therefore, when Adam sinned by breaking God's law, he (and all humanity with him) became lawless, i.e., not having the law. "For when Gentiles, who do not have the law, by nature do what the law requires, they are a law to themselves, even though they do not have the law. They show that the work of the law is written on their hearts, while their conscience also bears witness, and their conflicting thoughts accuse or even excuse them" (Rom. 2:14-15).

So, we see that Gentiles, who did not have the law (as it was delivered by God on Mount Sinai), may sometimes do what the law requires. How so? Because they have the *work of the law* on their hearts. This work of the law is what we are calling the "rule of righteousness." This is the same covenant of works that now condemns them as sinners. Again, Westminster Confession of Faith in Chapter 19:

5   God gave to Adam a law, as a covenant of works, by which he bound him and all his posterity to personal, entire, exact, and perpetual obedience; promised life upon the fulfilling, and threatened death upon the breach of it; and endued him with power and ability to keep it.

6   This law, after his Fall, continued to be a perfect rule of righteousness; and, as such, was delivered by God upon mount Sinai in ten commandments, and written in two tables; the first four commandments containing our duty toward God, and the other six our duty to man.

Notice that though the law as a covenant of works still stands, it was not delivered on Mount Sinai as a covenant of works but as "a rule of righteousness." (We'll cover this a bit more later.) Since the fall, no human being is able to personally, entirely, exactly, and perpetually be obedient to the covenant of works, which is "a perfect rule of righteousness," no one except the sinless Jesus Christ. John Calvin says,

> Now if the Gentiles have by nature God's righteousness imprinted on their minds, we cannot call them wholly blind in their understanding of how life is to be lived. People, to be sure, are generally aware that the natural law to which the apostle refers provides man with adequate guidance in the manner of right living. However, we must ask for what purpose the knowledge of the law was given to men. Only then may we judge how far it can take us toward the goal of reason and truth. This we may discover from what Paul says if we examine the course of his argument in the passage quoted [i.e., Rom. 2:14-15]. A little while before he had written that 'those who have sinned under the law will be judged by the law, and those who have sinned without the law will perish without the law' (Rom. 2:12). In case we think this last idea unreasonable – that poor, ignorant folk, deprived of the light of truth, should immediately perish – Paul adds that their conscience is able to serve them as law, and

therefore is enough rightly to condemn them. Thus the purpose of natural law is to make man inexcusable.[82]

With the above in mind, what non-Christian does not think that God will let people into Heaven because they are maybe not quite perfect but have been trying to be good? Even if they deny God or even worship or follow another god, their own consciences are reminding them to be good in line with the "rule of righteousness." For notice that is according to conscience, i.e., the work of the law, that either accuses or excuses our works of the law.

Therefore, the law that is spoken of here is the same moral law that God had already written on Adam's and humanity's hearts. It is the same moral law that was written on the tablets of stone and given to the Israelites in the wilderness, which is the same moral law that God writes anew on the hearts of His elect (Heb. 8:10), as per the covenant promise of Jeremiah 31:33, "But this *is* the covenant that I will make with the house of Israel after those days, says the LORD: I will put My law in their minds, and write it on their hearts; and I will be their God, and they shall be My people."

So, every sinner, whether Jew and Gentile, God, after He converts them, brings them into the house of Israel and writes His moral law anew and afresh on their hearts and teaches them to obey all that He, i.e., the covenant head of the house of Israel,

---

[82] John Calvin, *Institutes of the Christian Religion*, Translated from the first French edition of 1541 by Robert White, The Banner of Truth Trust, Edinburgh, U.K., reprinted 2017, 59-60.

the household of God (Rom. 11:11-27), has commanded (Matt. 28:20).

Thus, pre-fall, God's moral law was written on the hearts of humanity. Post-fall and pre-conversion only *the work of the law* remained on humanity's heart. Post-conversion the moral law is once more written on the renewed heart, with the Spirit enabling the Christian to keep it. Says Herman Witsius,

> It is moreover to be observed, that this law of nature is the same in substance with the decalogue; being what the apostle calls την εντολην την εις ζωην, "a commandment, which was ordained to life," Rom. 7:10; that is, that law, by the performance of which life was formerly obtainable. And, indeed, the decalogue contains such precepts, "which, if a man do, he shall live in them," Lev. 18:5. But those precepts are undoubtedly the law proposed to Adam, upon which the covenant of works was built. Add to this what the apostle says, that that law, which still continues to be the rule of our actions, and whose righteousness ought to be fulfilled in us, "was made weak through the flesh," that is, through sin, and that it was become impossible for it to bring us to life, Rom. 8:3, 4. The same law, therefore, was in force before the entrance of sin; and, if duly observed, had the power of giving life. Besides, God in the second creation inscribes the same law on the heart, which in the first

creation he had engraven on the soul. For what is regeneration, but the restitution of the same image of God, in which man was at first created? In fine, the law of nature could be nothing but a precept of conformity to God, and of perfect love, which is the same in the decalogue.[83]

It is because the "law of righteousness", as in nature's law or the law of nature, remains on the soul as the "work of the law" that fallen humanity remains condemned as sinners without excuse before God. "For the wrath of God is revealed from heaven against all ungodliness and unrighteousness of men, who by their unrighteousness suppress the truth. For what can be known about God is plain to them, because God has shown it to them. For his invisible attributes, namely, his eternal power and divine nature, have been clearly perceived, ever since the creation of the world, in the things that have been made. So they are without excuse. For although they knew God, they did not honour him as God or give thanks to him, but they became futile in their thinking, and their foolish hearts were darkened" (Gen. 1:18-21). Says John Calvin.

That there exists in the human minds and indeed by natural instinct, some sense of Deity [*sensus divinitatis*], we hold to be beyond dispute, since God himself, to prevent any

---

[83] Herman Witsius, *Economy of Covenants Between God and Man*, 2 Vols, Book I, Chapter I, VII, (First published 1677, reprinted 1822, Kindle version 2014), 59.

man from pretending ignorance, has endued all men with some idea of his Godhead, the memory of which he constantly renews and occasionally enlarges, that all to a man being aware that there is a God, and that he is their Maker, may be condemned by their own conscience when they neither worship him nor consecrate their lives to his service ... This is not a doctrine which is first learned at school, but one as to which every man is, from the womb, his own master; one which nature herself allows no individual to forget.[84]

Those ancient and somewhat corny Dracula films from the 60s and 70s used to terrify us when we were youngsters. If you watched them now, you'd just laugh at their antiquatedness, and their lack of decent special effects. Nevertheless, I remember that Dracula: Prince of Darkness was the name of one. Dracula dwelled in the shadows, always in the darkness. One of the curious things was that Dracula had no reflection in the mirror. Imagine wanting to brush your fanged teeth or comb your widow's peak hair without being able to see your face in the mirror. You'd cut yourself shaving! You'd be walking around with lots of little pieces of toilet-paper patching up bleeding nicks to your face.

Seriously, when God came to see His image in the garden, He was unable to see His reflection, because His little likeness was hiding his face from Him. Adam had God's character, His

---

[84] John Calvin, *Institutes of the Christian Religion*, Beveridge Edition, Book 1:3:1&3.

Commandments, stamped on him. Therefore, God's moral law is God's reflection. It reveals what God looks like. When we look at God's moral law, we see how distorted His image in us has become. There is nothing wrong with His law. It is we that are the problem. Like Bram Stoker's Dracula, "Everyone who does evil hates the light, and will not come into the light for fear that their deeds will be exposed" (John 3:20). Thus, the reason why Adam and humanity run and hide from the face of God. But God is merciful.

The proclamation and spread of the gospel throughout the nations is the Lord God doing what He did with Adam immediately after he had broken the everlasting covenant. The gospel call is God saying to humanity, "Where are you? Who told you that you were naked? Have you eaten from the tree of which I commanded you that you should not eat?"

So, the blame-game begins as man imputes his guilt to everyone and everything but himself. Some blame Adam, some blame God, and others the devil. But who blames themselves? Only those sinners who confess their sins and keep on forsaking them instead of trying to cover them. For these have been shown God's mercy.

The Serpent

What about those sinners who refuse till death to confess and forsake their sins and believe in the gospel? Westminster Larger Catechism,

> Q. 89. What shall be done to the wicked at the day of judgment?

A. At the day of judgment, the wicked shall be set on Christ's left hand, and, upon clear evidence, and full conviction of their own consciences, shall have the fearful but just sentence of condemnation pronounced against them; and thereupon shall be cast out from the favourable presence of God, and the glorious fellowship with Christ, his saints, and all his holy angels, into hell, to be punished with unspeakable torments, both of body and soul, with the devil and his angels forever.

Paul the apostle was concerned that Christians guard themselves against the serpent, "But I am afraid that as the serpent deceived Eve by his cunning, your thoughts will be led astray from a sincere and pure devotion to Christ" (1 Cor. 11:3). Notice who the serpent is: "And the great dragon was thrown down, that ancient serpent, who is called the devil and Satan, the deceiver of the whole world—he was thrown down to the earth, and his angels were thrown down with him" (Rev. 12:9). Notice the ultimate fate of the great deceiver, and the length of his torments, "The devil, who deceived them, was cast into the lake of fire and brimstone where the beast and the false prophet *are*. And they will be tormented day and night forever and ever" (Rev. 20:10). Notice who else joins the serpent in his everlasting torments, "And anyone not found written in the Book of Life was cast into the lake of fire" (Rev. 20:15). What will happen and when will this take place? "This will happen when the Lord Jesus is revealed from heaven in blazing fire with his powerful angels. He will punish those who do not know God and do not obey the gospel of our Lord Jesus. They will be punished with everlasting destruction and shut out from the presence of the Lord and from the glory of his might" (1 Thess. 1:7b-9).

Viewed in the light of hell and eternity, it would be hard to overstate the seriousness and sinfulness of sin. Therefore, Adam and Eve eating the forbidden fruit had eternal consequences because they had broken the eternal covenant. The covenant with its blessings and curses came from eternity past and it goes on for eternity.

On a lighter note, we mentioned vampires above, and where would a vampire be without a bat? The old saying, "blind as a bat" is technically incorrect. Bats' eyes are not much use to them when flying around in darkness, but that's what bats do. However, they use an inbuilt system of echolocation to pinpoint insects and avoid objects. When Adam and Eve listened to the serpent and thereby sinned, they died spiritually. Their sin made all humanity spiritually blind, with eyes that cannot see in spiritual darkness. "The god of this age has blinded the minds of unbelievers, so that they cannot see the light of the gospel that displays the glory of Christ, who is the image of God" (2 Cor. 4:4).

The world would be far more cruel and chaotic had not God by His common grace left fallen humanity with a conscience to help restrain sin. Though it can become more and more "seared" and thus desensitised (Eph. 4:9; 1 Tim. 4:2), or overly sensitive (Rom. 14:14; 1 Cor. 8:7), the conscience of the spiritually blind is as it were that echolocation device that warns of objects of sin and helps to avoid crashing into a total abandonment of all things evil prior to physical death.

We see Adam's "sin sonar device" kick into use where his own conscience warned him of danger right after he had sinned. This was illustrated by both his feeling of being naked, and his fleeing for cover to try to hide his sinfulness from God. What ought he have done? He ought to have confessed and forsaken his sins. For "He who covers his sins will not prosper, but whoever confesses and forsakes *them* will have mercy" (Prov. 28:13). Job makes reference to Adam, "If I have covered my transgressions as Adam, by hiding my iniquity in my bosom..." (Job 31:33). In this we see that Adam was the first to fear the wrath of God and to try to keep a lid on the truth of God, "For the wrath of God is revealed from heaven against all ungodliness and unrighteousness of men, who suppress the truth in unrighteousness" (Rom. 1:18).

The Puritan Richard Sibbes wrote in the 17th century, "The conscience is the soul reflecting upon itself."[85] Man mirrors God and the conscience mirrors man. These mirrors, of course, were buckled in the heat of the fall. However, just as man still is God's image (Gen. 9:6; James 3:9), so the conscience still reflects man as God created him (Rom. 1:19, 2:15). Let us again look at man imaging God in covenantal terms. Kenneth Gentry says,

---

[85] Richard Sibbes, *Commentary on 2 Corinthians Chapter 1*, *Works of Richard Sibbes*, Edinburgh, Banner of Truth, 1981 reprint, 3:208.

Furthermore, each party to the covenant was to have a copy of the covenant contract. That is why the covenantal Ten Commandments were on *two* tables of stone. Each stone held a complete copy of the Ten Commandments for each party, God and man.[86]

Adam pre-fall had a copy of the Ten Commandments on his heart as did the triune God who made him. Thus, two complete copies.

God and His law are still perfect, but even if fallen man were willing to be like God and perfectly obey His law, the weakness of the flesh would prevent it. As Jesus said to His disciples in the Garden of Gethsemane, "Watch and pray, lest you enter into temptation. The spirit indeed *is* willing, but the flesh *is* weak" (Matt. 26:41).

The subtle serpent tempted Eve to eat of the forbidden fruit through deception. "Now the serpent was more cunning than any beast of the field which the LORD God had made. And he said to the woman, "Has God indeed said, 'You shall not eat of every tree of the garden'?" And the woman said to the serpent, "We may eat the fruit of the trees of the garden; but of the fruit of the tree which *is* in the midst of the garden, God has said, 'You shall not eat it, nor shall you touch it, lest you die.'" Then the serpent said to the woman, "You will not surely die." (Gen. 3:1-4).

It's curious that Eve adds the words "nor shall you touch it" to the outward test God gave Adam. This suggests that Adam had passed onto Eve what

---

[86] Kenneth, L. Gentry, *The Greatness of the Great Commission*, Institute for Christian Economics, Tyler, Texas, 1993, 17.

God had said to him, "Of every tree in the garden you may freely eat, but of the tree of the knowledge of good and evil you shall not eat, for in the day you eat of it you shall surely die" (Gen. 2:16-17), telling Eve to not even touch the forbidden fruit. Anyway, the serpent lied to her when he said, "You will not surely die."

God said they would surely die, but the serpent said they would not surely die. God tested Adam, now Adam was testing God. He ate the fruit and died, proving God true and Satan a liar. But in what way did Adam and Eve die? First, they died spiritually, then physically, and, if not rescued by God, eternally, (none of which means soul-sleep or annihilation). Says R.C. Sproul,

> All people will have their bodies raised in the last judgment. The redeemed will have their bodies raised so that they may enjoy the glorious, honourable resurrection for all eternity. The bodies of the unjust will also be raised by Christ, but to dishonour. In recent decades annihilationism has gained some adherents within the evangelical world. The annihilation of the wicked has been the position of some sects and cults … According to the confession, Christ raises the bodies of the damned and preserves them to endure everlasting punishment. That is difficult to fathom or even to contemplate. One of the metaphors used in the New Testament is that hell is the place where the worm does not die. This suggests the possibility of a parasite that

lives off the flesh of another creature. If the flesh is completely consumed, the parasite dies. The ghastly image is that in hell the worm always has more flesh to eat. That means that the body of the damned has to be preserved by the power of God to endure the punishment that it is to receive ... Jesus talked more about hell than heaven. Almost everything we know about hell comes from the lips of Jesus.[87]

Conclusion

That Jesus does not believe in souls sleeping pre-resurrection of all the dead can be seen by what He said to the repentant thief on a cross next to His. "And Jesus said to him, "Assuredly, I say to you, today you will be with Me in Paradise" (Luke 23:43). About the resurrection He says, "Marvel not at this: for the hour is coming, in the which all that are in the graves shall hear his voice, and shall come forth; they that have done good, unto the resurrection of life; and they that have done evil, unto the resurrection of damnation" (John 5:28-29).

And that Jesus does not believe in post-resurrection annihilation can be seen by what He says about the final state of those who are resurrected unto damnation,

> If your hand causes you to sin, cut it off. It is better for you to enter into life maimed, rather

[87] RC Sproul, *Truths We Confess: A Layman's Guide to the Westminster Confession of Faith*, Volume 1, P&R Publishing, Phillipsburgh, New Jersey, 2006, 183-84.

than having two hands, to go to hell, into the fire that shall never be quenched—where 'Their worm does not die and the fire is not quenched.' And if your foot causes you to sin, cut it off. It is better for you to enter life lame, rather than having two feet, to be cast into hell, into the fire that shall never be quenched—where 'Their worm does not die and the fire is not quenched.' And if your eye causes you to sin, pluck it out. It is better for you to enter the kingdom of God with one eye, rather than having two eyes, to be cast into hell fire—where 'Their worm does not die and the fire is not quenched.' And if your hand causes you to sin, cut it off. It is better for you to enter life crippled than with two hands to go to hell, to the unquenchable fire. And if your foot causes you to sin, cut it off. It is better for you to enter life lame than with two feet to be thrown into hell. And if your eye causes you to sin, tear it out. It is better for you to enter the kingdom of God with one eye than with two eyes to be thrown into hell, 'where their worm does not die and the fire is not quenched' (Mark 9:43-48; cf., Isaiah 66:22-24).

Sometimes the word hell is used for Hades, the grave or place of departed souls. However, here, hell, as used by Mark, means *Gehenna* – "a valley of Jerusalem used figuratively as a name for the place (or state) of everlasting punishment: – hell"[88]

---

[88] James Strong, *The New Strong's Exhaustive Concordance of*

COVENANT DIVORCE

Introduction

Having seen that the temporal penalties for adultery (if there is no reconciliation) are divorce and perhaps death. And having seen that on judgment day the ancient serpent, who is called the devil and Satan, the deceiver of the whole world is to be cast into the lake of fire and brimstone where the beast and the false prophet *are*, to be tormented day and night forever and ever along with anyone not found written in the Book of Life, and having seen something of what it means to be cursed and forsaken by God, we are now ready to look at the Saviour in terms of covenant divorce.

The Saviour

Adam and Eve forsook God when they sinned against Him in the garden. They rejected God by breaking His covenant and instead bonding with Satan. God could have divorced them forever for their adulterous affair with idolatry. They were now in a spiritually dead state, meaning that their sin had separated them from the comfortable presence of God. However, it is worthy of notice that God didn't curse them but mitigated the curse by cursing the earth for their sake (Rom. 8:20-22). However, God cursed the serpent. And it was only subsequently that God cursed a human being, i.e., Cain, Adam and Eve's first child.

---

the Bible, Thomas Nelson Publishers, Nashville, Tennessee, 1984.

Eve is the "woman" being referred to and Christ our Saviour is the "Seed of the woman". However, it would seem that Adam and Eve were also of the Seed of the woman, while Cain their firstborn was of the seed of the serpent. "In this the children of God and the children of the devil are manifest: Whoever does not practice righteousness is not of God, nor *is* he who does not love his brother. For this is the message that you heard from the beginning, that we should love one another, not as Cain *who* was of the wicked one and murdered his brother. And why did he murder him? Because his works were evil and his brother's righteous. Do not marvel, my brethren, if the world hates you" (1 John 3:10-13).

So, like the devil, the children of the devil too are cursed. And regarding the cursed, our Saviour Jesus on judgment day, "Will also say to those on the left hand, 'Depart from Me, you cursed, into the everlasting fire prepared for the devil and his angels' … And these will go away into everlasting punishment, but the righteous to eternal life" (Matt. 25:41,46). This everlasting punishment is what John in the Book of Revelation calls the second death. "The one who conquers will have this heritage, and I will be his God and he will be my son. But as for the cowardly, the faithless, the detestable, as for murderers, the sexually immoral, sorcerers, idolaters, and all liars, their portion will be in the lake that burns with fire and sulphur, which is the second death" (Rev. 21:7-8).

The second death is speaking of already spiritually dead humanity entering into the eternal torments in hell. Therefore, the first death is to die physically. "And as it is appointed for men to die once, but after this the judgment" (Heb. 9:27). The Book of Revelation also speaks of a *first* resurrection. "Blessed and holy is the one who shares in the first resurrection! Over such the second death has no power" (Rev. 20:6a).

In the simplest of terms, the first resurrection is when, we who are spiritually dead, are made spiritually alive by the Spirit by being born again. As Jesus said to Nicodemus, "Do not marvel that I said to you, 'You must be born again'" (John 3:7). And as Paul says, "But because of his great love for us, God, who is rich in mercy, made us alive with Christ even when we were dead in transgressions—it is by grace you have been saved" (Eph. 2:5). So, those who have undergone the first resurrection have been saved from the second death. Says Nigel Lee,

> Note that the emphasis throughout is here on the salvation of the elect – rather than on the damnation of the wicked. The latter is, of course, the real alternative to the former. For death alias the grave, and even for Hell – all of their inhabitants will be destroyed (though never annihilated). "The death and the grave (and even Hell) were cast into the Lake of Fire. This is the second death. And whosoever was not found written in the *Book of Life* – was cast into the Lake of Fire (Rev. 20:14f.). Yet Life and Heaven are indestructible! Those who had not merely unannihilable existence (like the wicked), but who by God's grace had

been given everlasting life before they died – will then be further enriched, on the new Earth yet to come. Observe that the wicked, after the Final Judgment, are removed from the Earth forever – and henceforth hurled with the grave and even with hell itself into the Lake of Fire, where they will thenceforth be kept incarcerated for all eternity. Yet the present Earth itself is to be cleansed, and to become the everlasting abode of the righteous – when, after the Final Judgment, Heaven comes down and is merged with earthly life forever.[89]

So, we see then what the Saviour has saved us from. All who are spiritually regenerated by the Holy Spirit have been saved from the eternal torments of hell. To suggest that judgment day for the wicked is merely to be resurrected for annihilation (even after being beaten) rather than the everlasting judgment of God, is to cheapen the gospel. For it is to diminish what Christ went through on the cross. Says David Dickson.

Christ our surety, beside all the sufferings which He suffered in His body, did suffer also sorrow, grief, anguish, torment and desertion in regard of comfort in His soul, for this and other expressions prove so much. Our sins deserved that we should been utterly forsaken of God, for it behoved our Redeemer

[89] Francis Nigel Lee, *John's Revelation Unveiled*, Ligstryders, Lynnwoodrif, South Africa, 2000, 288.

to taste a little of the hell of being *forsaken* ere we could be redeemed.[90]

The law or the covenant of works cannot save us but rightly condemns us. It condemns us to hell. However, it also shows us our need of a saviour, the Saviour (Rom. 1:18, 2:15; Gal. 3:24; 1 Tim. 1:15). Thus, gospel preachers and teachers are duty-bound to tell covenant-breakers, i.e., sinners, of their need of the Saviour as the only one who can save them from the curse and judgment of the law, which means also warning them about the fires of hell.

The Westminster Standards include *The Practical use of Saving Knowledge, Contained in Scripture, and holden forth briefly in the foresaid Confession of Faith and Catechisms*. We find the following in paragraph III. *For convincing a man of judgment by the law*, consider 2 Thessalonians 1:7-10,

> "The Lord Jesus shall be revealed from heaven with his mighty angels, In flaming fire taking vengeance on them that know not God, and that obey not the gospel of our Lord Jesus Christ: Who shall be punished with everlasting destruction from the presence of the Lord, and from the glory of his power; When he shall come to be glorified in his saints, and to be admired in all them that believe."

---

[90] David Dickson, *Matthew*, The Banner of Truth, Edinburgh, (First published 1647), 1981, 398.

Wherein we are taught, that our Lord Jesus, who now offers to be Mediator for them who believe in him, shall, at the last day, come armed with flaming fire, to judge, condemn and destroy all them who have not believed God, have not received the offer of grace made in the gospel, nor obeyed the doctrine thereof; but remain in their natural state, under the law or the covenant of works.

Hence let every man reason thus: "What the righteous Judge hath forewarned me shall be done at the last day, I am sure is just judgment: But the righteous Judge hath forewarned me, that if I do not believe God in time, and obey not the doctrine of the gospel, I shall be secluded from his presence and his glory at the last day, and be tormented in soul and body for ever: Therefore I am convinced that this is a just judgment: And I have reason to thank God heartily, who hath forewarned me to flee from the wrath which is to come."

Thus every man may be, by the law or covenant of works, convinced of judgment, if he shall continue under the covenant of works, or shall not obey the gospel of our Lord Jesus.[91]

The Suffering

Enter, then, the Last Adam. "And the LORD God commanded the man, saying, 'Of

---

[91] *The Confession of Faith, The Larger and Shorter Catechisms, with the Scripture Proofs at Large: together with The Sum of Saving Knowledge*, Free Presbyterian Publication, Glasgow, Fourth reprint 1985, 327-8.

every tree of the garden you may freely eat; but of the tree of the knowledge of good and evil you shall not eat, for in the day that you eat of it you shall surely die'" (Gen. 2:16-17). The first Adam chose the curse of death over the blessing of life. He was free to eat of the tree of life, but instead ate of the tree of death. After which "The LORD God said, "Behold, the man has become like one of Us, to know good and evil. And now, lest he put out his hand and take also of the tree of life, and eat, and live forever" (Gen. 3:22). Westminster Shorter Catechism,

> Q. 19. *What is the misery of that estate whereinto man fell?*
> A. All mankind, by their fall, lost communion with God, are under his wrath and curse, and so made liable to all miseries in this life, to death itself, and to the pains of hell for ever.

We have already seen something of what it would be like to "live forever" in a spiritually dead state. It means the first death (physical) will be followed by the second death (eternal). For, as we have seen, whether perishing without the law, i.e., the work of the law written on your conscience, or perishing with the law, i.e., the Ten Commandments (and the judicial and ceremonial laws), to not have Jesus as your Saviour means that you die under the curse of the law. "For all who rely on works of the law are under a curse; for it is written, 'Cursed be everyone who does not abide by all things written in the Book of the Law, and do them'" (Gal. 3:10). Westminster Larger Catechism,

> Q. 149. *Is any man able perfectly to keep the commandments of God?*
> A. No man is able, either of himself, or by any grace received in this life, perfectly to keep the commandments of God; but doth daily break them in thought, word, and deed.

We saw something of our own salvation when we looked at the thief on the cross. He went from reviling Him (Matt. 27:14; Mark 15:32), to saying, "Lord, remember me when You come into Your Kingdom.' And Jesus said to him, 'Assuredly, I say to you, today you will be with Me in Paradise'" (Luke 23:42-43). The spiritually dead thief had become spiritually alive, i.e., born again, on the cross. Therefore, unlike the unrepentant thief, he escaped the second death and went Paradise with Jesus with the exhalation of his very last breath. Notice that the repentant thief went to the bliss of Paradise that very day, and the unrepentant thief went to the torments of hell. Therefore, heaven and hell are already populated with people awaiting the final judgment.

Judgment day is resurrection day. It is when *all* human beings get their bodies back. In Adam, a person's spirit is dead, and when their body returns the dust, their soul is in torments forever. For them the resurrection means getting their bodies back, then remaining both body and soul in the spiritually dead state of torments forever. For the Christian, however, their spirit is made alive by God before they physically die. Therefore, for them, the resurrection means everlasting bliss for the whole man. "Now may the God of peace himself sanctify you completely, and may your whole spirit and soul and body be kept blameless at the coming of our Lord Jesus Christ" (1 Thess. 5:23).

The first Adam died spiritually when He sinned thus separating himself from the favourable presence of God. When God imputed our sin to Him, the last Adam died spiritually as it were, not as God but as man. However, unlike the first Adam who forsook God after which God cried out to him in the garden, the Last Adam was obedient even unto death, still crying out to God who had forsaken Him as He took our curse upon Himself, "My God, My God, why have You forsaken Me?" Mark 15:34. Says Arthur Pink,

> [T]he counterpart of God's original threat to Adam, namely, spiritual death (for he did not die physically that same day), which is the separation of the soul from God, is witnessed in the solemn of all cries, 'My God, My God, Why hast Thou *forsaken* Me?' (Matt. 27:46). How absolutely did our blessed Saviour identify Himself with those which were lost, took their place and suffered the Just for the unjust! How apparent it is, that Christ in His own body, *did* bear the Curse entailed by the Fall.[92]

[92] Arthur Pink, *Gleanings in Genesis*, Moody Press, Chicago, Illinois, Fifteenth Printing, 1978, 54.

Why would Jesus mention being forsaken by God at this point as He hung on the cross? Well, keep in mind that there was a great exchange taking place on that cross. The New Living Translation of the Bible does well in explaining what was happening here where it says, "For God made Christ, who never sinned, to be the offering for our sin, so that we could be made right with God through Christ" (2 Cor. 5:21). The great exchange is that when God sacrificed His Son Jesus He was at the same time reconciling Himself to us and us to Him. Yes, He was also reconciling us to Him. Jesus, the perfect Man, was the only thing that could represent us. Bulls, sheep and goats could never substitute for human beings. And, because Jesus is also God as well as human, His human sacrifice is of infinite worth. In Lord's Day 16 of The Heidelberg Catechism, we read the following in reference to a line in The Apostles' Creed,

> 44. Q. Why is there added, *He descended into hell?*
> A. That in my greatest temptations I may be assured, and wholly comfort myself in this, that my Lord Jesus Christ, by His inexpressible anguish, pains, terrors, and hellish agony, in which He was plunged during all His sufferings, but especially on the cross, hath delivered me from the anguish and torment of hell. (Isa. 53; Matt. 26:36-46; 27:45-46; Luke 22:44; Heb. 5:7-10).

Commenting on this G.I. Williamson says,

[W]hen God warned our first parents that the wages of sin is death – and by this, of course, he meant an eternal death. Death does not mean nonexistence. It means eternal existence away from God and away from all the blessings that come from God. It has to be eternal because sin against an infinite God requires an infinite penalty. The only way a finite creature can pay an infinite penalty is to keep on paying it forever. But here is the good news: because Jesus is infinite (being divine) as well as finite (being human), he was able to suffer the infinite penalty in a finite period of time. He suffered only for a time, but because he was infinite, he was able to suffer an infinite amount. As a matter of fact, his suffering was the equivalent of eternal damnation. Therefore, he is able to save us from eternal death.[93]

Jesus is God and Man in one divine Person forever. He is not two persons, but one person with two distinct natures, the divine and the human. This is where we need to get ready to start talking about God being triune in nature, i.e., Father and Son and Holy Spirit, three Persons, but one God. The question then becomes: Can any Person in the Godhead forsake any of the Other Persons? Can the Father *really* forsake the Son who said, "My God, My God, why have You forsaken Me"?

---

[93] G.I. Williamson, *The Heidelberg Catechism, A Study Guide*, P & R Publishing, Philippsburg, New Jersey, 1993, 74.

We must realize that God cannot look upon sin, even my sin and your sin. Scripture says of God, "Your eyes are too pure to look on evil; You cannot tolerate wrongdoing" (Hab. 1:13a). Jesus had become a sin-offering to God on the cross. God had imputed or transferred our sins to Jesus on the cross. Then He poured out His wrath, i.e., hellfire, on His Son consuming all of our sins. It was this wrath of God that killed Jesus as it was poured out upon Him (instead of believers). Thus, Jesus experienced the torments of hell, in body and soul and spirit while on the cross. As our Saviour He went into the fires of hell to rescue us from the flames. E.g., "Is not this man a burning stick snatched from the fire?" (Zech. 3:2b).

So then, what's wrong with Jesus feeling forsaken even though technically He wasn't being forsaken by God? Have you ever *felt* forsaken? Well, apparently so has Jesus! Let's tease this out a little more.

As God accounted our sins to Jesus as He hung there on the cross, Jesus could feel in His humanity that there was now, for the first time, a barrier between Him and God. He felt as if He had the full weight of our sin on His shoulders. That's why He cried out, "My God, My God, why have You forsaken Me?" It shows us that He really did take our sins upon Him as He hung there representing the elect (Isa. 53:5-6).

The apostle Paul minced no words when he discovered the Galatians sinning. "O foolish Galatians! Who has bewitched you? It was before your eyes that Jesus Christ was publicly portrayed as crucified" (Gal. 3:1). The preincarnate Christ, the One who walked in the garden with His image Adam, the One who delivered His Ten Commandments on Mount Sinai, was clearly portrayed on the cross by Paul. But, like Adam smashing the image of God clearly portrayed on his heart, as had Israel by breaking the Ten Commandments after him, so were the foolish Galatians before whose eyes Paul had presented the express image of God crucified. Like Israel of old, the Galatians had turned aside quickly from the way of the Lord. As Moses said to Israel,

> So I turned and came down from the mountain, and the mountain was burning with fire. And the two tablets of the covenant were in my two hands. And I looked, and behold, you had sinned against the LORD your God. You had made yourselves a golden calf. You had turned aside quickly from the way that the LORD had commanded you. So I took hold of the two tablets and threw them out of my two hands and broke them before your eyes" (Deut. 9:15-17).

And as our covenant representative, Christ our covenant became Christ the *broken* covenant on the cross. At the Last Supper Jesus broke bread as a picture of His body being broken on the cross, saying, "Take; this is My body." On the cross He was to become what Adam had become after eating the forbidden fruit. Jesus said at His last supper, "I will not drink again of the fruit of the vine until that day when I drink it new in the kingdom of God" (Matt.

26:29). "For He made Him who knew no sin *to be* sin for us" (2 Cor. 5:21). And "Christ has redeemed us from the curse of the law, having become a curse for us (for it is written, "Cursed *is* everyone who hangs on a tree)" (Gal. 3:13).

We begin to understand a bit more why it is so dangerous to partake of the covenant meal when we view the pre-fall tree of life as a covenant sacrament, "Then the LORD God said, "Behold, the man has become like one of Us, to know good and evil. And now, lest he put out his hand and take also of the tree of life, and eat, and live forever" (Gen. 3:22). Compare this with, "For he who eats and drinks in an unworthy manner eats and drinks judgment to himself, not discerning the Lord's body" (1 Cor. 11:29). Says Robert Jamieson,

> This tree being a sacramental sign of pledge of that immortal life with which obedience should be rewarded, man lost, on his fall, all claim to this tree; and therefore, that he might not delude himself with the idea that eating of it would restore the inner life of the soul, the Lord sent him forth from the garden. Although incapable, through want of faith, of deriving any spiritual virtue from the eating of its fruit, he might, if permitted to remain, have attempted, by continuing the use of it, to profane the ordinance of God, and was therefore righteously debarred from the sight, when he had forfeited the thing signified … An earth immortality would, in the condition

of the fallen pair, have been a curse instead of a blessing.[94]

The pre-fall Adam was the image of God. That image was broken by his sin. When God imputed our sin to His Son on the cross, the Last Adam became the image of the fallen Adam. He poured out His wrath on His Son instead of the elect. It was total torment and absolute agony of soul for Jesus Christ – an excruciating feeling of forsakenness, abandonment. Hell is to be forsaken by God for *eternity*. And because Jesus is God and Man in one Divine Person forever, His suffering went out into all eternity and has eternal consequences – everlasting life for all who believe in Him. Says David Thomas,

> What greater misery can be imagined than a consciousness of being forsaken by God? Saul felt this; and in the dark cave of Endor, trembling before a wicked enchantress, he cried, 'I am sore distressed, for God hath departed from me, and answereth me no more, neither by prophets nor by dreams.' This feeling is the hell of the lost. Conscious banishment from God is perdition. Christ was now permitted to have this feeling, and in this feeling there was a mysterious hell.[95]

---

[94] Robert Jamieson, *Jamieson, Fausset, Brown, A Commentary, Critical, Experimental, Practical*, Vol. 1, Eerdmans Publishing, Grand Rapids, Michigan, reprinted 1989, 61-2.
[95] David Thomas, *Gospel of Matthew, Expository and Homiletical*, Kregel Publications, Grand Rapids. Michigan, Reprint of 1873 edition, 1979, 542.

Now, we really do need to be careful here. God the Father never for an instant stopped loving God the Son. God cannot deny Himself. Therefore, what Jesus was experiencing was a *feeling* of forsakenness *only* in His *human* nature. As God as it were turned His face away from Him, Jesus experienced agony of soul as He hung there in the darkness (Matt. 27:45). Thus, He experienced hell on the cross. For isn't hell utter darkness? Forsakenness? God holocausted all our sins as He slew His Son, the sacrificial Lamb, by hanging Him upon the cursed tree, i.e., the cross. God cannot die. Therefore, it was in regard to His human nature, not His divine nature, that Jesus felt forsaken and subsequently died.

The Saviour suffered the eternal torments of hell on behalf of the elect as their covenant head, their federal representative. Those who die without the Saviour perish under the curse of the law. They remain cursed forever. The never get out of debtor's prison (Matt. 18:31-35), hell, because they never pay back their debt to God, i.e., perfect, personal, and perpetual keeping of God's law. Also, unlike the Saviour, they are unable to pay the penalty they each owe for breaking God's covenant. Says Robert Dabney,

> Finally, passing over for the time, the unanswerable argument, that sin has infinite ill desert, as committed against an excellent, perfect, and universal law, and an infinite lawgiver, I may argue that even though the desert of a temporary season were only

temporary penalties, yet if man continues in hell to sin forever, he will suffer forever. While he was paying off a previous debt of guilt he would contract an additional one, and so be forever subject to the penalty.[96]

On Adam reaching out his hand and taking of the fruit on the tree of life in Genesis 3:22 Keil and Delitzsch say,

> Had he continued in fellowship with God by obedience to the command of God, he might have eaten of it, for he was created for eternal life. But after he had fallen into sin, into the power of death, the fruit which produced immortality could only do him harm. For immortality in a state of sin is not the ζωή αἰώνιος [everlasting life] which God designed for man, but endless misery, which the Scriptures call 'the second death' (Rev. 2:11, 20:6, 14, 21:8). The expulsion from paradise, therefore, was punishment inflicted for man's good, intended, while exposing him to temporal death, to preserve him from eternal death.[97]

[96] Robert Lewis Dabney, *Systematic Theology*, first published 1872, Banner of Truth, Edinburgh, Reprinted 1996, 857.
[97] Keil and Delitzsch, *Old Testament Commentaries*, Vol. 1, Associated Publishers, Grand Rapids, Michigan, no date, 82-3.

The Sentencing

Resurrection day is judgment day. "He has appointed a day on which He will judge the world in righteousness by the Man whom He has ordained. He has given assurance of this to all by raising Him from the dead" (Acts 17:31).

> When the Son of Man comes in His glory, and all the holy angels with Him, then He will sit on the throne of His glory. All the nations will be gathered before Him, and He will separate them one from another, as a shepherd divides *his* sheep from the goats. And He will set the sheep on His right hand, but the goats on the left. Then the King will say to those on His right hand, 'Come, you blessed of My Father, inherit the kingdom prepared for you from the foundation of the world' … "Then He will also say to those on the left hand, 'Depart from Me, you cursed, into the everlasting fire prepared for the devil and his angels' … And these will go away into everlasting punishment, but the righteous into eternal life' (Matt. 25:31-34, 41, 46).

Notice that Jesus calls the sheep "you blessed of My Father" and the goats, "you cursed". Blessed and cursed are covenant terms: blessed by being obedient to God and refraining from eating of the forbidden fruit and cursed for disobeying God and eating it. Adam was judged by God on the day he ate the forbidden fruit, and he died that day, first spiritually, which resulted in his temporal or physical death. "For the wages of sin is death..." (Rom. 6:23a). No one escapes, "For all have sinned and fall short of the glory of God" (Rom. 3:23).

So, we all die physically. But what happens after we die? Where do we go? The answer is that we go to either heaven or to hell. So, the question becomes: Why is there going to be a judgment day if people have already died and have gone to heaven or to hell? Well, judgment day is all about sentencing. We labour this point because of the erroneous idea of soul-sleep. The error is that it is our body that sleeps when we are dead, not our soul. The Westminster Larger Catechism summarises what we are talking about,

> Q. 86. What is the communion in glory with Christ, which the members of the invisible Church enjoy immediately after death?
> A. The communion in glory with Christ, which the members of the invisible Church enjoy immediately after death, is, in that their souls are then made perfect in holiness, and received into the highest heavens, where they behold the face of God in light and glory; waiting for the full redemption of their bodies, which even in death continue united to Christ, and rest in their graves, as in their beds, till at the last day they be again united with their souls. Whereas the souls of the wicked are at their death cast into hell, where they remain in torments and utter darkness; and their

bodies kept in their graves, as in their prisons, until the resurrection and judgment of the great day.

So, both the sheep and the goats have a conscious existence after physical death as they await the resurrection of their bodies. Therefore, there is a period between the death of the body and its resurrection. We refer to as this period the Intermediate State.

As we have already seen, the Intermediate State is different for believers than for unbelievers. As believers await the resurrection of their bodies, the Intermediate State is a state of bliss for them. But unbelievers await their resurrection in order to be cast body and soul into hell where they remain forever in a state of torment – just as the parable of the Rich Man and Lazarus attests.

> There was a certain rich man who was clothed in purple and fine linen and fared sumptuously every day. But there was a certain beggar named Lazarus, full of sores, who was laid at his gate, desiring to be fed with the crumbs which fell from the rich man's table. Moreover the dogs came licking his sores.
>
> So it was that the beggar died and was carried by the angels to Abraham's bosom. The rich man also died and was buried. And being in torments in Hades, he lifted up his eyes and saw Abraham afar off, and Lazarus in his bosom. Then he cried and said, 'Father

Abraham, have mercy on me and send Lazarus that he may dip the tip of his finger in water and cool my tongue; for I am tormented in this flame.'

But Abraham said, 'Son, remember that in your lifetime you received your good things, and likewise Lazarus evil things; but now he is comforted and you are tormented. And besides all this, between us and you there is a great gulf fixed, so that those who want to pass from here to you cannot, nor can those from there pass to us.'

Then he said, 'I beg you therefore, father, that you would send him to my father's house. For I have five brothers, that he may testify to them, lest they also come to this place of torment.'

Abraham said to him, 'They have Moses and the prophets; let them hear them.' And he said, 'No, father Abraham; but if one goes to them from the dead they will repent.' But he said to him, 'If they do not hear Moses and the prophets, neither will they be persuaded though one rise from the dead' (Luke 16:19-31).

Notice that neither the Rich Man nor Lazarus was unconscious. Notice that neither was asleep. There is no such thing as soul sleep. The Bible tells us far more about the Intermediate State for Christians than it does for that intervening state for non-Christians. The repentant thief on the cross died the same day as Jesus Christ. The thief must have been fortified very much as he was dying by the words Jesus spoke to him, saying, "Assuredly, I say to you, today you will be with Me in Paradise" (Luke 23:43). Thus, we see that the repentant thief was not expecting soul-sleep but was expecting to go directly to heaven and be awake enough to see Jesus there.

To be sure the dead body sees corruption, but the souls of believers go to Paradise where they behold the face of God in light and glory while awaiting the full redemption of their bodies. So, at death the Christian's spirit is made perfect, and he or she sees God in heaven.

But what about the non-Christian? Well, the non-Christian too has, or better, is, an immortal soul, i.e., every human is a soul spirit with a body. However, the non-Christian, like the Rich Man in the Parable, goes to a place of torments. In the Parable of the Rich Man and Lazarus we're told that there is a great gulf fixed between the two places, i.e., the place of bliss, heaven, and the place of torments, hell (Luke 16:26).

Jude speaks of the angels who did not keep their proper domain, but left their own abode, "being reserved in everlasting chains under darkness for the judgment of the great day, as Sodom and Gomorra, and the cities around them in a similar manner to these, having given themselves over to sexual immorality and gone after strange flesh, are set forth as an example, suffering the vengeance of eternal fire" (Jude 6-7). The NIV makes it explicit when it says, "They serve as an example of those who suffer the punishment of eternal fire" (Jude 7b). So, the Rich

Man is in hell as an example of one of those already suffering the punishment of eternal fire.

It's clear that the Parable of the Rich Man and Lazarus is teaching us about the Intermediate State, because the Rich Man wanted his five brothers testified to "lest they also come to this place of torment" (Luke 16:28). Thus, his five brothers hadn't even entered into the Intermediate State, never mind the Final State. The picture does present the urgency for people to repent and believe in the gospel before they die.

So, we see then that all true Christians immediately go to be with the Lord upon the death of the body, where they experience conscious bliss in heaven. And the non-Christian goes to a place of conscious torment called hell upon the death of the body. Therefore, judgment day/resurrection day is all about sentencing. For the unbeliever, first it is jail (Intermediate State), then comes the trial (Judgment Day), and finally it is prison forever (Final State).

"Do not marvel at this; for the hour is coming in which all who are in the graves will hear His voice and come forth—those who have done good, to the resurrection of life, and those who have done evil, to the resurrection of condemnation" (John 5:28-29).

Those who receive "the resurrection of life" will be acquitted on account of what the last Adam has done for them. This is grace. And those who receive "the resurrection of condemnation" will remain in Adam, i.e., outside of the last Adam. This is justice. However, those "sheep" who have received God's mercy will know that they have been saved by grace alone through faith alone, and therefore that they should be condemned with the goats. And the "goats" who receive God's justice will know that that is what their sins deserve.

Sheep and goats, blessing and curses are descriptions of God's grace and His justice. Thus, if God promised Adam the bliss of eternal life in heaven for obedience to the covenant of works, then He threatened the torments of eternal death in hell for disobedience. "For our God *is* a consuming fire" (Heb. 12:29).

Conclusion

Once more we remember the self-maledictory oath fully illustrated by God when He cut His covenant with Abraham. "And it came to pass, when the sun went down and it was dark, that behold, there appeared a smoking oven and a burning torch that passed between those pieces" (Gen. 15:17). God was saying in effect, "May what was done to these animals be done to Me should I ever break My covenant."

Christ on the cross, paradoxically, was the representative covenant keeper while at the same time being the representative covenant breaker. "For Christ also suffered once for sins, the righteous for the unrighteous, that he might bring us to God, being put to death in the flesh but made alive in the spirit" (1 Pet.3:18). As quoted earlier, Hermann Witsius was correct when he said,

> God likewise signified … that all the stability
> of the covenant of grace was founded on the
> sacrifice of Christ, and that the soul and body

of Christ were one day to be violently separated asunder.[98]

Jesus, as the great High Priest, "the Lamb of God" offered up Himself to God as the perfect sacrifice (John 2:36; Heb. 9:11-15, 28). Says J.V. Fesko,

The remedy for the broken covenant of works is the work of Christ. Christ's passive obedience addresses the covenant's transgression, but his active obedience addresses the fulfillment of the covenant of works.[99]

[98] Herman Witsius, *Economy of Covenants Between God and Man*, 2 Vols, Book I, Chapter I, VII, First published 1677, reprinted 1822, Kindle version 2014, 37.
[99] J.V. Fesko, *Adam and the Covenant of Works*, Mentor Imprint by Christian Focus Publications Ltd., Geanies House, Fearn, Ross-shire, 2021, 346.

PART THREE
The Covenant of Grace

"'For the mountains may depart
and the hills be removed,
but my steadfast love shall not depart from you,
and my covenant of peace shall not be removed,'
says the LORD, who has compassion on you" (Isa.
54:3).

INTRODUCTION

Having seen that because the covenant of redemption is trinitarian, we noted that it is impossible to study it without also considering its relationship to the covenants of works and of grace. Therefore, because we have already studied the covenants of redemption and of works, we already know something of the covenant of grace, which of course is our focus in the following.

Most people should be able to understand God's grace as God *freely* giving people what they do not deserve and not giving them what they do deserve. However, what is difficult for most Christians to understand is the word *freely* in the previous sentence. As fallen sinners we deserve only God's justice not His mercy. Yet God by His free grace is pleased to justify, i.e., declare as righteous, as right with Him, hell-deserving sinners on account of what Jesus did. His grace to us is freely given because of Christ.

The Father placed the order for the gift. The Son purchased the gift. And the Holy Spirit delivers the same gift into the hands and hearts of undeserving sinners. God does all the work. Believers simply receive His gift of grace with thanksgiving. Yes, before the fall the covenant was a promise suspended upon a condition, which promise was to be attained by Adam's works on our behalf. After the fall the covenant remains as a conditional promise. However, its promised reward is attained by the works of the last Adam on behalf of the elect of God, i.e., all true believers. Says J. Nicholas Reid,

In short, the essential difference between the covenant of works and the covenant of grace is not the presence or absence of conditions. In the covenant of works, the conditions precede the blessing of justification. In the covenant of grace, the blessing of justification precedes the conditional evangelical fruit.[100]

Even though we are saved by grace alone through faith alone in Christ alone according to the Scriptures alone to the glory of God alone, it would seem true that there is a Pharisee hiding in every believer's heart. Every Christian wrestles with legalism. In other words, works and grace often get confused. Sometimes it's the belief that we are saved by our owns works. And sometimes this belief is softened by the equally erroneous belief that we are and stay right with God because of His grace plus our own works. In this we can see that, though people may not outwardly acknowledge the doctrine of the covenant of works or even claim to reject it, they demonstrate by their words and by their actions that they actually do believe in it! They do this by acting as if they are still on probation. Martyn Lloyd-Jones helps rescue us from such bondage where he says,

We are no longer in a state of probation and liable to fall; but that was Adam's position.

---

[100] J. Nicholas Read, *The Mosaic Covenant*, Edited by Waters, Reid, and Muether, *Covenant Theology: Biblical, Theological, and Historical Perspectives*, Crossway, Wheaton, Illinois, 2020, 171.

He was made in the image of God, he was innocent, he was perfect, he was without sin, but he was on probation. There was a possibility of his falling, and he fell.

In Him the tribes of Adam boast
More blessings than their father lost.

I say that in Christ we are not in a state of probation, and that there is no possibility of our falling from grace. We are beyond that. Our glorification is guaranteed.[101]

We have already stated that the covenant of grace is simple the gospel by another name. Since the fall, sinners have always been saved by God's grace alone. Where do good works fit in? Good works are the result of grace and not the producer of it. "For by grace you have been saved through faith. And this is not your own doing; it is the gift of God, not a result of works, so that no one may boast. For we are his workmanship, created in Christ Jesus for good works, which God prepared beforehand, that we should walk in them" (Eph. 2:8-10).

Another way of saying that some people place themselves under the yoke of the covenant of works instead of the freedom of the covenant of grace is that they confuse the law and the gospel. These must be kept distinct from each other. Which is not to say that they are not interconnected. However, any attempt to keep God's law without understanding the gospel is

---

[101] Martyn Lloyd-Jones, *Romans*, *Exposition of Chapter 5, Assurance*, The Banner of Truth Trust, Edinburgh, (1971), Reprinted 1988, 236.

to misunderstand the intention of the law. It is to put the proverbial cart before the horse.

The law is designed to lead us to Christ by showing fallen humanity our need of a Saviour (Gal. 3:24). "What purpose then *does* the law *serve?* It was added because of transgressions, till the Seed should come to whom the promise was made; *and it was* appointed through angels by the hand of a mediator" (Gal. 3:19).

Theologians speak of the threefold use of the moral law,

1. It is the standard for society, i.e., it is binding on all men, restraining evil and promoting good.
2. It is the rule of life revealing sin, and may lead to repentance for non-Christians (and backslidden Christians), that's why the law ought to be preached with the gospel to show the clear need of Christ for salvation.
3. It is the rule of righteousness for believers, i.e., those who are sanctified and are growing in holiness through the proper use of the law.

The moral law helps Christians restrain their own corruptions by showing them what sin is, and by its forbidding it. The threatenings for the breaking of it show us what our sins deserve and therefore encourage us to keep it. And the sin and misery in the world show us the type of sufferings expected in this life because of humanity's sins. But we must always keep in mind that true Christians have been freed from the curse threatened by the law. And, when we consider the promised blessings, we are able to see that God approves of our obedience to His law. Says John Calvin,

> The law is like a mirror. In it we contemplate our weakness, then the iniquity arising from this, and finally the curse coming from both – just as a mirror shows us spots on our face. For when the capacity to follow righteousness fails him, man must be mired in sins. After the sin forthwith comes the curse. Accordingly, the greater the transgression of which the law holds us guilty, the graver the judgement to which it makes us answerable. The apostle's statement is relevant here, "Through the law comes knowledge of sin" (Rom. 3:20).[102]

None of these three uses of the law are contrary to the grace of the gospel. The fact is that they are in complete harmony with it. For it is the Spirit of Christ who enables Christians to freely and cheerfully do the will of God revealed in His law as it is required to be done.

Now, this is where we must be careful. We have already spoken of three covenants, viz., the covenants of redemption, works, and now grace. By now it should be clear to us that the covenants of works and grace are simply two different and distinct administrations of the eternal covenant of redemption. When we talk about the covenant of works, we mean the *first* covenant. And by covenant of grace, we

---

[102] John Calvin, *The Institutes of the Christian Religion*, Book 2:7:7, Battles Edition, The Westminster Press, Philadelphia, 355.

mean the *second* covenant. However, when referring to first and second covenants we must not confuse the covenant of works with the Mosaic covenant. Says Robert Cara,

> In Hebrews, the term διαθηκη is used to refer to both the first/old covenant and the second/new/better/eternal covenant (e.g., 7:22; 8:7, 13; 13:20), that is, the Mosaic covenant and the new covenant.[103]

By Old Testament we mean those thirty-nine books (Genesis to Malachi) that speak of the first administrations of the covenant of grace. And by New Testament we mean those twenty-seven books (Matthew to Revelation) that reveal the transition of the first/old covenant into the second/new/better/eternal covenant. However, as will become clear, the same covenant of grace was at various times differently administered in the Old Testament (or the old covenant economy or dispensation) than in the New Testament (or new covenant economy). With Christ at its heart, the covenant of grace is a system of promise and fulfillment. Says Michael J. Kruger,

> The Mosaic covenant, also known as the 'old' covenant, refers to the legal arrangement that God made with the nation of Israel on Mount Sinai upon her deliverance from Egypt.

[103] Robert J. Cara, *Covenant in Hebrews, Covenant Theology: Biblical, Theological, and Historical Perspectives*, Crossway, Wheaton, Illinois, 2020, 248.

Central to the Mosaic covenant was, of course, the law of God – not only the moral law in the Ten Commandments but also the ceremonial law, which would govern the cultic life of Israel and the manner in which they would worship Yahweh. In order to be ritually 'clean,' Israelites were required (among other things) to engage in various washings, abstain from certain foods, and offer the appropriate animal sacrifices. The Gospels present the ministry of Jesus as completing or fulfilling various aspects of the Mosaic covenant...[104]

Westminster Confession of Faith 7, *Of God's Covenant with Man*, provides the following handy summary which will help to remind us of where we've been and where we're going.

1. The distance between God and the creature is so great, that although reasonable creatures do owe obedience unto Him as their Creator, yet they could never have any fruition of Him as their blessedness and reward, but by some voluntary condescension on God's part, which He hath been pleased to express by way of covenant. (Isa. 40:13–17, Job 9:32–33, 1 Sam. 2:25, Ps. 113:5–6, Ps. 100:2–3, Job 22:2–3, Job 35:7–8, Luke 17:10, Acts 17:24–25)

---

[104] Michael J. Kruger, *Covenant and Gospels,* Edited by Waters, Reid, and Muether, *Covenant Theology: Biblical, Theological, and Historical Perspectives*, Crossway, Wheaton, Illinois, 2020, 219-20.

2. The first covenant made with man was a covenant of works, (Gal. 3:12) wherein life was promised to Adam; and in him to his posterity, (Rom. 10:5, Rom. 5:12–20) upon condition of perfect and personal obedience. (Gen. 2:17, Gal. 3:10)

3. Man, by his fall, having made himself incapable of life by that covenant, the Lord was pleased to make a second, (Gal. 3:21, Rom. 8:3, Rom. 3:20–21, Gen. 3:15, Isa. 42:6) commonly called the Covenant of Grace; wherein He freely offereth unto sinners life and salvation by Jesus Christ; requiring of them faith in Him, that they may be saved, (Mark 16:15–16, John 3:16, Rom. 10:6–9, Gal. 3:11) and promising to give unto all those that are ordained unto eternal life His Holy Spirit, to make them willing, and able to believe. (Ezek. 36:26–27, John 6:44–45)

4. This covenant of grace is frequently set forth in Scripture by the name of a Testament, in reference to the death of Jesus Christ the testator, and to the everlasting inheritance, with all things belonging to it, therein bequeathed. (Heb. 9:15–17, Heb. 7:22, Luke 22:20, 1 Cor. 11:25).

We see then that just as there are requirements or conditions attached to the promises in the covenant of works, so there are also in the covenant of grace. Whereas perfect works was the condition in the pre-fall covenant, God grace is the post-fall covenant's condition. Come judgment day, without grace we are left to bargain with God with our own works, works that God has already called filthy rags, i.e., used menstrual rags (Isa. 64:6).

We cannot make a silk purse from a sow's ear, nor can we make garments of righteousness from our sin-soiled graveclothes. We have broken the covenant of works, and the stench of death that clings to us can only be removed by the cleansing blood of Christ through God's grace. We must seek to be forgiven by His grace alone and not because of any of our own works. "If we confess our sins, He is faithful and just to forgive us *our* sins and to cleanse us from all unrighteousness" (1 John 1:9).

There are so many wonderful promises of future good things in Isaiah that the whole book could be called "The Gospel According to Isaiah"! All the promises are in accordance with God's covenant of grace, with Christ as their fulfillment. Consider the following sample,

"Comfort, yes, comfort My people!" Says your God. "Speak comfort to Jerusalem, and cry out to her, that her warfare is ended, that her iniquity is pardoned; for she has received from the LORD's hand double for all her sins."

The voice of one crying in the wilderness: "Prepare the way of the LORD; make straight in the desert a highway for our God. Every valley shall be exalted and every mountain and hill brought low; the crooked places shall be made straight and the rough places smooth; the glory of the LORD shall be revealed, and all flesh shall see *it* together; for the mouth of the LORD has spoken."

The voice said, "Cry out!" And he said, "What shall I cry?" "All flesh *is* grass, and all its loveliness *is* like the flower of the field. The grass withers, the flower fades, because the breath of the LORD blows upon it; surely the people *are* grass. The grass withers, the flower fades, but the word of our God stands forever."

O Zion, you who bring good tidings, get up into the high mountain; O Jerusalem, you who bring good tidings, lift up your voice with strength, lift *it* up, be not afraid; say to the cities of Judah, "Behold your God!" Behold, the Lord GOD shall come with a strong *hand,* and His arm shall rule for Him; behold, His reward *is* with Him, and His work before Him. He will feed His flock like a shepherd; He will gather the lambs with His arm, and carry *them* in His bosom, a*nd* gently lead those who are with young" (Isa. 40:1-10).

So, we see then that all the covenant promises of God will come to pass because God's word stands forever. His word is His bond, His oath, His promise, His covenant. Another way of saying the same thing is that Jesus Christ is God's Word in the flesh, and He is God's covenant with us. It is He that John the Baptist paved the way for (Matt. 3:1-12; Mark 1:1-12; Luke 3:1-22; John 1:19-42).

The LORD God first began to reveal His covenant of grace immediately after Adam broke the covenant of works (Gen. 3:15). The covenant of grace included the Redeemer, who would redeem a people and a place, i.e., His cursed people and His cursed creation. Says Herman Bavinck,

> The covenant of grace differs from the covenant of works in method, not in its ultimate goal. It is the same treasure that was promised in the covenant of works and is granted in the covenant of grace. Grace restores nature and takes it to its highest pinnacle, but it does not add to it any new and heterogenous constituents.[105]

The covenant of grace progressed through the Old Testament in four main phases until reaching its fulfillment in the New, viz., the Noahic, the Abrahamic, the Mosaic (which includes the Davidic). These covenants were simply older administrations of the same covenant of grace that pointed to and climaxed in the new covenant with Christ (Luke 22:20; 1 Cor. 11:25).

The Noahic covenant promises a people and a place for them to dwell, i.e., a renewed earth (foreshadowing the new creation). It was a general covenant but still included prohibitions and promises. The Abrahamic covenant was more specific in its promises of a people, i.e., Abraham's seed of whom Christ was the ultimate Seed (Gal. 3:16), and a place (the promised land). It also had prohibitions and promises but emphasizes gospel or grace over law.

---

[105] Herman Bavinck, *Reformed Dogmatics*: *Sin and Salvation in Christ*, Vol. 3, Baker Academic, 2006, 577.

The Mosaic covenant emphasizes law over gospel or grace which reveals in the Davidic covenant an everlasting throne upon which an everlasting King will sit ruling in the midst of His people. Moses was a prophet, while Aaron his brother was a priest, and David was a king. The new covenant fulfills God's promises of a believing people (i.e., the spiritual children of Abraham) (Gal. 3:7, 29), and a land in which He will dwell as Prophet, Priest, and King with them forever. The promised land was simply a token for the renewed creation.

The period of grace, as per the covenant of grace, began immediately upon the fall of man. God could have destroyed humanity and His creation when Adam fell. However, as we already know, God had a plan from eternity. Martyn Lloyd-Jones reminds us of that eternal plan where he says,

> What is the story of the establishment of the reign of grace, and the inauguration of the kingdom of grace? The answer is given in many places in the Bible. For instance, in the First Epistle of Peter, chapter 1, verse 20, we read of One 'Who verily was foreordained before the foundation of the world'. That is when the kingdom was established and inaugurated, 'before the foundation of the world'. Grace was set upon its throne in the eternal Council, held before time began, between the Father, the Son, and the Holy Spirit. The problem of sin arose, and the question was how to deal with it. Was man to be destroyed because of sin? The divine

decision was that grace was to be introduced, and in due time grace was established and set upon the Throne. As the old theologians used to put it, a covenant was entered into between the Father and the Son, the 'Covenant of Redemption'. That was the setting up of the kingdom of grace. The moment the decision was taken that all men were not to be destroyed, grace was set upon the Throne. Such was the great inauguration – the Covenant of Redemption. And that involved the division of offices as between the three blessed Persons in the Most Holy Trinity – the gracious purpose and plan of the Father, the willing subordination of the Son to carry it out, and the work of the Holy Spirit in applying it to the needs of sinners.[106]

What we are looking at in the following is the progression and application of the covenant of grace through time.

---

[106] Martyn Lloyd-Jones, *Romans, Exposition of Chapter 5, Assurance*, The Banner of Truth Trust, Edinburgh, Scotland, (1971), Reprinted 1988, 320.

COVENANT COMFORT

Introduction

Having already studied the covenants of redemption and of works and having seen how Adam's failure to keep the covenant of works has cursed and condemned all of us to Hell unless God saves us, we are now ready to focus our attention on God's covenant of grace.

The first prophetic promise that Christ was coming to destroy the works of the devil (1 John 3:8) by tying up the strongman so that He can plunder his house (Mark 3:27) was given right after the fall when the LORD God said to the serpent, "And I will put enmity between you and the woman, and between your seed and her Seed; He shall bruise your head, and you shall bruise His heel" (Gen. 3:15). This is the beginning of the revelation of the covenant of grace. It is the conditional promise of the gospel.

Adam and Eve would have taken comfort in this promise, and more so when they observed the Lord sacrifice an animal and then clothe them with its skin (Gen. 3:21), putting on them the Lord Jesus Christ as it were (Rom. 13:14), the Lamb of God who takes away the sin of the world (John 1:29). As the LORD God, i.e., the preincarnate Christ, "sent him out of the garden to till the ground from which he was taken" (Gen. 3:23), perhaps He could have said to Adam, "Let not your heart be troubled; you believe in God, believe also in Me. In My Father's house are many mansions; if *it were* not *so,* I would have told you. I go to prepare a place for you" (John 14:1-2).

Adam and Eve knew that the promised Redeemer would come from their loins. He was the promised Seed of the woman. Could the promised Saviour be Abel, their first son? The Lord's revelation in Scripture of the coming Saviour was given progressively by prophetic statements and the use of typology all prefiguring the doing and dying of Jesus, including His resurrection.

The Old Testament is full of Christ, but He is seen only in the shadows as it were. We have to wait till the New Testament, till the canon of Scripture is complete, before we can see Him clearly in all of Scripture. For only then are we able to carry the New Testament as a lamp to go back through the Old Testament and shine it into all the nooks and crannies to illuminate Christ in every shadow. "Then I said, 'Behold, I have come—In the volume of the book it is written of Me—To do Your will, O God'" (Heb. 10:7). Says Michael Horton,

> What Adam and Israel failed to do – namely, drive the serpent from God's holy garden and extend his reign to the ends of the earth – the Last Adam and True Israel will accomplish once and for all. The serpent's head is crushed and the powers of evil are disarmed (Ro 16:20; Col 2:14-15). Death and hell no longer have the last word.[107]

Eve gave indication of her faith in the Lord by acknowledging Him when, in obedience to the cultural mandate to be fruitful and multiply, she gave

---

[107] Horton, Michael, *The Christian Faith, A Systematic Theology for Pilgrims on the Way*, Zondervan, Grand Rapids, Michigan, 2011, 501.

birth to Cain, "Now Adam knew Eve his wife, and she conceived and bore Cain, and said, 'I have acquired a man from the LORD.' Then she bore again, this time his brother Abel" (Gen. 4:1-2a). Says John Calvin,

> Although Moses does not state that Cain and Abel were twins, it yet seems to me probable that they were so; for, after he said that Eve, by her first conception, brought forth her first-born, he soon after subjoins that she also bore another; and thus, while commemorating a double birth, he speaks only of one conception.[108]

The first-born human being was of the seed of the serpent and murdered his brother who was in and of the Seed of the woman. Herein we see already the beginning of the separation of the sheep and the goats, i.e., the distinction between the children of the promise and the children of the flesh (Rom. 9:8) which is the distinction between the elect of God and those whom God has by-passed in His covenant of redemption. This theme is restated later with other twins, where the Lord says, "Jacob I have loved, but Esau I have hated" (Rom. 9:13 quoting Mal. 1:2-3). So we see that the same womb can give birth to the elect and non-elect, even if they are twins.

The two Adams were without sin. Adam, as the pre-fall son of God, was without sin. The new Adam, as the post-fall Son of God, was without sin.

---

[108] John Calvin, *Genesis*, the Banner of Truth Trust, London, England, (1554) 1965, 189-90.

However, Adam so to speak slew his "twin" by eating the forbidden fruit. To be sure, like Abraham offering up Isaac (Gen. 22:10), the Father offered up His Son – by the hands of sinful men. And just as Cain rose up and murdered Abel, so Adam by his rebellion had as good as murdered Jesus. For, "Him, being delivered by the determined purpose and foreknowledge of God, you have taken by lawless hands, have crucified, and put to death" (Acts 2:23). Thus, the sovereignty of God and the responsibility of man is kept in strict tension here and throughout Scripture, including the fall. In the words of Westminster Confession of Faith chapter 6, paragraph 1, "This their sin God was pleased, according to His wise and holy counsel, to permit, having purposed to order it to His own glory." As Scripture says, "For God has committed them all to disobedience, that He might have mercy on all" (Rom. 11:32).

As it became more and more populated (Gen. 5:1-5), the world only grew worse after the initial fall of humanity. "Then the LORD saw that the wickedness of man *was* great in the earth, and *that* every intent of the thoughts of his heart *was* only evil continually" (Gen. 6:5). Is it any different in our own generation?

Back in 1962 there was a thing called The Cuban Missile Crisis. The Soviet Union had placed ballistic missiles in the country of their Cuban ally, pointing at the USA. As kids in the 60s we didn't really care very much about politics, or Khrushchev or Kennedy. We only cared about mushroom clouds and the end of the world, the world that had just been rebuilding itself after WWII which had ended just seventeen years earlier in 1945.

So, there were dark clouds of fear encircling the planet back then. Does any of this sound familiar? As the great baseball philosopher Yogi Berra would say tongue-in-cheek, "It's like déjà vu all over again!" In our own time, it's fear of anything from Covid-19 to global warming to nuclear bombs (yet, again!) that is causing *some* people to panic.

We've been here before. Think of Noah. Let's see what we can learn from him. Genesis 9:13: "I have set my rainbow in the clouds, and it will be the sign of the covenant between me and the earth."

The Panic

The world had just ended! Noah, his wife, their three sons, and their three wives were the only humans left alive on the planet. Think about it: God had just destroyed the antediluvian world with a global flood.

The world had become as it was before God had formed the dry land on the third day of creation (Gen. 1:9-13). If it wasn't a *global* flood, then why wouldn't Noah and the rest of humanity and all the animals not just have headed for high ground, just as you and I would have? Anyway, God says that He covered the mountains with flood waters. "They rose greatly on the earth, and all the high mountains under the entire heavens were covered. The waters rose and covered the mountains to a depth of more than fifteen cubits [eight metres]" (Gen. 7:19-20). A cubit is about eighteen inches or 45.72cm.

As Noah and all his family, with all the animals, exit the ark to start rebuilding the world, God knows exactly how Noah feels. God had warned Noah about the great deluge that He was going to send. God gave him instructions about the ark he was to build. Obedient to God, by putting faith in God into practice, Noah involved himself in the cultural activity of shipbuilding. He also involved himself in the cultural activity of homiletics, as in preaching. For Peter says, "[God] did not spare the ancient world when he brought the flood on its ungodly people, but protected Noah, a preacher of righteousness, and seven others" (2 Pet. 2:5). Noah also involved himself in animal husbandry with the animals on the ark, and the cultural activity of horticulturalism by planting a vineyard when he got off the boat, not to mention the cultural activity of winemaking, *vinification*, and, of course, wine-tasting!

No doubt, there are many more cultural activities that could be listed, such as carpentry, but you can see that there is a strong cultural connection between the cultural mandate given to Adam in Genesis 1:26-28 and its reissue with Noah. Indeed, Noah is the new world's new Adam, pointing to the last Adam, Jesus Christ. Noah was a carpenter as was Christ.

When I lived in Winnipeg, (affectionately known as 'Winterpeg'), on account of its severe winters of minus 40C weather for months on end, every September I would have a sense of foreboding. Fear! We called it 'winterizing' the house, after the usually warm and beautiful but too short summer.

You had to make sure windows and doors and what-have-you would close and seal properly, among other things, before the cruel winter snows and plummeting temperatures arrived. Otherwise, you'd have ice and snow creeping into your house, like when your old freezer badly needs to be defrosted and you can't get the door to shut!

When Noah was building the ark, he would've had a feeling of foreboding. He knew that a flood that was going to destroy the earth and everything that lived and breathed on it, including all the ungodly people.

God warned Noah, and, in turn, Noah warned the ungodly to flee the wrath of God to come. You don't hear many preachers nowadays telling their congregations to flee the wrath of God to come! I guess they would have called Noah 'a fire and brimstone' preacher.

And just in case you think that the coming judgment in Noah's day was simply death by flood, consider how the writer to the Hebrews says it, "People are destined to die once, and after that to face judgment" (Heb. 9:27). The real judgment of God comes *after* you die, not before. Therefore, people, including Christian people, need to be warned to flee to God in Jesus Christ to escape the fires of Hell.

Nowadays people would be sending Noah graphs and statistics showing him how wrong he was about the coming flood. They would tell him that the science was settled. Here's a fairly recent quote,

> In 2007, [then Climate Commission chief, Tim] Flannery predicted cities such as

Brisbane would never again have dam-filling rains, as global warming had caused 'a 20 per cent decrease in rainfall in some areas' and made the soil too hot, 'so even the rain that falls isn't actually going to fill our dams and river systems.'[109]

You could hear the same sorts of people attacking Noah back in his day. Noah would be ostracised for talking about the coming rains. He'd be banned from social media for not going with the flow. But Noah just kept on swinging his hammer and warning the God-deniers about their impending doom.

One of the benefits of being a Christian is that you are no longer under the covenant of works in Adam but are instead under the covenant of grace in the new Adam. This means that you need not live your life in fear, including fear of death and judgment. "Inasmuch then as the children have partaken of flesh and blood, He Himself likewise shared in the same, that through death He might destroy him who had the power of death, that is, the devil, and release those who through fear of death were all their lifetime subject to bondage" (Heb. 2:14-15). Christians have been released from the power of the devil and the fear of death and judgment. "This is how love is made complete among us so that we will have confidence on the day of judgment: In this world we are like Jesus. There is no fear in love. But perfect love drives out fear, because fear has to do with

[109] Andrew Bolt, *Sun Herald*, Australia,14/7/2011.

punishment. The one who fears is not made perfect in love" (1 John 4:17-18).

Panic? Yes, those who do not know Jesus Christ ought to panic. Jesus says, "But I will show you whom you should fear: Fear Him who, after He has killed, has power to cast into hell; yes, I say to you, fear Him!" (Luke 12:5). "And do not fear those who kill the body but cannot kill the soul. But rather fear Him who is able to destroy both soul and body in hell [*Gehenna*]" (Matt. 10:28).

Jesus will return in the clouds to judge. Daniel 7:13 is speaking of Christ's ascension *into* heaven after His resurrection, where it says, "Behold One like the Son of Man coming with the clouds of heaven! He came *to* the Ancient of Days…" And we believe that Matthew 24:30 is speaking of the same time, where it says, "Then the sign of the Son of Man will appear in heaven, and then all the tribes of the earth will mourn, and they will see the Son of Man coming on the clouds of heaven with power and great glory." This was when He came in judgment and destroyed the Temple at Jerusalem, thus abolishing the old covenant system of worship and establishing the new covenant system we're now under. But, still speaking of clouds, when Christ comes again, "Then we who are alive *and* remain shall be caught up together with them in the clouds to meet the Lord in the air" (1 Thess. 4:17; see also Rev. 1:7; 14:14).

Clouds and darkness surround Him;
Righteousness and justice *are* the foundation of His throne.
A fire goes before Him,

And burns up His enemies round about.
His lightnings light the world;
The earth sees and trembles (Psa. 97:2-4).

Adam and then Noah are types of Christ. In other words, when you look at Adam and Noah you can see Christ in them. Adam pre-fall and Noah post-fall have to do with God's everlasting covenant. "I have set my rainbow in the clouds, and it will be the sign of the covenant between me and the earth" (Gen. 9:13).

Now, God's pre-fall covenant of works has as much to do with Jesus Christ as His post-fall covenant of grace with Noah has to do with Him. Both covenants point to Jesus. The sign of God's covenant pre-fall with Adam was the Tree of Life. The sign of His covenant post-fall with Noah was and is the rainbow.

What does all this have to do with panic and panicking? Well, if *you* had seen the dark clouds gathering as *you* were entering the ark, and *you* had heard the roar of thunder and then the clatter of heavy rains, if *you* had felt the boat *you* had just built rising as the floodwaters grew higher and higher, if *you* had thought about all humanity, the world and everything in it, being submerged in the great deluge, what would *you* think?

If you had seen carcasses of drowned animals, if you had perhaps seen the dead bodies of human beings, you would be wondering why God had saved a wretch like you, and if you had survived all that terror and were now standing on solid dry ground after the devastation of the great flood, and then you saw dark clouds forming *again* in the sky, what would you think? Would you need a glass of wine perhaps?

Would your heart start beating a little faster? Would a sense of foreboding come over you? Would you start to panic just a little as you looked at the dark clouds? Well, God is saying to Noah, don't panic! "I have set my rainbow in the clouds, and it will be the sign of the covenant between me and the earth." We tend to focus too much on the depressing dark clouds, the imagined mushroom clouds, the covid, the climate, yes, every supposed catastrophe, instead of the rainbow, instead of the covenant.

When we were kids we would say, "First to see the rainbow!" Whoever saw it first, got to make a wish. Instead of making a wish, I wish we had been taught to say a prayer thanking God for Jesus Christ. Because that is who the rainbow is to remind us of.

Never ever forget to factor God into all your equations. Back when we were being told it would never rain again, we would meet for prayer and ask God to send rain and end the drought. Which He did. Bless Him!

The Promise
Whether with Adam pre-fall or Noah post-fall, God's covenant is all about His promises. God's pre-fall covenant with Adam included issuing the cultural mandate. And God's post-fall covenant with Noah includes the same cultural mandate. We are to fill the earth and subdue it to God's glory.

Before the fall we read, "So God created mankind in his own image, in the image of

God he created them; male and female he created them. God blessed them and said to them, "Be fruitful and increase in number; fill the earth and subdue it. Rule over the fish in the sea and the birds in the sky and over every living creature that moves on the ground."

And keeping in mind that Adam and Eve were forbidden from eating the fruit of only one tree, the Tree of the Knowledge of Good and Evil, "Then God said, "I give you every seed-bearing plant on the face of the whole earth and every tree that has fruit with seed in it. They will be yours for food" (Gen. 1:29).

After the fall, "Then God blessed Noah and his sons, saying to them, 'Be fruitful and increase in number and fill the earth. The fear and dread of you will fall on all the beasts of the earth, and on all the birds in the sky, on every creature that moves along the ground, and on all the fish in the sea; they are given into your hands. Everything that lives and moves about will be food for you. Just as I gave you the green plants, I now give you everything. But you must not eat meat that has its lifeblood still in it'" (Gen. 9:1-4).

So, it looks like our diet as humans was only fruit and vegies pre-fall and only got supplemented by animal flesh post-fall. There was the forbidden fruit pre-fall, as per the covenant then, and there is the forbidden blood post-fall, as per the covenant then. We see then that God's covenants whether before or after the fall have prohibitions attached to them as well as promises.

The lifeblood was to be drained from the animal before being cooked and eaten. Why? Well, we learn a bit more from the upcoming sacrificial system of Israel, "For the life of a creature is in the blood, and I have given it to you to make atonement for yourselves on the altar; it is the blood that makes atonement for one's life" (Lev. 17:11).

So, like the Tree of Life, like the rainbow in the clouds, shedding the blood of animals for food or for sacrifice, were signs. They were reminders of God's covenant. They are signs pointing to the promises of God fulfilled in and by Christ. The writer to the Hebrews says, "In fact, the law requires that nearly everything be cleansed with blood, and without the shedding of blood there is no forgiveness" (Heb. 9:22). And John says, "the blood of Jesus, his Son, purifies us from all sin" (1 John 1:7).

So, during the fruit and vegie diet of Adam pre-fall, redemption through the shedding of blood was not needed. But post-fall, when redemption through the shedding of blood was needed, God added animal flesh to our diet. It all pointed forward to Jesus, the promised Seed of the woman, the Lamb of God who takes away the sin of the world.

But where then is the human aspect in God's covenant with Noah? It's part of the cultural mandate, "And for your lifeblood I will surely demand an accounting. I will demand an accounting from every animal. And from each human being, too, I will demand an accounting for the life of another human being. Whoever sheds human blood, by humans shall their blood be shed; for in the image of God has God made mankind. As for you, be fruitful and increase in number; multiply on the earth and increase upon it" (Gen. 9:5-7).

So, here in Genesis 9 we see God instituting the death-penalty for murder. To murder a human being is heinous because we are made in God's image. Says Richard P. Belcher,

> In Genesis 1:26-28 human beings are made in God's image and the implication of the sanctity of life is affirmed in Genesis 9:6. Human life is so significant that the taking of human life by one person requires their life be taken in return, 'for God made man in his own image.' This lays the foundation of government and establishes capital punishment as an appropriate response to murder.[110]

Again, including even the death-penalty, it all pointed forward to the covenant promise, the rainbow in the clouds, Jesus Christ, the One who would shed His own blood to bring us forgiveness, and to cleanse us of all our sins. All of God's promises point to Jesus (2 Cor. 1:20).

He wasn't coming to drown in a global flood. He wasn't coming to die by strangulation. As the last Adam He was coming to have His innocent lifeblood shed by the hands of murderers, by being hung on a cross, which is a tree of life of whose fruit we must partake if we are to be clothed in Christ's righteousness.

---

[110] Richard P. Belcher, Jr., *The Fulfillment of the Promises of God: An Explanation of Covenant Theology*, Mentor Imprint by Christian Focus Publications Ltd., Geanies House, Fearn, Ross-shire, 2020, p. 54.

The LORD God clothed or covered the first Adam's nakedness after he had partaken of the forbidden fruit (Gen. 3:21). Two of Noah's sons covered Noah's nakedness after he had partaken of the fruit of the vine (Gen. 9:21-23). Two of His followers covered the last Adam's nakedness after He had partaken of the fruit of the vine (Matt. 27:59; John 19:38-40).

What does this have to do with the price of fish? It's all redemptive history. As the Bible progresses, by use of signs, types, and foreshadows throughout, it shows you that, not only was Christ coming to redeem His cursed people, He also was coming to redeem His cursed creation (Rom. 8:21).

Noah's ark was like a floating garden of Eden. To be in the garden was to be safe. Outside was dangerous. To be in the ark was to be safe. Outside, danger. To be in Christ is safety. Outside, trouble. The ark was a type of Christ.

As a Christian, if you can't see Christ in everything, then you're looking at the clouds and not Jesus! "I have set my rainbow in the clouds, and it will be the sign of the covenant between me and the earth" (Gen. 9:13). Jesus is the rainbow in the clouds, every cloud. Always keep your eyes on Jesus. As William Cowper wrote,

> God moves in a mysterious way,
> His wonders to perform;
> He plants His footsteps in the sea,
> And rides upon the storm.

Isaiah says, "Behold, the LORD rides on a swift cloud" (Isa. 19:1). The psalmist says, "He makes the clouds his chariot and rides on the wings of the wind" (Psa. 104:3). "He mounted the cherubim and flew; he soared on the wings of the wind. He made darkness his covering, his canopy around him—the dark rain clouds of the sky. Out of the brightness of his presence clouds advanced, with hailstones and bolts of lightning" (Psa. 18:10-12).

One of the things I loved about living on the Manitoba prairie was watching the summer thunderstorms sweep across the land. Mind you, I've seen some awesome thunderclouds since moving to Queensland, some that have looked like a giant light bulb in the sky switching on and off. Others have looked dark green in colour, so saturated with water. Who hasn't sat through a deafening thunderstorm wondering if the lightning was going to strike you?

After newly arriving in Australia, I remember walking down a street with Dorothy and our young family after an awesome thundershower and being amazed at the steam rising off the hot streets! God is awesome! And thunderstorms are a picture of His awesomeness. Black clouds, thunderbolts and lightning, hailstones rattling off your roof. God sure gets your attention during a thunderstorm. Cowper again,

> You fearful saints, fresh courage take;
> The clouds you so much dread
> Are filled with mercy and shall break
> In blessings on your head.

Judge not the Lord by feeble sense.
But trust Him for His grace;
Behind a frowning providence
Faith sees a smiling face.

Look, it doesn't matter what the science says. If it is science without factoring in God, then it is not true science. Doing science without God is doing Atheism, not science. For Scripture says, "We destroy arguments and every lofty opinion raised against the knowledge of God, and take every thought captive to obey Christ" (2 Cor.10:5), and, "Trust in the LORD with all your heart, and do not lean on your own understanding. In all your ways acknowledge him, and he will make straight your paths" (Prov. 3:5-6), Thus, as Christians whose hearts have been renewed, we are to trust in God with all our heart. Says Herman Dooyeweerd,

> In Adam not only all humankind fell, but also that entire temporal cosmos of which the human was the crowned head. And in Christ, the Word become flesh, the second Covenant Head, God gave the new root of His redeemed creation, in Whom true humanity has been implanted through self-surrender, through surrender of the center of existence, the heart.[111]

Be it biology, physics, climatology, virology, chemistry, medicine, nuclear, political, meteorological, theology, no matter which the branch

---

[111] Herman Dooyeweerd, *The Christian Idea of the State*, Craig Press, Nutley, New Jersey,1968, 5.

of science, doing science without God is to ignore the One who makes science possible. He gave us His cultural mandate, first, to humanity before the fall, and then He repeated His mandate after the fall. So, whether it's corona virus, climate change, nuclear bombs, no matter what the storm clouds are, remember that God says, "I have set my rainbow in the clouds, and it will be the sign of the covenant between me and the earth" (Gen. 9:13). Therefore, don't look at the clouds. Look at the rainbow. Take comfort in His covenant. Take courage in His covenant. Look to Christ.

The People & Place

Let's focus on the nature of the rainbow covenant. "It will be the sign of the covenant between me and the *earth*" (Gen. 9:13). In Genesis 9:9a it's, "I now establish my covenant with *you*", in 9b it's, "and with your *descendants* after you. And in 9:10, it's "with *every living creature* that was with you—the birds, the livestock and all the wild animals, all those that came out of the ark with you—every living creature on earth." And in 9:11 it's, "I establish my covenant with you."

So, we've got the picture that this is God's covenant with Noah, his family, and all of God's creatures. It is God's covenant with the *earth*. Therefore, the earth and all the people are not going to be destroyed by a global flood, or by a virus, or by nuclear bombs. How do we know? Because of God's covenant, i.e., His covenant with His creation. Says Geerhardus Vos,

The representation with regard to the sign of the rainbow is anthropomorphic, but for that very reason more impressive than it could possibly be otherwise. The idea is not, as usually assumed, that by the bow man will be reminded of the divine promise, but that God Himself, were it possible for Him to forget, will by the sign Himself be reminded of His oath: 'When I bring a cloud over the earth, it shall come to pass that the bow shall be seen in the cloud, and I will remember My *berith* [covenant]'. With the rainbow it is as later on it was with circumcision; both existed before, and at a certain time, the appointed time, were consecrated by God to serve as signs of His *berith*. The sign here is connected in its character with the ominous force of nature from which it pledges protection. It is produced against the background of the very clouds that had brought destruction to the earth. But is produced upon these by the rays of the sun by which in the symbolism of Scripture represents the divine grace.[112]

Like a sweet musical refrain, the "people and place" leitmotif runs through all the Bible from Adam through Noah through Abraham, Isaac, and Jacob through Moses through David to Christ and the new heaven and new earth. The people are the elect of God, i.e., those chosen before the foundation of the

---

[112] Geerhardus, Vos, *Biblical Theology, Old and New Testaments*, The Banner of Truth Trust, Edinburgh, Scotland, 1948 (Reprinted 1985), 55.

world by the Father to be given to the Son as a bride upon His perfectly fulfilling every condition of the covenant of works. The place is not somewhere up in the clouds but on the New Earth, i.e., this earth after its renewal.

Christ was coming to redeem His creation that had become fallen and cursed when Adam sinned, "For the creation was subjected to frustration, not by its own choice, but by the will of the one who subjected it, in hope that the creation itself will be liberated from its bondage to decay and brought into the freedom and glory of the children of God. We know that the whole creation has been groaning as in the pains of childbirth right up to the present time" (Rom. 8:20-22).

So, the creation moans and groans, through droughts, floods, and fires, global viruses, and even wars between nations. These are all part of the birth pangs as we await the birth of the new creation (Rev. 21:1), of which the resurrected Christ is its firstfuits (1 Cor. 15:23).

Conclusion

Isaiah says, "'As the new heavens and the new earth that I make will endure before me,' declares the LORD, 'so will your name and descendants endure. From one New Moon to another and from one Sabbath to another, all mankind will come and bow down before me,' says the LORD." [That was the good news of the rainbow. Now the bad news of the clouds] 'And they will go out and look on the dead bodies of those who rebelled against me; the worms that eat them will not die, the fire that burns them will not be quenched, and they will be loathsome to all mankind'" (Isa. 66:22-24).

Remember what it was like for Noah and his family exiting the ark right after the flood – the dead bodies of those who rebelled against God. It was the same when the Lord destroyed Jerusalem and the Temple 66-70 AD, "For wherever the carcass is, there the eagles will be gathered together" (Matt, 24:28). Why should it be any different for us whom God is saving from His judgment? But remember, don't panic. Remember the covenant promise. Don't look at the clouds. Look at the rainbow in the clouds, our covenant, i.e., the Lord Jesus Christ.

COVENANT CONTINUITY & CONTRASTS

Introduction

Having seen that the Lord God began revealing His covenant of grace immediately after Adam broke the covenant of works, and that God's covenant with Noah revealed in broad terms His promise of a people and a place for them to dwell, and that the pre-fall cultural mandate was reissued with the addition of animals for food and sacrifice and the death-penalty for murder, we are ready to look at the continuity of the covenant of grace from Adam to Christ.

The covenant of grace was not needed before the fall. Therefore, it applies to the fallen world. Let's revisit Cain and Abel, Adam and Eve's first two children. Cain slew Abel. "Do not be like Cain, who belonged to the evil one and murdered his brother. And why did he murder him? Because his own actions were evil and his brother's were righteous" (1 John 3:12). We see by Abel's faithful actions an indication that he was of the Seed of the woman, and by Cain's unfaithful actions that he was of the devil's seed. "By faith Abel offered to God a more acceptable sacrifice than Cain, through which he was commended as righteous, God commending him by accepting his gifts. And through his faith, though he died, he still speaks" (Heb. 11:4). Thus, the first murder was when Cain slew Abel.

"Then the LORD said to Cain, 'Where is your brother Abel?' 'I don't know,' he replied. 'Am I my brother's keeper?' The LORD said, 'What have you done? Listen! Your brother's blood cries out to me from the ground. Now you are under a curse and driven from the ground, which opened its mouth to receive your brother's blood from your hand'" (Gen 4:9-11).

So, we see that Abel's shed blood cries out for justice to be done and that by placing His curse upon him, the LORD held Cain responsible for his actions in the murder of his brother. This foreshadows the death-penalty instituted with the restating of the cultural mandate with Noah (Gen. 9:5-6), "And the LORD said to him, 'Therefore, whoever kills Cain, vengeance shall be taken on him sevenfold.' And the LORD set a mark on Cain, lest anyone finding him should kill him" (Gen. 4:15).

If we keep in mind that God did not introduce the death-penalty for murder till after Noah came out of the ark, we won't get entangled in speculating why God didn't immediately kill or have Cain killed for his heinous sin. Also, much has been made of the "mark of Cain." It appears that it may have been a physical mark that others could see. It would seem that this "mark", like the "mark of the beast" mentioned in Revelation 16:2; 19:20; 20:4, was the opposite of the sign of the covenant of grace, (i.e., Old Testament circumcision and New Testament baptism). Thus, the actions of Cain and the mark of Cain showed that Cain was of the seed of the serpent and therefore was cursed by God.

Also, Abel was a keeper of sheep, some of which he would offer to God. God accepted Abel's sacrifices because his heart was right with God. Therefore, human beings were sacrificing and eating animal flesh prior to God making the practice official in Genesis 9. Therefore, the sacrificial system was in practice long before God institutionalized it in the Mosaic covenant with the nation of Israel, as were observing the Sabbath, circumcision, and many other things that became part of the Mosaic covenant. Thus, we see the continuity of the covenant of grace in Old Testament times as all these promises and prohibitions progressed towards their fulfillment with Christ in the new covenant administration.

Abrahamic Administration

We already know a lot about God cutting a covenant with Abraham (Gen. 15). Therefore, we won't need to spend too much time with Abraham here.

Adam named animals in the garden of Eden (Gen. 2:19-20). Noah saved animals in the ark (Gen. 8:15-19). However, Abraham slew animals in the land that God had promised to his seed (Gen. 15:9-11). The slain animals were substitutes, representations of what would happen to those cursed by God, as illustrated by the theophany of the smoking fire pot and flaming torch that passed between the pieces of animals (Gen. 15:17). The fiery wrath of God would come upon them.

To be sure, we have already noted that this was God's conditional promise of what He would do to Himself should He ever break His covenant of grace. Thus, all death whether human or animal, pointed forward to the death of death by the death of Christ as per the covenant of grace. "Christ has redeemed us from the curse of the law, having become a curse for us (for it is written,

"Cursed *is* everyone who hangs on a tree)" (Deut. 21:23; Gal. 3:13).

God had Abraham cut representative and substitutionary animals in two and place the pieces side by side. "And it came to pass, when the sun went down and it was dark, that behold, there appeared a smoking oven and a burning torch that passed between those pieces" (Gen. 15:17). Thus, God cut His covenant with Abraham, which same covenant in time would be ratified by the coming Prophet, Priest, and King as promised throughout the Old Testament.

God had lawless hands crucify His Son (Acts 2:23). Then He cut His temple curtain in two and, from His smoking oven as it were, as if He were His enemy, heaped hot coals of fire upon His Son's head as He bore our sins. "Then the sun was darkened, and the veil of the temple was torn in two. And when Jesus had cried out with a loud voice, He said, "Father, 'into Your hands I commit My spirit.' Having said this, He breathed His last" (Luke 23:45-46). It was then that by the Spirit Christ passed between the rent veil with His own blood. "Not with the blood of goats and calves, but with His own blood He entered the Most Holy Place once for all, having obtained eternal redemption" (Heb. 9:12).

Lest we confuse the heavenly with earthly, that which is symbolized for the symbol, the antitype with the type, Matthew Poole helps us understand what happened here,

> He entered in once into the holy place; with this blood of the covenant he entered, immediately upon the breathing out of his soul

on the cross, (the veil of the temple being rent asunder, and room made for the great High Priest to fulfil his type), into the holy of holiest in heaven, where never angel came, nor any but himself, till his now piercing through, rending the veil, and laying it open (Heb. 10:19; compare Isa. 57:15); and came with it to God's throne of justice there, and made the everlasting atonement for sin, and so turned it into a throne of grace, fulfilling his type, and as the high priest did before the sacrifice was burnt or consumed (Lev. 16:1-34). For the expiation of sin was not deferred by Christ to his ascension, forty-five days after his death, but was immediately on his giving up the Ghost by him performed; and in this he fulfilled all righteousness (Matt. 3:15).[113]

"Therefore, brethren, having boldness to enter the Holiest by the blood of Jesus, by a new and living way which He consecrated for us, through the veil, that is, His flesh" (Heb. 10:19-20). Thus, God ratified His covenant with Abraham and his Seed.

Christ, by His death, has redeemed all those who were chosen by the Father in eternity past in accordance with the covenant of redemption. These are God's elect (Eph. 1:1-14), who, because of God's gift of faith (Eph. 2:8), are also known as "the children of Abraham."

---

[113] Matthew Poole, *A Commentary on the Holy Bible*, Banner of Truth.

Abraham is the prime example of God's gift of faith. "By faith Abraham obeyed when he was called to go out to the place which he would receive as an inheritance. And he went out, not knowing where he was going. By faith he dwelt in the land of promise as *in* a foreign country, dwelling in tents with Isaac and Jacob, the heirs with him of the same promise; for he waited for the city which has foundations, whose builder and maker *is* God" (Heb. 11:8-10). Thus, Abraham is the father of the faithful.

Regardless of whether you are physically descended from Abraham or not, if you do not believe in the Messiah, then you are of the seed of the serpent. For example, Jesus met some Jews who had faith that their physical descendancy from Abraham made them right with God, rather than the grace of God through faith in the promised Messiah. Jesus said to them, "You are of *your* father the devil, and the desires of your father you want to do. He was a murderer from the beginning, and does not stand in the truth, because there is no truth in him. When he speaks a lie, he speaks from his own *resources,* for he is a liar and the father of it" (John 8:44). The apostle Paul says it plainly, "Therefore know that *only* those who are of faith are sons of Abraham" (Gal. 3:7), "And if you *are* Christ's, then you are Abraham's seed, and heirs according to the promise" (Gal. 3:29).

It is in God's covenant dealings with Abraham that the picture of the Father's covenant of redemption's promises to the Son of a people and a place become much clearer to us. Abram means "exalted father." In line with His covenant promise, the Lord subsequently would change Abram to Abraham meaning "father of a multitude." In line with the cultural mandate commands to "be fruitful and multiply", with God's blessings, the offspring of Abraham would become as numerous as the stars in the sky and the sand on the seashore. Jesus, of course, is Abraham's greatest Son, and, as we saw earlier, His bloodline traces back through David to Abraham even to Adam (Luke 3:23-28).

Though we are saved by grace alone through faith alone, James explains that true biblical faith is much more than just acknowledging God. Says James, "You believe that there is one God. You do well. Even the demons believe—and tremble! But do you want to know, O foolish man, that faith without works is dead?" (James 2:19-20).

So, Abraham, the example of faith (Heb. 11:8), was obedient to God's commands to him. "Now the LORD had said to Abram: 'Get out of your country, from your family and from your father's house, to a land that I will show you. I will make you a great nation; I will bless you and make your name great; and you shall be a blessing. I will bless those who bless you, and I will curse him who curses you; and in you all the families of the earth shall be blessed'" (Gen. 12:1-3).

We see that Abraham was a type of Christ. Those who bless Him are blessed and he who curses Him is cursed. The blessed are those who, like Abraham, have faith in the Seed of the woman. The cursed are the serpent and his seed. In short, the blessed are the obedient and the cursed are the disobedient. To be sure, as one reads the Biblical narrative, we can see that Abraham's obedience was less than perfect. However, as He does for all true believers, God imputed Abraham's faith for righteousness (Gen. 15:6; Rom. 4:3, 9, 22).

At the mention of God's blessings and curses through Abraham, we hear echoes of the pre-fall covenant of works, i.e., promised blessings for obedience and threatened curses for disobedience. God's covenant of grace promise to Abraham was "in you all the families of the earth shall be blessed." It would have been the same for Adam if had been obedient to the covenant of works. The difference being that Adam's pre-fall righteousness would have been his own rather than the post-fall righteousness of Christ, i.e., the righteousness of the obedient Christ that God credits to Abraham and to all his faithful children.

God instituted circumcision with Abraham and his household as a sign and seal of His covenant with him (Gen. 17:9-14; Rom. 4:9-12). Subsequently, male circumcision was incorporated into the Mosaic covenant as part of the ceremonial law pointing to Christ. Now, don't miss the obvious, the covenant mandate of procreation ("multiply, fill the earth") was included in the sacrament of circumcision. And don't miss how much circumcision was a reminder to Israel not to break the 7th Commandment! For to commit physical adultery was also to commit spiritual adultery (Matt. 5:28).

Jesus was the seed of Abraham coming to put off the body of sinful flesh (Col. 2:11). And notice to whom the promised Abrahamic blessings were made, "The promises were spoken to Abraham and to his seed. Scripture does not say 'and to seeds,' meaning many people, but 'and to your seed,' meaning one person, who is Christ" (Gal. 3:16). The Abrahamic covenant is fulfilled by and in Christ.

Mosaic Administration

God changed Jacob's name to Israel and repeated to him the "be fruitful and multiply" refrain of the cultural mandate.

> Then God appeared to Jacob again, when he came from Padan Aram, and blessed him. And God said to him, "Your name *is* Jacob; your name shall not be called Jacob anymore, but Israel shall be your name." So He called his name Israel. Also God said to him: "I *am* God Almighty. Be fruitful and multiply; a nation and a company of nations shall proceed from you, and kings shall come from your body. The land which I gave Abraham and Isaac I give to you; and to your descendants after you I give this land (Gen. 35:9-12).

The promise of the "nation and a company of nations" that were to proceed from Jacob/Israel began to form and become structured in the forty years of wilderness wanderings with Moses. The promised "kings" that would come from his body had to wait until Israel was established in the land that God had promised to Abraham, Isaac, and Jacob. A covenant people and a covenant place. Thus, with God's oversight, Israel developed into a well-structured and well-ordered society of families (12 tribes) under Moses.

God had redeemed them from slavery in Egypt, and subsequently had handed down the summary of His moral law to them from Mount Sinai during their travels. These are the Ten Commandments, the Decalogue, and had been written by the finger of God on two tablets of stone. Before this had taken place, Moses told the people of Israel what God had said, and they responded by stating that they wanted to be obedient to God. "Then all the people answered together and said, 'All that the LORD has spoken we will do.' So Moses brought back the words of the people to the LORD. And the LORD said to Moses, 'Behold, I come to you in the thick cloud, that the people may hear when I speak with you, and believe you forever' So Moses told the words of the people to the LORD" (Exod. 19:8-9).

After learning that the moral law would be accompanied by civil/judicial laws and ceremonial laws, Israel was still intent on obeying the covenant. "When Moses went and told the people all the LORD's words and laws, they responded with one voice, "Everything the LORD has said we will do" (Exod. 24:3). Says Robert Cara,

> The Mosaic covenant includes a significant amount of legislation. The Christian tradition has often summarized this legislation with three categories: moral (e.g., the Ten Commandments, Ex. 20:2-17; Deut. 5:6-21), ceremonial (e.g., sacrificial offering, priestly

regulations, Lev. 1–8), and civil/judicial (e.g., divorce, roof regulations, Deut. 22:8; 24:1–4) [WCF 19.3–4].[114]

The judicial law was administered by the *civil* authorities and the ceremonial law was attended to by the *religious* authorities of Israel, though there could be some general overlap. The triune God alone was their authority. He promised covenant blessings for obedience to Him (via His law), and threatened covenant curses for disobedience. These blessings for faithful obedience and curses for unfaithful disobedience are spelled out by God in great detail in Deuteronomy 27 and 28.

Though Israel under the Mosaic administration was not under a covenant administration as a means of gaining everlasting life, it was, however, *reminiscent* of the covenant of works: blessings for obedience, curses for disobedience. All of this, of course, pointed forward to the Christ to come. Says Nicholas Reid,

> While a proper covenant of works was impossible for sinful humanity, the Mosaic administration of the covenant of grace was a covenant of works for Christ.[115]

---

[114] Robert J. Cara, *Covenant in Hebrews, Covenant Theology: Biblical, Theological, and Historical Perspectives*, Crossway, Wheaton, Illinois, 2020, 258.

[115] J. Nicholas Read, *The Mosaic Covenant*, Edited by Waters, Reid, and Muether, *Covenant Theology: Biblical, Theological, and Historical Perspectives*, Crossway, Wheaton, Illinois, 2020, 169.

So, it was important right from Adam and Eve's expulsion from the garden of Eden that humanity understands that the way of salvation is not through personal obedience, but rather by God's grace alone through faith alone, which faith will be accompanied by obedient works that God has prepared for believers beforehand (Eph. 2:10). Says Ray Sutton,

> The principle is that law is at the heart of God's covenant. The primary idea is that God wants His people to see an *ethical* relationship between cause and effect: be faithful and prosper.[116]

It is during the Mosaic period that we see the duties of prophets, priests, and kings, as they are developed by God, become distinguished from each other. For example, the prophet Samuel told Saul that God was removing his kingship because he disobediently acted as if he were a priest and presented burnt and peace offerings to the LORD (1 Sam. 13:8-15). David was called by God to replace Saul as king.

Israel under the Mosaic covenant was a theocracy. Family, Church, and State, it was one nation under God. The prophets spoke forth the Word of the LORD as they reminded Israel of God's covenant with them, and the blessings for obedience to His covenant law, and curses for disobedience. The

---

[116] Ray R. Sutton, *That You May Prosper, Dominion by Covenant*, Institute for Christian Economics, Tyler, Texas, 1987, 17.

priests were to minister in the mobile tabernacle which became the fixed temple at Jerusalem, interceding for the people with the various sacrifices according to the ceremonial law. And the kings were the rulers, to rule in civil matters in accordance with the judicial law.

We should note that the jurisdictions of ceremonial law and civil law, as in Old Testament church law (religious authority) and state law (civil authority), meet in the moral law's fourth Commandment, "Remember the Sabbath day, to keep it holy" (Exod. 20:8). And if we remember that the word sabbath does not mean seven, but rest, as in cessation of labour in order to worship God, we will easily see that though the jurisdictions between church and state are distinct, in terms of the covenant of grace, they must never be separated lest those who labour forget God.

God's moral law was the basis for order in Old Testament Israel. Whereas the priestly focus was to be on the first four commandments which show our duty to God, the kingly focus was to be an the last six which show our civil duties to each other. The prophet was to help ensure that the moral law as it applied to the nation of Israel was kept. (See above example with Samuel and Saul.)

It only takes a little thought to see that the distinctions among a prophet, a priest, and a king in the Old Testament are the same as the distinctions between knowledge, holiness, and righteousness respectively. God had created Adam with knowledge of God, holiness, and righteousness. God restores this when He converts the sinner, with the result that he or she now knows God, is holy, and is righteous.

Let's remind ourselves what righteousness and holiness are. To be righteous is to be declared right with God because of Christ. This is a legal transaction. This is justification. Being justified by God does not change your nature. However, to be holy is to be separated unto God. It is to be made what God has declared the justified person to be, i.e., righteous. Holiness is both definitive, meaning that you now *are* holy, (i.e., you have been given a new nature), and progressive, meaning that you are being made even more holy. This is sanctification. Though you can't have one without the other, justification and sanctification must be kept distinct and should never be confused. But what about knowledge?

Well, how do we know God? We know God through the things He has made, i.e., creation, and ourselves as part of His creation, especially through our conscience, and by the Spirit speaking to us with His Word, i.e., His written revelation.

We've gone to great lengths already explaining that we were created as the image of God. We are supposed to be little mirrors of God, but we became tarnished in the fall. The promise in the Mosaic covenant is that God will put His laws in our minds and write them on our hearts and that we will know the LORD, the least of us to the greatest (Jer. 31:31-34; Heb. 8:7-13). This is the promise of the second or new or better covenant, making the first or the old covenant with Israel obsolete (Heb. 8:13).

So, God declares us righteous, and He makes us holy. How? By the Spirit regenerating us and writing the two tables of His law anew on our new hearts. This law on renewed hearts is what James calls the "law of liberty" and the "royal law" (James 1:25; 2:8-12). God's law no longer condemns us (Rom. 8:1), as it did before we were converted by God's grace through faith (Rom. 3:20).

If we keep in mind that God's moral law that is written on our renewed hearts is revelation of His character, it is interesting to note that both James and Paul talk about us looking into a mirror. James compares the disobedient non-Christian to be like someone who sees his reflection but forgets what kind of person he or she saw, with the one who looks into the perfect law of liberty and obediently continues in it. The former is only a hearer of the Word. The latter is a hearer and a doer of it and will be blessed in what he or she does (James 2:23-25).

Paul, as per the "Love Passage" as traditionally read out at weddings, says, "For now we see through a glass, darkly [αἰνίγματι]; but then face to face: now I know in part; but then shall I know even as also I am known" (1 Cor. 13:12). The "darkly" in the "glass, darkly" is where we get the word "enigma" from. Paul sees in the looking glass enigmatically what he shall see face to face. To be sure, when we see Christ return in glory we shall be like Him (1 John 3:2) and see Him face to face. This is the usual understanding of seeing through the glass, darkly, i.e., looking in a mirror rather through a window. And let's not argue with the truth of that! However, Christ who is the express image of God was seen only in the shadows (types, theophanies, the ceremonial law etc.) of the Old Testament. But now, in New Testament times, the Light of the World has lit Himself up, i.e., He has revealed Himself to us in the new covenant in His blood. Also, the Bible, the Book of the Covenant, is now no longer "in part" but is complete. The Spirit works with the Word as the elect look into its mirror and see Christ revealed therein.

Let us remember that God's covenant of redemption in eternity past was revealed to us progressively. First, partially in the covenant of works. Then fully the covenant of grace. Redemption, works, grace, in that order. matching the order of the Trinity, Father, Son, and Holy Spirit. The Father proposes redemption in eternity, the Son procures redemption on the cross, and the Spirit applies the grace of this redemption to those chosen by the Father to be the Son's bride. Now, with this in mind, think of the moral, ceremonial, and civil law in the Mosaic administration of the covenant of grace.

We know that the Ten Commandments reveal the character of God. The first four of which were administered by the priests, and the last six by the kings. The prophets were to remind Israel of the blessings and curses that would come from obedience or disobedience to the covenant law. Thus, prophets, priests, and kings. This also is revelation of God who is triune. Thus, under the Mosaic administration of the covenant of grace Israel had its legislative, executive, and judicial branches of government, reflecting and progressively revealing the character of God.

Post-fall the first four commandments pertain to redemption found in God (the Father). The last six how that redemption is accomplished by God (the Son). And all Ten Commandments (which are incomplete without the inclusion of the important preamble) reveals that that redemption is graciously given by God (the Spirit). Thus, the covenants of redemption, works, are revealed in the covenant of grace, even in its Mosaic administration. Progressive revelation.

The prophet reflects the Father by pointing to God's legislation, i.e., the covenant law. The king reflects the Son by enforcing that legislation as executor. And the priest reflects the Spirit judicially interceding (see e.g., John 16:8) on behalf of those who have broken the covenant and pointing to the God who forgives by grace alone. Thus, the Mosaic covenant by its legislative, executive, and judicial branches of administration, reveals the promised prophet, priest, and king to come, i.e., Christ Jesus, who is the complete revelation of the triune God (Col. 2:9; Heb. 1:3).

The Mosaic covenant, as in the Old Testament application of the two tables of the law, (the first table in the ceremonial law and the second in the civil law), was to be done away with by Christ fulfilling the roles as Prophet, Priest, and King in His life, death, resurrection, ascension, and session at the right hand of His Father. The Mosaic covenant is now fulfilled in and by Christ.

Davidic Administration

God had said to Jacob, "I *am* God Almighty. Be fruitful and multiply; a nation and a company of nations shall proceed from you, and kings shall come from your body" (Gen. 35:11). David was one of the kings that came from Jacob's body. Yet even though God had made this covenant promise, like the fall of man, it came to pass through disobedience.

> Then all the elders of Israel gathered together and came to Samuel at Ramah, and said to him, 'Look, you are old, and your sons do not walk in your ways. Now make us a king to judge us like all the nations.' But the thing displeased Samuel when they said, 'Give us a king to judge us.' So Samuel prayed to the LORD. And the LORD said to Samuel, 'Heed the voice of the people in all that they say to you; for they have not rejected you, but they have rejected Me, that I should not reign over them. According to all the works which they have done since the day that I brought them up out of Egypt, even to this day—with which they have forsaken Me and served other gods—so they are doing to you also. Now therefore, heed their voice. However, you shall solemnly forewarn them, and show them the behavior of the king who will reign over them' (1 Sam. 8:4-7).

Here, one is reminded of that well-known verse, "And we know that all things work together for good to those who love God, to those who are the called according to *His* purpose" (Rom. 8:28). Whether the fall of Adam or the sin of Israel, God is working all things together for good according to His purpose, i.e., His covenant of redemption from eternity past.

> Thus says the LORD: 'If you can break My covenant with the day and My covenant with the night, so that there will not be day and night in their season, then My covenant may also be broken with David My servant, so that he shall not have a son to reign on his throne, and with the Levites, the priests, My ministers. As the host of heaven cannot be numbered, nor the sand of the sea measured, so will I multiply the descendants of David My servant and the Levites who minister to Me' (Jer. 33:20-22).

God raised up prophets, priests, and kings down through the ages as forerunners of Jesus Christ, the Prophet, Priest, and King. He was foreshadowed by those who came before Him. Yet none of His predecessors could measure up to the rule of righteousness even as spelled out in the Mosaic covenant. Moses and the rest of prophets fell short. Aaron and the Levitical priesthood too, as did David and the rest of the kings. Only Christ could keep the Mosaic covenant perfectly.

The preincarnate Christ was David's Lord. Psalm 110 has the title, *A Psalm of* David. Note the difference between LORD and Lord, "The LORD said to my Lord, 'Sit at My right hand, Till I make Your enemies Your footstool'" (Psa. 110:1). Jay Green is helpful where he translates the original Hebrew, "A statement of Jehovah to my Lord, Sit at My right hand, until I set Your enemies (as) Your footstool."[117]

So, what we have is a reminder of the promises the Father made to the (to be incarnated) Son in the covenant of redemption in eternity past, which covenant promise was honoured when Jesus fulfilled it by His passive and active obedience through His life and death. For Him it was a covenant of works, which for all believers (whether Old or New Testament) is the covenant of grace. The apostle Paul applies this verse to Jesus where he says, "For He must reign till He has put all enemies under His feet. The last enemy *that* will be destroyed *is* death" (1 Cor. 15:25-26). Jesus, the Son of David, applied that verse to Himself, "While the Pharisees were gathered together, Jesus asked them, saying, 'What do you think about the Christ? Whose Son is He?' They said to Him, '*The Son* of David.' He said to them, 'How then does David in the Spirit call Him "Lord," saying: "The LORD said to my Lord, 'Sit at My right hand, Till I make Your enemies Your footstool'? If David then calls Him "Lord," how is He his Son?' And no one was able to answer Him a word, nor from that day on did anyone dare question Him anymore" (Matt. 22:41-46). Thus, Jesus, whose genealogy came from David, and, as per the covenant of grace, because He was the Word who became flesh, was able to stop the mouths of the Pharisees.

So, we see that David's greater Son, his Lord, is none other than the man Christ Jesus, who now sits

---

[117] Jay Green, *The Interlinear, Hebrew/Greek/English Bible*, Volume Three, Associated Publishers and Authors, Inc, Evansville, Indiana, 1978, 1497.

as the King of kings upon the throne of David in Heaven (Isa. 9:7; Rev. 19:16). Jesus is the great Prophet by whom God speaks. (Hebrews 1:2). Jesus is the Great High Priest who ministered once for all in the Holy of Holies. He sprinkled His own shed blood on the Mercy Seat in the Temple (Heb. 9:11-12). Thus, Jesus Christ is Prophet, Priest, and King.

As Prophet, He calls His elect from all the ends of the earth. He is King of kings because as Mediator all authority has been given to Him in heaven and on earth (Matt. 28:18; 1 Tim. 2:5). And if He has all authority in heaven and on earth, then He can, by the Holy Spirit, spiritually regenerate, and as High Priest, sprinkle His shed blood on whom He wants, including even David retroactively.

That David was a sinner in need of redemption from God's justice is clearly seen in the episode with his adultery with Bathsheba and the murder of her husband Uriah (2 Sam. 11:1-17). David escaped the ultimate punishment for adultery and murder, i.e., the death-penalty, through true repentance (Psa. 32). Again, we see that in the covenant God works even our disobedience for good. Though David's son of adultery dies in infancy, he went on to father the wisest king Solomon by Bathsheba.

It is interesting to note that David's repentance for his sins of adultery and murder came about after hearing a parable from the Lord's prophet Nathan. It was about the unjust theft and death of a poor family's only lamb, a beloved pet, at the hands of a rich man who had "exceedingly many flocks and herds" (2 Sam. 12:2). Though David repented, he still lost his son to Bathsheba because of his sin. "So David said to Nathan, 'I have sinned against the LORD.' And Nathan said to David, 'The LORD also has put away your sin; you shall not die. However, because by this deed you have given great occasion to the enemies of the LORD to blaspheme, the child also *who is* born to you shall surely die'" (2 Sam. 12:13-14). The death of a lamb and the death of a son. God will not be mocked (Gal. 6:7).

Jesus, the Lamb of God, the Son of David came to die for sinners such as king David. The Davidic covenant is now fulfilled in and by Christ.

New Testament Administration

The whole crux of covenant theology is that, as per the covenant of redemption, the death of the first Adam, as per the covenant of works, guaranteed the death of the last Adam, as per the covenant of grace. In other words, the death of Adam signalled and ensured the death of the Testator and the release of all the covenant blessings. Paradoxically, the life that God promised to Adam for keeping the covenant of works was received through the death that was threatened for its transgression. In other words, Adam (if he is one of God's elect) receives the blessings promised in the covenant of works through Christ's death.

The New Testament administration begins where the Old Testament administration ends, i.e., with the resurrection of Christ from the dead. The demolition of the Temple in 70 AD signalled the end of the old covenant administration and the inauguration of the new.

The ceremonial law and the civil law of Old Testament Israel which centred on the Temple in Jerusalem where God dwelled in the holy of holies, gave way to the new place where God dwelled, i.e., in Christ, and He, by His Spirit and therefore by extension, in His holy catholic or universal church. No longer were quarterly pilgrimages to the Temple necessary to meet God, now God could be met wherever two or three are gathered in Christ's name, i.e., at a church gathering.

The New Testament administration is currently being fulfilled in and by Christ.

COVENANT HEART CHECK

Introduction

Having seen that the Lord God began revealing His covenant of grace immediately after the fall, and that the covenants with Noah, Abraham, Isaac, Jacob, Moses, and David were various administrations of the covenant of grace demonstrating its continuity from Adam to Christ, in the following we shall have a closer look at how Christ in the covenant of grace applies to believers.

Just as those moving from a sedentary to a rigorously physical life should have a heart check-up, so should those who have been given new life in Christ, lest we fall in a ditch clutching our chest.

Heart Treatment

Isn't it wonderful when mothers instruct their daughters, fathers their sons, and parents their children? Of course, sadly, some children grow up without either a mother, or a father, or even any parents. However, here we have a father instructing his son. And this is not just any father. This father is the wisest man in the world! The following is King Solomon instructing his son. Therefore, his advice is worth paying attention to.

> My son, pay attention to what I say; turn your ear to my words. Do not let them out of your sight, keep them within your heart; for they are life to those who find them and health to one's whole body. Above all else, guard your heart, for everything you do flows from it.

287

Keep your mouth free of perversity; keep corrupt talk far from your lips. Let your eyes look straight ahead; fix your gaze directly before you. Give careful thought to the paths for your feet and be steadfast in all your ways. Do not turn to the right or the left; keep your foot from evil (Prov. 4:20-27 NIV).

We see here in Proverbs 4:20 that Solomon starts with, "My son, pay attention to what I say." Then he mentions some parts of the human body, and even the whole body itself. But he mentions the ears, the mouth, the lips, the eyes, the feet, and the thing I want us to focus on, i.e., the heart.

We are to listen to Solomon's words with our ears, we are to store them within our hearts, we are to keep our mouths from speaking perverse things, and our lips far from corrupt talk, and our eyes on the straight and narrow, and our feet on the well-lit the paths of righteousness. Wow! How are we going to manage to do all this? That is why I want us to focus on the following, "Above all else, guard your heart, for everything you do flows from it" (Prov. 4:23).

You are being instructed to guard your heart. Why? Because your life depends on it. Notice that Solomon says, "Above all else." Yes, ears, mouths, lips, and feet are important aspects of who we are. But the heart is the thing, the main thing. We can survive with things wrong with most other parts of our bodies, but definitely not the heart. Once the heart stops pumping, then everything that flows from it ceases too.

I saw a doctor. He placed his cold stethoscope on my chest and listened to my heart. He told me that my heartbeat was irregular. He tapped the rhythm with a pen on his desk. "Wow! Reggae?" said I. When I got home, I plugged my ears and listened to my own heartbeat. It sounds more like the old Queen song, "We Will Rock You!" Boom, boom, chish! Boom, boom, chish! Anyway, while at the doctor's office I mentioned that, when I was in the army, because of high blood pressure I had asked the army doctor if he expected me to have a heart attack if I kept on running and playing sports. He said, "Probably not." I asked the civilian doctor, "What do you say?" He replied, "Just make sure you don't exercise alone."

You look to the experts for advice, and all you get is a "probably not" and a "don't exercise alone"! Well, at least I know I need to keep an eye on my heart. Why? Because I know that something's not quite right with it.

Why would Solomon need to tell us to guard our hearts if nothing can go wrong with them? "Above all else, guard your heart." More than your Superannuation, more than your house, more than your car, your job, your chooks, your goldfish, your hair, your appearance, your ears, mouth, lips, and feet, above all else, guard your heart. Why? Because "everything you do flows from it." Or, as the NKJV puts it, "for out of it spring the issues of life."

Hold on a wee minute! Is Solomon talking about the thing that pumps blood around our bodies, or is he using the heart to teach us a spiritual lesson? Now, that may seem like a redundant question, but remember what Jesus said to Nicodemus, "If I told you earthly things and you do not believe, how will you believe if I tell you heavenly things?" (John 3:12).

Cardiologists use many medical technological marvels to probe our hearts, but God uses His Word. "For the word of God is living and active, sharper than any two-edged sword, piercing to the division of soul and of spirit, of joints and of marrow, and discerning the thoughts and intentions of the heart" (Heb. 4:12).

I startled a little lizard in my backyard one time. Its little tail fell off as the wee lizard shot through. As he made a run for it, I watched the little tail as it wriggled frantically, no doubt as a decoy, as the tailless lizard fled to safety. I watched the tail as it did its wriggly thing, eventually slowing down to a complete halt some seven or so minutes later. Amazing stuff!

I remember one of my friends, an ambulance guy, an "Ambo", telling me that if you slice a little sliver from a living human heart, (kids, don't try this at home!) the sliver keeps on beating – a least for a while. Don't quote me, but I think he called it the "intrinsic factor".

What do lizards and heart slivers have to do with what we're looking at? What happened to Adam when he ate the forbidden fruit in the Garden? God had told Adam, "when you eat from it you will certainly die" (Gen. 2:17). Well, Adam died immediately, but his heart kept on beating – at least for a while. Therefore, just because your heart's beating doesn't mean that you are alive. It's like the lizard's tail. The beating heart is merely a decoy.

After eating the forbidden fruit, Adam and Eve made a run for it into the bushes to hide. What was wrong with them? Their hearts were still beating but they were now dead spiritually. They had become dead in their trespasses and sins (Eph. 2:1). And so had all their posterity. "Therefore, just as sin entered the world through one man, and death through sin, and in this way death came to all people, because all sinned" (Rom. 5:12).

Think about it: Everything every human being does flows from a defective heart. Do you wonder why there're wars in the world? A defective heart! Do you wonder why people argue with each other? A defective heart! Do you wonder where hate comes from? Why people say bad things about others? Why people lie and cheat? Why you sometimes even lie to yourself? Yes, it's because everything you and I do flows from a heart defect!

This is why Solomon is telling his son, (and us), to guard his heart above all else. Why? Because "From out of it spring the issues of life." Our physical hearts pump blood to every part of our body. It's like our hearts are bubbling springs that water everything we do. And James gives us this warning,

> But no human being can tame the tongue. It is a restless evil, full of deadly poison. With the tongue we praise our LORD and Father, and with it we curse human beings, who have been made in God's likeness. Out of the same mouth come praise and cursing. My brothers

and sisters, this should not be. Can both fresh water and salt water flow from the same spring? (James 3:8-11).

Therefore, the heart treatment is that, first off, we know our heart's arrhythmic condition. And then take steps to protect it. We do this by guarding our hearts. How do we guard our hearts? By paying attention to wise instruction. By inclining our ears to Solomon's sayings, by storing them within our hearts, by keeping our mouths from speaking perverse things, and our lips far from corrupt talk, our eyes on the straight and narrow, and our feet on the well-lit paths of righteousness.

The Psalmist says, "I have hidden Your word in my heart that I might not sin against You" (Psa. 119:11). The LORD urges us to do the same thing by the graphic and memorable, "Therefore circumcise the foreskin of your heart, and be stiff-necked no longer" (Deut. 10:16).

Heart Trouble

Adam and Eve were supposed to love the LORD their God with all their heart, soul, strength, and mind, and love their neighbour as themselves. When Adam failed to do this, we all failed to do this, for when Adam sinned, we all sinned (Rom. 5:12). When Adam hid from God, we all hid from God. When Adam tried to cover up his shame, we all try to cover up our shame. But what about the "intrinsic factor"? Well, it's all the lizard's twitching tail, isn't it? You think you're alive because your heart is beating. But that horse has long since bolted. When

Adam got heart trouble, we all got heart trouble. When Adam's heart blackened, all our hearts blackened.

James says that "the body without the spirit is dead". It's simply the "intrinsic factor" that is at play. The spirit is dead, but the ears, mouth, lips, and feet keep moving, indeed the whole body keeps moving because the heart keeps beating – at least for a while. Eventually, Adam died (Gen. 5:5).

All human beings die because our spirits are dead. When Adam sinned, he immediately died spiritually and proved that he was spiritually dead by running off to try to hide from God. "God is spirit" (John 4:24). Spiritual things are spiritually discerned. Your spirit is dead to God, and it leaves you when you expire, when you take your last breath, and then your last breath leaves you.

In the Bible, the words breath, wind, spirit are all the same words. Context determines whether Old Testament *ruach* and New Testament *pneuma* are translated as breath or wind or spirit. Remember, it was God who gave breath to Adam (and all humanity). "Then the Lord God formed a man from the dust of the ground and breathed into his nostrils the breath of life, and the man became a living being" (Gen. 2:7). And what did God say that He was going to do at the time of Noah's Flood? "I am going to bring floodwaters on the earth to destroy all life under the heavens, every creature that has the breath of life in it. Everything on earth will perish" (Gen. 6:17).

If you think all of this is a bit drastic, then you haven't understood the sinfulness of sin. Why did God destroy all humanity, except for those in the ark?

"The LORD saw how great the wickedness of the human race had become on the earth, and that every inclination of the thoughts of the human heart was only evil all the time" (Gen. 6:5).

Did you get that? "Every inclination of the thoughts of the human heart was only evil all the time." That's your heart and my heart that's being spoken of. The Lord through His prophet Jeremiah says, "The heart is deceitful above all things and beyond cure. Who can understand it?" (Jer. 17:9). Paul says to the Romans,

> As it is written: 'There is no one righteous, not even one; there is no one who understands; there is no one who seeks God. All have turned away, they have together become worthless; there is no one who does good, not even one.' 'Their throats are open graves; their tongues practice deceit.' 'The poison of vipers is on their lips.' 'Their mouths are full of cursing and bitterness.' 'Their feet are swift to shed blood; ruin and misery mark their ways, and the way of peace they do not know.' 'There is no fear of God before their eyes' (Rom. 3:10-18).

We could pile up Bible verses showing us what's wrong with our hearts, but if you are thinking that none of this refers to you, then you are proving that the heart is deceitful above all things. We lie to ourselves! You may easily understand people lying to others. But lying to yourself? That's just crazy! Plumb loco! One of the biggest lies we tell ourselves is that we are good at heart. "Yeah, I may not be perfect, but at least I'm not like an axe-murderer. Yes, I thank God that I'm not like other men, such as tax-collectors." (see e.g., Luke 18:11).

Thinking of your own goodness, your own righteousness is simply the lizard's detached wriggling and writhing tail. It's a decoy. It's of the devil. Beware! Any form of self-righteousness is the Great Dragon's twitching tail of distraction.

Do you see why Solomon is saying, "Above all else, guard your heart"? It's because "everything you do flows from it." Therefore, being a Christian is all about self-control and not self-righteousness. Thus, Christian revival must begin in the individual Christian's heart before it will spread.

But listen to this piece of good news regarding Christians, "But God, being rich in mercy, because of His great love with which He loved us, even when we were dead in our transgressions, made us alive together with Christ (by grace you have been saved)" (Eph. 2:4-5). And remember God's covenant promise to do for His people, including you and me, i.e., as Christians, "I will give you a new heart and put a new spirit within you; and I will remove the heart of stone from your flesh and give you a heart of flesh" (Ezek. 36:26).

Heart Transplant

The first-ever human heart transplant was done by the South African Christiaan Barnard on December 3, 1967. But sadly, the recipient died some eighteen days later of pneumonia. Poor guy! However, God has been renewing hearts since the fall of man in the Garden. Sure, God is not transplanting the physical pump. That will have to wait until the great resurrection at the Last Day. However, God has been renewing the hearts of His people down through history till today.

Look at any of the genealogies that run from Adam down to Solomon's greatest ancestor Jesus Christ. God gave each of these a new heart. About Solomon's father, King David, Scripture says, "After removing Saul, he made David their king. God testified concerning him: 'I have found David son of Jesse, a man after my own heart; he will do everything I want him to do.' From this man's descendants God has brought to Israel the Savior Jesus, as he promised" (Acts 13:22-23).

Could you imagine being a man or a woman after God's own heart? Who is more like a man after God's own heart than Jesus Christ? Referring to Himself, Jesus told His people that One greater than Solomon is here. "The Queen of the South will rise at the judgment with the people of this generation and condemn them, for she came from the ends of the earth to listen to Solomon's wisdom; and now something greater than Solomon is here" (Luke 11:31).

The name Solomon is derived from the Hebrew word *shalom*, meaning peace. As Solomon was the King of Peace, so Jesus, his greatest Son, is the Prince of Peace. "And he will be called Wonderful Counselor, Mighty God, Everlasting Father, Prince of Peace. Of the greatness of his government and peace there will be no end" (Isa. 9:6b-7a).

If a sinner like David was a man after God's own heart, then what does that make the righteous Jesus? He is the Great Physician who has given everyone who believes in Him a heart transplant. As the lizard grows a new tail, so the Christian, by God's grace, grows a new heart. How does the Christian know that he or she has a new heart? You no longer rule, but the Spirit of Christ rules in your heart.

God removes your stony heart and gives you a heart of flesh. He throws away the old brick dangling from a frayed piece of rope and gives you a solid gold pendulum that the Holy Spirit keeps going forever. "For the eyes of the LORD range throughout the earth to strengthen those whose hearts are fully committed to him" (2 Chron. 16:9). And in Hebrews 10 we see,

> But when this priest had offered for all time one sacrifice for sins, he sat down at the right hand of God, and since that time he waits for his enemies to be made his footstool. For by one sacrifice he has made perfect forever those who are being made holy. The Holy Spirit also testifies to us about this. First he says: 'This is the covenant I will make with them after that time, says the LORD. I will put my laws in their hearts, and I will write them on their minds.' Then he adds: 'Their sins and lawless acts I will remember no more.' And where these have been forgiven, sacrifice for sin is no longer necessary (Heb. 10:12-18).

You, the Christian, are no longer an enemy of God. You and God have been reconciled. You're no longer trying to hide from God. You have come into the light, and by coming into the light your sins have been exposed. But God has given you the promise that, because of what Christ did on the cross by shedding His blood for you, He will remember your lawless acts no more.

Sin is lawlessness. "Everyone who sins breaks the law; in fact, sin is lawlessness" (1 John 3:4). But God has given you a new heart with His law written on it. It is this new heart that you are to keep healthy, as Solomon says, "Above all else, guard your heart, for everything you do flows from it." As Jesus says in Luke 6:45, "A good man brings good things out of the good stored up in his heart, and an evil man brings evil things out of the evil stored up in his heart. For the mouth speaks what the heart is full of."

Conclusion

Follow Solomon's clear instruction. Keep his words in your heart. In other words, cram your head full of Scripture. Read the Bible carefully and often. Listen to good sermons. Read good books that explain the Bible. Saturate yourself with solid Bible teaching. Be spiritually discerning. Learn how to apply Biblical principles to every situation, everything you do, be it politics, education, child-rearing, business dealings, economics, marriage, music, architecture, science, law, everything!

Yes, "Above all else, guard your heart, for <u>everything</u> you do flows from it."

COVENANT ANGEL

Introduction

Having seen that the covenant of grace was put into place immediately after the fall, and that Noah, Abraham, Isaac, Jacob, Moses, David, and Christ were involved in the continuity of various administrations of the covenant of grace and its application to believers, and that Christians need to guard their renewed hearts, let us now look at one of the ways Christ was present with believers since the fall to His incarnation.

In the following we'll be looking at someone referred to in Scripture as *the Angel of His Presence,* and we'll see that this Angel, like the Father and the Holy Spirit, is also Jehovah.

> In their affliction He [i.e., Jehovah or LORD] was afflicted, and the Angel of His Presence saved them; in His love and in His pity He redeemed them; and He bore them and carried them all the days of old (Isa. 63:9).

Covenant Messenger

Who is the Angel of His Presence? First off, we know that an angel is a "messenger." That's what the word "angel" means, "messenger." Therefore, whoever this angel is, he's a messenger of the LORD. It would appear, also, that the Angel of His Presence is not the Holy Spirit.

The Holy Spirit is a title, a name, as is the Angel of His Presence. Yet the Holy Spirit and the Angel of His Presence are closely related. They're both referred to as His (i.e., Jehovah's), Holy Spirit and the Angel of His, (i.e., Jehovah's), Presence. So, we could say, then, that the LORD is in possession of the Holy Spirit and the Angel. Yet, as we shall see more clearly, the Angel is not Jehovah the Holy Spirit. For, as we know from other places in Scripture, the Holy Spirit is the One who *sanctifies.* To be sanctified is to be set apart for a holy use. E.g., the Sabbath is a "holy" day. It is set apart. The Holy Spirit is the One who *sanctifies* those who are saved by the LORD. They're called "holy people" in Isaiah 63:18 because they are sanctified by the Holy Spirit in their midst. However, the Angel of His Presence, as we see in Isaiah 63:9, "saved them."

Whereas the Holy Spirit is their Sanctifier, the Angel of His Presence is their Saviour. Yet it was the LORD who *both* saved and sanctified His set-apart or "holy people." For we see that the LORD Himself is clearly referred to as their "Saviour", "So He became their Saviour" (Isa. 63:8).

The LORD, then, is the One who *sent* the Angel of His Presence to save them. And it was the LORD who *sent* His Holy Spirit among them or upon or within them (Isa. 63:11). Therefore, three Persons are to be distinguished here. First, there's the LORD. This is the One whom Isaiah on behalf of the people refers to in Isaiah 63:16 as "our Father." For Isaiah says there twice, "You, O LORD, are our Father." He is saying, "You, O *Jehovah*, are our Father." And Jehovah is the One who sends His Messenger, i.e., the Angel of His Presence. And finally, of course, He also sends His Holy Spirit.

So, we see here then, the Father, the Angel, and the Holy Spirit, i.e., three Persons or *Elohim,*

(Hebrew אֱלֹהִים), but One *Jehovah* or LORD (Hebrew: יְהֹוָה YHWH). "Hear, O Israel: The LORD [יְ ה וָ ה] our God, the LORD *is* one!" (Deut. 6:4).

It can be a little confusing sometimes when distinguishing the roles of the three Persons of the Godhead, however, our main interest at the moment is in the middle Person, the Angel of His Presence. And we've already established that He is the people's Saviour. For Isaiah 63:9 says He is the Angel of the LORD's Presence who saved them.

Now we're ready to look a little more closely into the nature of His Being. We know already that He is a messenger because that's what the title "angel" means. But a "messenger of what? Well, He is the Messenger of the LORD's Presence. Now then, if I said, "Take my presence back to your place for dinner today", what would you have to do to comply? You'd have to take *me* myself with you, wouldn't you? So, who would you have to take, to take the LORD's Presence home with you? You'd have to take the LORD Himself with you, wouldn't you? But is He *just* the LORD's Messenger? What is He the Messenger of? He's the Angel of, the Messenger of, the LORD's *Presence*. Therefore, wherever this Messenger goes, the LORD Himself goes.

We see then that this Angel actually carries the LORD with Him or in Him. Wherever this Angel is, there too is the Presence of the LORD God, *Jehovah Elohim*. The face of this Angel then, is the face of the LORD God. And isn't that what the Hebrew word "presence" is literally, i.e., "face" (Hebrew: פָּנִים *panim*). He is the Messenger of the LORD God's face. He is the same Angel God sent before Israel's conquest of the Promised Land. "Behold, I send an Angel before you to keep you in the way and to bring you into the place which I have prepared. Beware of Him and obey His voice; do not provoke Him, for He will not pardon your transgressions; for My name *is* in Him" (Exod. 23:20-21).

What does this mean? Well, it most certainly means that God reveals Himself in this Messenger. For this Angel is the express image of the One who sent Him. He comes from the face of God, and He represents the face of God. But more importantly, He *is* the face of God, because He is God! Think about it, here is a Messenger who carries God's face with Him wherever He goes! To look into the face of this Angel is to look into the face of God.

This Angel is not like any other angel. All other angels were created, but not this Angel. This Angel has to be the eternally begotten Son of the Father. For to have Him present with you is to have God present. He's the One, then, who brought good news, the gospel of salvation to Adam and Eve after they fell. Adam and Eve heard the sound or *voice* (for it's the same word) of the LORD God literally walking up and down in the Garden. Now, didn't this Voice of the LORD God walking up and down in the Garden have a message? Didn't He have a message for three sentient beings, viz., the serpent or Satan, the woman and the man? If He carried a message does that make Him a messenger, even an angel? Of course, it does.

If you were to read Genesis 3:8 again, you'd see that Adam and Eve hid themselves from His

Presence! The New International Version misses it by saying, "And they hid from the LORD God." The King James Version and the New King James Version get it right, for they both say, "And Adam and his wife hid themselves from the presence of the LORD God." Adam and Eve, then, hid themselves from what? From the presence, i.e., from the face of the LORD God. Who carries the presence or the face of the LORD God with Him? The Angel of His presence.

And who was it that came to Cain after he slew his brother Abel? We're told in Genesis 4 that it was the LORD Himself who spoke to Cain. "And Cain said to the LORD, 'My punishment is greater than I can bear! Surely You have driven me out this day from the face of the ground; I shall be hidden from your <u>face</u>'" (Gen. 4:13-14). And Genesis 4:16, "Then Cain went out from the <u>presence</u> of the LORD." So, that was Cain's punishment then, banished from the face of God.

At least one of the three angels who visited Abraham was the Angel of the LORD (Gen. 18:1-3). The Messenger of the LORD told Abraham that He was about to destroy Sodom. And after Abraham bargained with the Angel about the number of righteous people in Sodom, we read this interesting verse, "Then the LORD rained brimstone and fire on Sodom and Gomorrah, from the LORD out of the heavens" (Gen. 19:24).

To state the obvious, a messenger is one who brings a message. And the messenger may be human, such as the Prophet Isaiah, or he may be a spirit being such as the angel Gabriel (who's mentioned by name twice in the Book of Daniel and once in Luke). But, as we've seen, the Messenger may even be the LORD Himself, as is the case of the Angel of His Presence.

So, we've seen then, that Isaiah knows who this Angel is. He knows it's the LORD Himself. He didn't have a copy of the New Testament, but Isaiah, as you can see, knows that God is Triune. Let me give just a couple of illustrations before we move on. Isaiah 6:3, "Holy, Holy, Holy is the LORD of hosts." The LORD is Holy three times, the Holy Father (John 17:11), and the Holy Son (Luke 1:35), and the Holy Spirit (Matt. 28:19). Now you might think that this would be scant evidence to use to prove the Trinity in the Old Testament. But not so when you lay it up against the rest of Scripture thus far not including the New Testament.

Isaiah 6:8, does this ring any bells? "Also I heard the voice of the Lord, saying, 'Whom shall I send, and who will go for Us?'" It would be ludicrous to think that Isaiah was ignorant of the Scriptures. He has read Genesis 1:1 and he has seen that God is a plurality of Persons. He has read Genesis 1:26 where the LORD God says, "Let Us make man in Our image." He has read where God said after Adam had fallen, "Behold, the man has become like one of Us." He has read where God said at the Tower of Babel, "Let Us go down there and confuse their language." He has read the Proverb where it's asked, "What is His [the Lord's] name, and what is His Son's name?" He has read all the Psalms. He's read, "Kiss the Son, lest He be angry ... Blessed are all those who put their trust in Him" (Psa. 1:12). The point I make is that Isaiah, along with all the Old Testament saints we'll see in heaven, trusted in the same Person we trust in for salvation, i.e., God the Son.

The Son is the Immanuel (i.e., God with us) that Isaiah speaks of in Isaiah 7:14. Think about it, the Old Testament saints had God with them as the Angel of His Presence. And another Old Testament Prophet, Malachi, says that the Old Testament believers "delighted" in the Angel. For Malachi says in 3:1b, "Even the Messenger of the covenant, in whom you delight, Behold, He is coming." (The NIV misses the fact that the Old Testament saints were "delighting" in the Angel at that point in time. (*Delighting* is present tense in the Hebrew). And I'm sure all of this has become clear to you. For we've seen that the Angel of His Presence is really Jehovah Himself, as represented by God the Son. And, of course, this kind of thing, though mind-boggling, is only possible because the LORD God is triune.

So, let us now consider the *special* role of the Angel of the LORD's Presence.

Covenant Mediator

The Apostle Paul said to Timothy, "For there is one God and one Mediator between God and men, the Man Christ Jesus" (1 Tim. 2:5). A mediator, as you all know, is a go-between between two or more parties. Paul says that there is only one Mediator between God and men. Then he names that Mediator. It's the Man Christ Jesus. Have you ever said to yourself about someone, "I know that name", but you can't put a face to the name? It's Jesus who puts a face to the name "God" i.e., *Elohim*. It's Jesus who puts a face to the name of the LORD, i.e., Jehovah.

Jesus puts a true and accurate face to the LORD God because He is the LORD God. He is *Jehovah Elohim!* He is *the* Messenger of the LORD. He is the One who speaks face to face with God. And He is also the One who speaks face to face with men. He is the Mediator between God and humanity, both in the Old Testament and the New Testament.

He appeared in temporary *Theophanies* (i.e., God-appearances) in the Old Testament, as He did to Isaiah. But now He has become, as the Westminster Confession of Faith 8, paragraph 2 puts it, "Very God and very man, yet one Christ, the only Mediator between God and man." And, according to what we've seen thus far, Christ has *always been* the Mediator. And doesn't He Himself say that no one comes to the Father except through Him? (John 14:6).

So, what about the Church in the Old Testament? How did the saints in those days come to the Father? Who was *their* Mediator? Who was *their* Messenger? Who did Moses speak to? It was the *preincarnate* Christ, wasn't it? He is the same yesterday, today and forever (Heb. 13:8). The LORD God doesn't change, and Christ is the LORD God, Jehovah *Elohim.*

We could go on and on quoting New Testament verses which show that Christ in the flesh is the same as the Angel of the LORD's Presence. But let's make no mistake that it was the same Christ who redeemed His people from Egypt. He is their Saviour. He is the One to whom Isaiah is referring. The Angel Isaiah is speaking of is the One who says, "I am the LORD your God who brought you out of the land of Egypt, out of the house of bondage" (Exod. 20:2).

This is the same LORD who says they are not to make any *images* because He's a jealous God. Therefore, if this Angel of the LORD's Presence is not God, are the people of God not in danger of worshiping an image? Yet Abraham worshipped this Angel of the LORD, as did His son Isaac. Indeed, it was this Angel of the LORD who commanded Abraham not to plunge the knife into his son Isaac (Gen. 22:9-14). And what did Jacob call the name of the place where he wrestled with a Man, who was none other than the Angel of the LORD? (Gen. 32:30). "And Jacob called the name of the place Peniel: 'For I have seen God face to face.'" "Peniel" literally means "Face of God." And what about Moses before the burning bush? "And the Angel of the LORD appeared to him in a flame of fire from the midst of a bush" (Gen. 3:2). Moses wanted to know His name and He was told it was "I AM WHO I AM." The name Jehovah or Yahweh comes from I AM. And, of course Jesus referred to Himself as the "I AM" (John 8:58).

The LORD said, "Behold, I send an Angel before you ... Beware of Him and obey His voice; do not provoke Him, for He will not pardon your transgressions; for My name is in Him" (Exod. 23:20). "And I will send My Angel before you" (Exod. 33:2). Then finally, Exodus 33:14ff, "And He [the LORD] said, 'My Presence will go with you' ... And he [Moses] said, 'If Your Presence does not go with us, do not bring us up from here. For how then will it be known that Your people and I have found grace in Your sight, except You go with us?" John in his Gospel says, "In the beginning was the Word, and the Word was with, [i.e., present with] God, and the Word was God."

Now, to be sure *the Word*, i.c., *the Logos, God the Son*, became flesh as John tells us (John 1:14). But this doesn't mean that the LORD God changed, not even in the slightest. He certainly humbled Himself, or made Himself of no reputation, as Paul says to the Philippians. But this emptying of Himself in no way compromised who He is, i.e., the eternal Second Person of the Trinity. "For in Him dwells all the fullness of the Godhead bodily" (Col. 2:9). John says, "And the Word became flesh and dwelt among us, and we beheld His glory as of the only begotten of the Father, full of grace and truth" (John 1:14). John says, "No one has seen God at any time. The only begotten Son who is in the bosom of the Father, He has declared Him" (John 1:18). Hebrews 1:1ff., "God, who at various times and in different ways spoke in times past to the fathers by the prophets, has in these last days spoken to us by His Son, whom He has appointed heir of all things, through whom also He made the worlds; who being the brightness of His glory and the express image of His person." The Apostle Paul, "For it is the God who commanded light to shine out of the darkness, who has shone in our hearts to give the light of the knowledge of the glory of God in the face of Jesus Christ" (2 Cor. 4:6).

Let us remind ourselves again, in the plain words of the Amplified Bible, Classic Edition, "Behold, I send My messenger, and he shall prepare the way before Me. And the Lord [the Messiah], Whom you seek, will suddenly come to His temple; the Messenger *or* Angel of the covenant, Whom you

desire, behold, He shall come, says the Lord of hosts"
(Mal. 3:1).

The face of Jesus Christ is the face of an
Angel. For Jesus Christ is the Messenger, the
Mediator, the Angel of the LORD's Presence, the
Angel of the Covenant. He is Immanuel, God with us.
Therefore, the New Testament Jesus and Old
Testament Jehovah is the same Person. Christ looked
after the Church in the Old Testament as the Angel of
His Presence. Therefore, Christ, our God, is the God
of Abraham, Isaac and Jacob not forgetting the
Prophet Isaiah. Says Herman Witsius,

> The second period of this covenant [between
> the Father and the Son] I place in that
> intercession of Christ, by which, immediately
> upon the fall of man, he offered himself to
> God, now offended, in order actually to
> perform those things to which he had engaged
> himself from eternity; saying, thou hast given
> them to me, and I will make satisfaction for
> them: and so he made way for the word of
> grace to be declared to, and the covenant of
> grace to be made with them. Thus Christ was
> actually constituted Mediator, and revealed as
> such immediately upon the fall; and, having
> undertaken the suretyship, he began to act
> many things belonging to the offices of a
> Mediator. As a Prophet, and the interpreter of
> the divine will, he even then, by his Spirit,
> revealed those things relating to the salvation
> of the elect, and by his ministers published
> them, Is. 48:15, 1 Pet. 1:11, and 3:19. Nay, he

himself sometimes appeared in the character of an angel, instructing his people in the counsel of God. As a King, he gathered his church, and formed to himself a people, in whom he might reign by his word and Spirit. For it was the Son of God who said to Israel, Ex. 19:6, "And ye shall be unto me a kingdom of priests," and who, with more than royal pomp, published his law on Mount Sinai, Acts 7:38, and whom Isaiah saw sitting as king upon a throne, chap. 6 compared with John 12:41. As a Priest, he took upon himself the sins of the elect, that he might expiate them by the sacrifice of his body, which was to be prepared for him in the fulness of time. In virtue of this, as a faithful surety, he likewise interceded for the elect, by declaring his will, that they might be taken into favour, saying, "Deliver them from going down to the pit, I have found a ransom," Job 33:24. But what angel could speak thus, but the Angel of the Covenant? Who even then was called an angel, before his coming in the flesh, because he was accomplishing what depended upon that future mission. He is one of a thousand, the captain of the host of angels, that guards each believer, the chiefest of (the standard bearer above) ten thousands, Cantic. 5:10.[118]

---

[118] Herman Witsius, *Economy of Covenants Between God and Man*, 2 Vols, Book I, Chapter I, VII, (First published 1677, reprinted 1822, Kindle version 2014), 196.

So, we see then that Christ has been with His people right from the beginning. We've seen that the Covenant Messenger and the Covenant Mediator is the same Person. He is the Angel of the Covenant, our Prophet, Priest, and King. He is our Saviour, the One who would take the sins of His people upon Himself on Calvary's cross. On the cross our affliction became His affliction. As Isaiah says, "In all their affliction He was afflicted" (63:9). Affliction is suffering. Therefore, He suffered on the cross that we might escape suffering forever. For by His stripes we are healed (Isa. 53:5).

"And the Angel of His presence saved them" (Isa. 63:9). The cross of Christ is the instrument God used to cut the veil in two so that we might see His presence in the Holy of Holies as we gaze upon the face of Christ. The message of the cross is the unveiling of the face of God. The gospel message is God come out from behind the Temple curtain. "In His love and His pity He redeemed them" (Isa. 63:9).

The message of Christ is the proclamation of God's love for His people to His people. The cross of Christ is God's pity for His people put on visual display. The Angel of the Covenant nailed to a tree is God's love and pity for His people pinned as it were to a billboard. The gospel is the declaration to the universe of God's plan for redeeming the people of His love and pity. "And He bore them and carried them all the days of old" (Isa. 63:9). The Angel of His Presence bore His people all the way to heaven. It was at Calvary's cross He had us inscribed on the palms of His hands (Isa. 49:16). And no one can snatch us out of His tender but strong hand (John 10:28-29).

The Old Testament church and the New Testament church is one covenant people. For the Angel of His Presence was none other than the One who became the Saviour of us all. The Covenant Messenger and Covenant Mediator is Jesus Christ who is the same yesterday, today, and forever. He is *Jehovah-Jesus*. And whoever believes in Him shall not perish but have everlasting life (John 3:16).

Conclusion
Your hand, O God, has guided
Your flock from age to age;
Your faithfulness is written
on hist'ry's open page.
Our fathers knew Your goodness,
and we their deeds record;
and both to this bear witness:
One church, one faith, one Lord.[119]

---

[119] Edward Hayes Plumtre, (1821-91).

COVENANT WORSHIP & SABBATH

Introduction

Having seen that immediately after the fall God revealed His covenant of grace and applied it to the Old Testament saints through various administrations, and we saw the need for believers to guard their hearts, and how Christ was present with them since the fall to His incarnation, let us now consider worship and the sabbath.

Covenant Worship

Unlike during Old Testament times, now that Christ has lived, died, risen, and ascended bodily into heaven, there are no places on earth any more spiritual or holy than any other places. Says Westminster Confession of Faith 21, paragraph 6,

> Neither prayer, nor any other part of religious worship, is, now, under the gospel, either tied unto, or made more acceptable by, any place in which it is performed, or towards which it is directed; but God is to be worshipped every where in spirit and in truth; as in private families daily, and in secret each one by himself; so more solemnly in the publick assemblies, which are not carelessly or wilfully to be neglected or forsaken, when God, by his Word or providence, calleth thereunto.

In Old Testament times God is the God who dwelt between the cherubim on the Ark of the

Covenant in the Holy of Holies in the Temple in Jerusalem in the Holy Land. Jerusalem was the holy city because God, as it were, dwelt there. Therefore, the people of God had to make pilgrimages to Jerusalem for feasts four times a year because that's where the Temple of God was: *spring*, Unleavened Bread/Passover (Matt. 26:17-20), *summer*, Harvest/Pentecost (Acts 2:1), *Autumn*, Ingathering/Tabernacles (John 7:2), *and winter*, Dedication/Lights (John 10:22).

But where is God now that the Word has become flesh, i.e., since the promised Immanuel has arrived? Is Jerusalem any more holy than Hobart or Glasgow or Winnipeg or Brisbane now that the gospel is going out from Jerusalem and into all the nations? What did Jesus say to His disciples at the end of His Great Commission sermon? "And lo, I am with you always, even to the end of the age" (Matt. 28:20). So, where is the Spirit of God, i.e., the Spirit of Christ, now since the Temple was destroyed in 70 A.D., just as Jesus said it would? (Matt. 24:1-2). Well, God no longer dwells between the cherubim in the Holy of Holies. The veil was rent when Jesus died on the cross and the Spirit has gone out into all the world with the gospel.

What is the great refrain of God's covenant? What is His one great summary promise to those who worship Him in spirit and truth? The Apostle Paul summarises it in the following, "For you are the temple of the living God. As God has said: *'I will dwell in them and walk among them, I will be their God, and they shall be My people"* (2 Cor. 6:16).

Therefore, the temple of the living God is now wherever God is worshipped in spirit and truth.

God dwells by His Spirit in the hearts of His people throughout all the earth. Therefore, the Almighty doesn't dwell in church buildings (Acts 17:24). Therefore, those who go into empty church buildings to get close to God could get just as close were they to stay at home! Indeed, God is to be worshipped also in homes because He is to be worshipped everywhere in spirit and truth (John 4:24). Therefore, we don't need to make pilgrimages to Jerusalem or anywhere else. We are to worship God in spirit and truth daily, privately as individuals, and at home with our families. And we are to worship God in spirit and truth corporately and publicly with other families. This we do on the Lord's Day, the Christian Sabbath, and at such other times when His providence calls us to it. James Bannerman says,

> Into whatever relation he enters, man carries with him the same paramount and unchanging law which binds him to honour, and love, and worship his Creator; and every relation of life, capable of being turned to such an end, underlies according to its character the same obligation of doing homage to God. Man in the closet, man in the family, man in the Church, is equally bound to the duties of the personal, the domestic, the public worship of God. Without this, there are many of the powers and faculties of man's nature as a social being, formed as they were for the glory of God, which he cannot bring to do their

proper work of glorifying Him. The worship of God, publicly and in society with others, is the proper expression towards God of man's social nature. The very law of light and nature tell us that the public worship of God is a standing and permanent ordinance for the whole human race.[120]

The LORD through His prophet Malachi spoke of people everywhere worshipping God, "'For from the rising of the sun, even to its going down, My name shall be great among the Gentiles; in every place incense shall be offered to My name, and a pure offering; for My name shall be great among the nations,' says the LORD of hosts" (Mal. 1:11). And the Apostle Paul underlines this where he says, "I desire therefore that the men pray everywhere, lifting up holy hands, without wrath and doubting" (1 Tim. 2:8). And, as Jesus said to the woman at the well, "Woman, believe Me, the hour is coming when you will neither on this mountain, nor in Jerusalem, worship the Father" (John 4:21). Which is to say that the worship of the Father will take place everywhere the covenant of grace, i.e., the gospel goes. Therefore, we worship God in spirit and truth everywhere, privately as individuals, privately as families, and publicly as congregations.

Jesus exhorts us to private worship individually by ourselves where He says, "But you, when you pray, go into your room, and when you have shut your door, pray to your Father who is in the

---

[120] James Bannerman, *The Church of Christ*, Still Waters Revival Books, *reprint* 1991, 324.

secret place; and your Father who sees in secret will reward you openly" (Matt. 6:6).

And when it comes to families worshipping God in spirit and truth, "And these words which I command you today shall be in your heart. You shall teach them to your children, and shall talk of them when you sit in your house, when you walk by the way, when you lie down, and when you rise up" (Deut. 6:6-7). Individual and family worship are exampled by Cornelius who was "A devout man and one who feared God with all his household, and who gave alms generously to the people, and prayed to God always" (Acts 10:2).

And why ought we to worship God privately as individuals and with our families daily? As Jesus taught us in the Lord's Prayer, "Give us this day our daily bread" (Matt. 6:11). You ought to pray to God daily to give thanks for your daily bread.

Now, when it comes to corporate or public worship, the writer to the Hebrews says, "And let us consider one another in order to stir up love and good works, not forsaking the assembling of ourselves together, as is the manner of some, but exhorting one another, and so the much more as you see the Day approaching" (Heb. 10:24-25). Each approaching Lord's Day reminds us that there is a coming Day of the Lord (2 Pet. 3:10).

Christian Sabbath

The writer to the Hebrews says that God's Son Jesus Christ is the "express image of His person" (Heb. 1:3). As such He reflected God perfectly in all His undertakings. Jesus undertook to attend the synagogue every Sabbath "as His custom was" (Luke 4:16). He regularly taught and preached in the synagogues (e.g., Matt. 4:23; 9:35; Mark 1:39; 6:2).

J. Gresham Machen reminds us of something often overlooked by Christians where he says, "From the Jewish synagogue has sprung the congregation of the Christian Church."[121] Luke records Jesus on a particular Sabbath day preaching a sermon on a portion of Isaiah He had read out beforehand (Luke 4:16-30). The Sabbath day was the day of worship. Jesus therefore worshipped on the Sabbath.

The Apostle Paul, after Christ's resurrection and ascension into heaven, followed Jesus' custom, also even teaching and preaching on occasion (e.g., Acts 13:14ff). The word synagogue (Greek συναγωγὴν) simply means "a bringing together" of persons. The "assembly" (i.e., *synagogue*,) in James 2:2 is "a bringing together" of Hebrew Christians. The day set apart for the bringing together for the purpose of public worship was changed upon the resurrection of Jesus Christ. The Westminster Confession of Faith 21, paragraph 7 summarizes what the Bible teaches regarding the change of the Sabbath day,

> As it is of the law of nature, that, in general, a due proportion of time be set apart for the worship of God; so in His Word, by a positive, moral, and perpetual commandment, binding all men in all ages, He hath

---

[121] J. Gresham Machin, *The New Testament – An Introduction to its History & Literature*, Banner of Truth, Edinburgh, Scotland, first published 1976, 1981, 37.

particularly appointed one day in seven for a sabbath, to be kept holy unto Him: which, from the beginning of the world to the resurrection of Christ, was the last day of the week; and, from the resurrection of Christ, was changed into the first day of the week, which in Scripture is called the Lord's Day, and is to be continued to the end of the world, as the Christian Sabbath.

Christians have continued to follow the custom of Jesus and have corporately gathered for worship one day in seven (now the Lord's Day, the Christian Sabbath), as per the Fourth Commandment (Exod. 20:8-11). Says Rudi Schwartz,

The ceremonial part of the fourth commandment is abolished. For this reason we call the Lord's Day the Christian Sabbath. The Sabbath of the Old Testament was the shadow, the New Testament Sabbath is the substance (Col 2:17). On the night he was betrayed, our Lord declared "This cup is the new covenant in my blood which is poured out for you." (Lk 22:20 NIV).[122]

Jesus has nowhere set aside the day that God, from the beginning of creation, blessed and sanctified, i.e., the sabbath (Gen. 2:2-3). For Adam and Eve their week began on the day after they had been formed by God, which is the day God rested.

---

[122] D. Rudi Schwartz, *The Lord's Day: Does it Really Still Matter?*, Ark House Press, Australia, 2021, 67.

Our week begins with the Lord's Day, Sunday, which is the day Christians are to keep holy, sanctified, or set apart for public worship. To forget to remember to keep holy the Christian Sabbath is to blacken out a beautiful picture of the world to come. Says Geerhardus Vos,

> Before all other important things…, the Sabbath is an expression of the eschatological principle on which the life of humanity has been constructed. There is to be to the world-process a finale, as there was an overture, and these two belong inseparably together. To give up the one means to give up the other, and to give up either means to abandon the fundamental scheme of Biblical history. Even among Jewish teachers this profound meaning of the Sabbath was not entirely unknown. One of them, being asked what the world to come would be like, answered that it would resemble the Sabbath.[123]

Does the New Testament teach us to observe the Sabbath? Indeed, the Bible from its beginning to its end teaches us to keep the Sabbath holy. The Westminster Confession of Faith 21, paragraph 8 explains how to keep the Sabbath Day holy,

> This Sabbath is then kept holy unto the Lord, when men, after a due preparing of their

---

[123] Geerhardus Vos, *Biblical Theology, Old and New Testaments*, The Banner of Truth Trust, Edinburgh, Scotland, 1948 (Reprinted 1985), 140.

hearts, and ordering of their common affairs before-hand, do not only observe an holy rest all the day from their own works, words, and thoughts about their worldly employments and recreations; but also are taken up the whole time in the publick and private exercises of his worship, and in the duties of necessity and mercy.

Without the Sabbath man would need to work seven days a week with no day set apart (sanctified, holy) for rest. This would more resemble Hell (where there is no peace for the wicked) (Isa. 48:22), than the kingdom of Heaven. However, in "The Directory for the Publick Worship of God", (as agreed upon by the Assembly of Divines at Westminster in 1645), one reads under the heading, *Of the Sanctification of the Lord's Day*, the following.

That all people meet so timely for publick worship, that the whole congregation may be present at the beginning, and with one heart solemnly join together in all parts of the publick worship, and not depart till after the blessing.

Notice in the aforementioned words that there is a beginning and an end to the public worship. It starts and it finishes. Therefore, one special day of worship is to be set aside in every seven, in which day there is also set aside time for "the publick and private exercises of... worship."

All worship, whether private, family, or corporate is to be done in the Mediator's name. "For through Him we both have access by one Spirit to the Father" (Eph. 2:17). For Jesus says, "I am the way, the truth, and the life. No one comes to the Father except through Me" (John 14:6).

The Reformed Church met from 1618-19 at the Synod of Dordt to discuss some theological issues, among these was one that had to do with the Fourth Commandment. Nigel Lee (N.L.) makes interesting comments regarding the Synod's adoption of the commission's report in the following,

1. In the fourth commandment of the law of God, there is something ceremonial, and something moral (N.L. – an unfortunate relic of Aquinas!).

2. The resting upon the seventh day after the creation, and the strict observation of it, which was particularly (N.L. – but not exclusively!) imposed upon the Jewish people, was the ceremonial part of that law (N.L. – neither the Edenic nor the Decalogical sabbath were ceremonial, but only the latter's Mosaic peculiarities were – e.g., death penalty for desecration).

3. But the moral part is, that a certain day be fixed and appropriated to the service of God, and as much rest as is necessary to that service and the holy meditation upon Him … (N.L. – apart from the fact that there is also a purely physical reason for rest, especially since the

fall, this and the following articles are excellent)...[124]

Nigel Lee goes on to make the following comparison between what the Canons of Dordt and the Westminster Standards have to say about the Christian Sabbath,

> Westminster is an improvement upon Dordt in that it prohibits Sunday recreations, and in that it regards the Fourth Commandment as wholly moral. But it is inferior to Dordt as regards its silence on much needed (Sunday) physical rest, and as regards its insistence that the whole Sunday be devoted specifically to worship. For the danger thereby of converting the day of rest into a religious (!) "working day", is by no means insignificant.[125]

Conclusion

As with any of the others of the Ten Commandments, or even the Decalogue itself, we must be careful not to make an idol of the sabbath. God's moral law is eternal and therefore eternally includes the Sabbath Commandment.

The Sabbath is a creation ordinance (Gen. 2:1-3). There were ceremonial aspects appended to keeping the Sabbath or Fourth Commandment before Christ came. However, since the coming of Jesus, all the Old Testament ceremonial ritual pointing to Him

---

[124] Francis Nigel Lee, *The Covenantal Sabbath*, The Lord's Day Observance Society, London, 1966, 258.
[125] Ibid, 260.

has been fulfilled in and by Him. However, as Scripture says, "There remains therefore a rest (σαββατισμος, *sabbatismos*) for the people of God" (Heb. 4:9). The Christian Sabbath or the Lord's Day is the weekly reminder of God's eternal Sabbath rest. Says Robert Lewis Dabney,

> If the Sabbath command was in full force before Moses, the passing away of Moses' law does not remove it… The reason that the ceremonial laws were temporary was that the necessity for them was temporary. They were abrogated because they were no longer needed. But the practical need for the Sabbath is the same for all ages. When it is made to appear that this day is the bulwark of practical religion in the world, that its proper observance everywhere goes hand in hand with piety and the true worship of God; that where there is no Sabbath there is no Christianity, it becomes an impossible supposition that God would make the institution temporary. The necessity for the Sabbath has not ceased, therefore it is not abrogated. In its nature, as well as its necessity, it is a permanent moral command.[126]

[126] Robert Lewis Dabney, *Systematic Theology*, Banner of Truth, Edinburgh, Scotland, first published 1872, *reprint* 1996, 379-380.

COVENANT BAPTISM

Introduction

Having seen that the covenant of grace since the fall applied to believers throughout the Old Testament, and that believers are to guard their hearts by obedience to God's instructions, and that Christ was present even with the Old Testament saints, and we, like them, are to worship God and keep His sabbath, let us now consider believers and their children in relation to New Testament baptism.

Now, we know that in the covenant of redemption the Father has made various promises to the Son upon His keeping certain conditions. The Old and New Testaments are the record of the Son perfectly fulfilling the covenant's conditions. We have already noted that the Father (in eternity past) is the proposer in the covenant and its details, the Son as the procurer, and that the Spirit is the covenant's perfector. The proposer, procurer, and perfector alliteration was simply another way of saying that, though all three Persons of the Trinity are always involved, the Father is usually designated as the Creator, the Son as Redeemer, and the Spirit as the Consummator. After the resurrected Christ ascended into heaven, He and the Father poured out Their Holy Spirit on the Church (Jews and Gentiles, i.e., all nations) (Acts 2; 11).

Just before He ascended, Jesus made mention of the "Promise of the Father" "And being assembled together with *them,* He commanded them not to depart from Jerusalem, but to wait for the Promise of the Father, 'which,' *He said,* 'you have heard from

Me; for John truly baptized with water, but you shall be baptized with the Holy Spirit not many days from now'" (Acts 1:4-5).

After the "Promise of the Father" had been poured upon them, Peter explained to whom God's covenant promise was made: "Then Peter said to them, "Repent, and let every one of you be baptized in the name of Jesus Christ for the remission of sins; and you shall receive the gift of the Holy Spirit. For the promise is to you and to your children, and to all who are afar off, as many as the Lord our God will call" (Acts 2:38-39).

The "Promise of the Father" is God's gift to believers and their children. This covenant promise is depicted by covenant baptism.

Covenant Children

Let me start by asking a hypothetical question, a difficult question. If you were asked by a Christian couple who just had given birth to a stillborn child where you thought their child was now, what would you tell them? Surely you wouldn't think twice about telling them their child is safe with the Lord in heaven. But what would make you say that? Just wishful thinking? Would you be able to give comfort to the grieving couple from Scripture? Surely you'd, for example, think of the words Jesus said, "Let the little children come to me, and do not forbid them; for of such is the kingdom of heaven" (Matt. 19:14, Luke 18:16). You'd say, "See! The Lord cares about our little children."

Isn't it a great comfort to know that God has promised to look after you and your children? For He says, "For the promise is to you and your children" (Acts 2:39). Why was the promise given also to the children? Well, for the same reason as to why we believe that all children of Christians who die in infancy go to heaven. It's because children are included in God's covenant. One of the creeds of the Reformation, The Canons of Dordt, First Head: Article 17, sums it up,

> Since we are to judge of the will of God from His Word, which testifies that the children of believers are holy, not by nature, but in virtue of the covenant of grace, in which they together with their parents are comprehended, godly parents ought not to doubt the election and salvation of their children whom it pleases God to call out of this life in their infancy (Gen 17:7; Acts 2:39; 1 Cor 7:14).

The Lord loves His little covenant children. He even rebuked His disciples for preventing them from coming to Him. And, Jesus said, "And whoever receives one little child like this in My name receives Me" (Matt. 18:5). Therefore, the Lord welcomes all who belong to Him. Only the Lord Himself knows for sure who are His own (2 Tim. 2:19). We can only guess at best. So, what does His church on earth have to go on? What we're looking at in the following is summed up in the words, *All those in God's covenant are to receive the sign and seal of the Covenant.*

What is the Covenant?

As we have already seen, a covenant is an agreement of sorts, but it is not necessarily a mutual agreement. A covenant can be sovereignly imposed.

Some apartment complexes have covenant agreements. They allow you to live in the covenant community so long as you agree to abide by the conditions of the covenant. Perhaps the covenant might stipulate no cats or dogs, no loud music, non-smokers only, this sort of thing. But what happens if a child is born into this covenant community? Would that child be shown the gate and told to come back when he's old enough to know what the covenant community is all about? I don't think so. The child would be brought up in the covenant community and taught how to behave in accordance with the covenant agreement. And so it is for the institutional church on earth, which is the covenant community of God. Thus, water baptism is the institutional church acknowledging that a person qualifies as a member of God's covenant community.

When we speak of the Biblical covenant, we are ordinarily referring to the covenant of grace. The covenant of grace is a sovereignly imposed covenant. It was imposed by God on certain fallen sinners. There are certain conditions attached to it. (Properly understood, all of these conditions are of course met by God and are part of His gift of salvation).

As we know, though we see it only in embryonic form right after the fall, it is seen in clearer terms where God deals with Abraham. Abraham cut in half a heifer, a goat, a ram, and along with a turtle dove and a pigeon he made a path through the middle of the pieces. Then God appeared in the pitch dark as smoke and fire and proceeded to go through the valley of the shadow of death as Abraham watched on (Gen. 15:18).

God "cut" a Covenant with Abraham

We are reminded that the idea in the covenant that God cut with Abraham was that should the person who cut the covenant ever break it, they would have done to them as the animals had done to them, i.e., death and division, i.e., they would lose their lifeblood. Thus, God's covenant with Abraham is a blood agreement. It is a conditional promise involving bloodshed.

God has, as it were, bonded, or married Himself to a people, i.e., a covenant community, "For better or for worse, in sickness and in health, till death us do part. And, if I the Lord should ever break My covenant with you, may what happened to these dismembered animals happen to Me. May My blood be poured out."

Therefore, the Lord has bound Himself to His people by His covenant with Abraham, the covenant of grace. He has promised to look after His wife and children and prepare a place for them to live, i.e., the house with many mansions (John 14:2).

The Lord has given certain promises to Abraham in the Covenant

God has promised a seed and a land, to name a couple for starters. Suffice to say, however, that all the promises of God begin and end with Jesus Christ (2 Cor. 1:20). Jesus is the One who was to come and crush the Serpent's head (Gen. 3:15). And we know that all the promises of forgiveness of sin, of a Redeemer, of eternal life, of the Holy Spirit etc. are included in the one big promise, i.e., Jesus Christ.

Jesus Christ is the major promise attached to the covenant. Christ *is* the covenant. Therefore, everything in the covenant must somehow point us to Him. It is the work of the Holy Spirit to point us to Christ, (John 15:26).

What is the Sign of the Covenant?

Everyone knows what a signpost is. A signpost is a device which points to something else. The sign of the covenant in the Old Testament was circumcision, which was replaced by baptism in the New Testament (Col. 2:11-14). Therefore, the sign is different now from what it was in the Old Testament. But is the covenant in the New Testament the same as the covenant in the Old Testament? Well, God says, "And I will establish My covenant between Me and you and your descendants after you in their generations, *for an everlasting covenant*, to be God to you and your descendants after you" (Gen. 17:7). So, we see that this is an "everlasting" covenant. It goes on forever. It is God's covenant. And it goes on forever even with the faithful children of Abraham.

Who are the children of Abraham? We have seen that Jesus rebuked some Jews that thought they were right with God because they were *physical* descendants of Abraham. These had received the covenant sign and seal of circumcision. Yet Jesus said to them, "If you were Abraham's children, you would do the work of Abraham" (John 8:39). Therefore, to be a child of Abraham must mean more than something just physical. There's the more important *spiritual* dimension, "Therefore know that only those who are of faith are sons [or children] of Abraham" (Gal. 3:7). In other words, God has an everlasting covenant only with believers and their children.

Abraham is the father of the faithful (Rom. 4:11). Are Christians the faithful? Therefore, believers today are children of Abraham and therefore are included in the everlasting covenant. But aren't things a bit different in the New Testament than they were in the Old Testament? Yes, but the covenant is no different. The Abrahamic covenant is the exact same covenant of grace that we know today. Only the signs and seals of the covenant have changed.

And what were the conditions for Abraham and his descendants? "I am Almighty God; walk before Me and be blameless" (Gen. 17:1b). Have these conditions changed any in the New Testament? Doesn't Jesus say, "Therefore you shall be perfect, just as your Father in heaven is perfect"? (Matt. 5:48). But this is the covenant of grace, isn't it? Grace means that Abraham and his descendants are saved by grace. Genesis 15:6 tells us, "Abraham believed in the Lord and the Lord accounted it to him for righteousness." That's salvation by grace. And the everlasting covenant of grace includes promises. And don't we need constant reminders of those promises of grace? So then, who do all the promises of the covenant begin and end with? Jesus Christ (2 Cor. 1:20).

All the shed blood of the sacrifices that were to take place were to remind Old Testament Israel what? God's covenant promises! And where was Israel being pointed? Christ. Think back to the Galatians 3:16 passage and you'll see that God made the promise to Christ. "Now to Abraham and his Seed were the promises made. He does not say, 'And to seeds,' as of many, but as of one, *'And to your Seed,'* who is Christ."

How did God remind the people in Old Testament times of the everlasting covenant God has with Christ? Well, we see in Genesis 17 that God is giving Abraham and his descendants a sign of the covenant. What is this sign? "This is My covenant which you shall keep, between Me and you and your descendants after you: Every male child among you shall be circumcised; and you shall be circumcised in the flesh of your foreskins, and it shall be a <u>sign</u> of the covenant between Me and you" (Gen. 17:10). A sign is a reminder. It points to something. So, the sign of the everlasting covenant from the time of Abraham on was male circumcision.

What did this sign mean? Well, first off it meant the shedding of blood. It's a covenant in blood and it had to do with cleansing. It meant the partial removal of the filth of the flesh. All those who belong to *father* Abraham were to put on the covenant. To have this covenant put on is to have your sins removed.

Circumcision reminded Israel that it would be through procreation that the promised One would come and crush the serpent's head (Gen. 3:15). Circumcision pointed to descendants, i.e., the promised Seed, Jesus Christ in particular (Gal. 3:16).

To whom is the Sign of the Covenant to be applied?

Who are to put on the covenant (which means to put on Christ spiritually)? Well, we've already read in Genesis 17 that all the males in Abraham's household were to receive the sign. (Keep in mind that not everyone in Abraham's household is descended from him or is even physically related.) We are told that this sign is to be applied on the eighth day after the male child is born. And we have been reminded by the following verse that it is a physical sign of something spiritual, "Therefore circumcise the foreskin of your heart, and be stiff-necked no longer" (Deut. 10:16). Then we read this warning, "And the uncircumcised male child, who is not circumcised in the flesh of his foreskin, that person shall be cut off from his people; he has broken My covenant" (Gen. 17:14). So, we see that it's a serious business to neglect the sign of the covenant, i.e., to spiritually put on Christ. However, Westminster 28. Paragraph 5 offers this reminder,

> Although it be a great sin to contemn or neglect this ordinance, (Luke 7:30, Exod. 4:24-26) yet grace and salvation are not so inseparably annexed unto it, as that no person can be regenerated, or saved, without it: (Rom. 4:11, Acts 10:2, 4, 22, 32, 45, 47) or, that all that are baptized are undoubtedly regenerated. (Acts 8:13, 23)

The person without the sign is to be viewed as one who is not in God's covenant and is to be viewed as a covenant breaker. Says John Murray,

> If infants are excluded now, it cannot be too strongly emphasized that this change implies a complete reversal of the earlier divinely instituted practice. So we must ask: do we find any hint of intimation of such reversal in either the Old or New Testament? More pointedly, does the New Testament revoke or does it provide any intimation of revoking so expressly authorized a principle as that of inclusion of infants in the covenant and their participation in the covenant sign and seal? This practice had been followed, by divine authority, in the administration of the covenant for two thousand years. Has it been discontinued? Our answer to these questions must be that we find no evidence of revocation. In view of the fact that the new covenant is based upon and is the unfolding of the Abrahamic covenant, in view of the basic identity of meaning attaching to circumcision and baptism, in view of the unity and continuity of the covenant of grace administered in both dispensations, we can affirm with confidence that evidence of revocation or repeal is mandatory if the practice or principle has been discontinued under the New Testament.[127]

[127] John Murray, *Christian Baptism*, Presbyterian and Reformed Publishing Co, Phillipsburg, New Jersey, 1980, 49-50.

Now, we of the Reformed Faith speak of the sacrament or ordinance of baptism as a sign and a seal of the covenant of grace, just as circumcision used to be a sign and a seal of the covenant of grace. The Apostle Paul speaks of the sign and a seal aspect of Old Testament circumcision. Of Abraham he says, "And he received the sign of circumcision, a seal of the righteousness of the faith which he had while still uncircumcised, that he might be the father of all who believe, though they are uncircumcised, that righteousness might be imputed to them also" (Rom. 4:11). At this point, and this is extremely important, notice in Romans 4:11 that circumcision was a sign and seal of righteousness. It was not a sign and seal of our faith. (I'll pick up on this in a moment).

So then, you're probably wondering what all of this has to do with baptism. Well, since Jesus came, unbloody water baptism has replaced bloody circumcision as the sign and seal of the covenant (Col. 2:11-14). The covenant of grace remains the same. It is everlasting. Only the sign has been changed by Jesus (Matt. 28:19).

Are there any similarities between Circumcision and Baptism?

Previously circumcision and now baptism are a sign of God's gracious promise. Both depict cleansing. Both signify blood, covenant-blood. Both picture the removal of the filth of the flesh, cleansing. Both speak of the One who does to us what these signs depict. Circumcision was a sign of the Christ to come, and baptism is a sign of the Christ who has come. Therefore, Old Testament circumcision and New Testament baptism mean one and the same thing, i.e., the covenant of grace, a.k.a. the gospel of Jesus Christ.

If you have received its sign on your body, then you are in God's covenant. Does the sign itself save you? No! A sign is only a reminder of the One who saves. The sign and seal of the covenant simply illustrate the conditional promise of salvation in picture form. The Lord wants you to *see* the gospel as well as *hear* it. Hence circumcision and now baptism. Therefore, circumcision was never the sign of an Israelite's faith. Rather, it has to do with the imputed righteousness of Christ. It was the gospel in pictures. And so it is with baptism. It is simply the sign of the covenant or, if you will, the gospel.

Don't miss this important aspect of God's eternal covenant. Water baptism, like physical circumcision before it, does not signify a person's faith. Notice that it signifies and seals righteousness, the righteousness that can only be received through faith. Ponder the following verse again, "And [Abraham] received the sign of circumcision, a seal of the righteousness of the faith which he had while still uncircumcised, that he might be the father of all who believe, though they are uncircumcised, that righteousness might be imputed to them also." Thus, the sacrament of baptism that replaces circumcision is the sign and seal of imputed righteousness. It is first and foremost a signpost pointing to Christ, not to someone's faith, which is only secondary. Water baptism is in accordance with God's covenantal promise, and not your faith or my faith. In other words, a person is not saved because of his or her faith but rather is saved, i.e., granted saving righteousness, by grace through faith (Eph. 2:8).

Regarding God's covenant signs, if we substitute the word water for bow in the following, what Geerhardus Vos said about God and the rainbow could equally be applied to covenant baptism,

> The idea is not, as usually assumed, that by the bow [or baptism] man will be reminded of the divine promise, but that God Himself, were it possible for Him to forget, will by the sign Himself be reminded of His oath.[128]

Thus, though Christians are strengthened in their faith by seeing it, the sign is a reminder to God of His promise, i.e., His promise in the covenant of redemption to His Son, Abraham's Seed (and those in Him). Like the rainbow, baptism points us to Christ.

But not only is water baptism an outward sign of the righteousness promised and revealed in the gospel, it actually seals the covenant or gospel-promise of salvation to the recipient. For water baptism seals or brings the baptized person into membership of the visible church or covenant community on earth, same thing. Thus, for the believer, baptism is the sign and seal of the conditional promise of the covenant. And that promise is to believers and to their children (Acts 2:39). The conditional promise is that if you repent

---

[128] Geerhardus, Vos, *Biblical Theology, Old and New Testaments*, The Banner of Truth Trust, Edinburgh, Scotland, 1948 (Reprinted 1985), 55.

and believe in the gospel, then you too will receive the promised righteousness depicted in the gospel, which righteousness is received through faith.

The condition of the covenant is, "Walk before Me and be blameless" and you shall be saved. "Be perfect as your Father in heaven is perfect" and you shall be saved. However, as we all say, "But Lord, none of us is blameless. None of us is perfect. All of us have sinned and have fallen short of Your glory. And the Lord as it were replies, "Well then, look to My covenant, the covenant I have made with you. Look to My promise as depicted in the sign and seal I've given you. Look unto Me and live. Look to Me and repent and believe in My covenant of grace which is My gospel. I have signed and sealed the good news, the gospel, My covenant of grace upon your body by the poured out water at your baptism. Now, like the one who is first to see the rainbow after a rainstorm, behave as one who has just received some good news, as one who has received the righteousness revealed in that good news. Therefore, walk before Me and be blameless. Be perfect. For that is what I have declared you to be on My righteous Son's account."

To witness water baptism is to see the gospel being applied to the recipient

You know how kings of old used to melt wax and seal letters? As mentioned before, they'd press their signet ring onto the hot wax, i.e., sealed in the name of the king – mine! That's what the sign and seal of the covenant is. It's the Lord letting you know what belongs to Him. "Sealed in the name of the Father and of the Son and of the Holy Spirit!"

And who are to receive the sign and seal of the covenant? We're not to prevent the Lord from placing His seal upon those who are in His covenant. Someone outside of the covenant community who wants to come in must become a believer first. Only then is he or she eligible to receive the sign and seal of the covenant. And when he or she is baptized the whole congregation is reminded of God's covenant promise.

And what of those who are born into the covenant community? Baptism is a visible sign of something invisible, i.e., something you and I cannot see. The physical sign is depicting something greater, something spiritual. Baptism is depicting God's promise of regeneration. For, that's what salvation to the individual is, regeneration.

The Bible speaks of at least two types of baptism. water baptism and Spirit baptism. Try not to confuse them. Water baptism is something we do visibly, whereas Spirit baptism is what God does invisibly. Water baptism is an outward sign applied outwardly to those who belong to the visible church which is the covenant community on earth. The Holy Spirit through water baptism seals the baptized as a member of the outward visible church. But Spirit baptism is an invisible baptism wherein the Spirit brings the Spirit-baptized person into membership of the invisible church. Therefore, water baptism signifies Spirit baptism. It signifies the shed blood of Christ, the blood that cleanses us of all iniquity, the blood of the everlasting covenant, being applied to the recipient by the Holy Spirit. Says Kenneth Gentry,

> In the pouring out of the waters of baptism upon the convert, we receive the sign of the coming of the Holy Spirit, Who effects our union with the Triune God, cleansing from sin, and faith in Christ. Baptism, then, speaks of blessing and forgiveness.[129]

In baptism the Lord is saying, as it were, "I'm married to you. You're My wife. See! I have given you a certain sign to remind you of My marriage to you. I've married Myself to you Abraham, and I have adopted your children. I promise to look after you and your children, including your little ones who die in infancy. Never will I leave you nor forsake you. Lo, I am with you always. Even with your faithful descendants until the end of the age."

Peter says, "For the promise is to you and to your children, and to all who are afar off, as many as the Lord will call" (Acts 2:39). The preceding verse tells us, "Then Peter said to them [the Hebrews], 'Repent and let every one of you be baptized in the name of Jesus Christ for the remission of sins; and you shall receive the gift of the Holy Spirit." And what does it mean to receive the gift of the Holy Spirit? It means that you belong to Christ. It means that you are in Christ. It means that you have put on Christ.

---

[129] Kenneth L., Gentry, *The Greatness of the Great Commission*, Institute for Christian Economics, Tyler, Texas, 1993, 84.

Old Testament circumcision was putting on the covenant, right? Well, so is New Testament baptism. Scripture says that Christ is our covenant. If you were to read, for instance, Isaiah 42:6 and Isaiah 49:8 you'd see clearly Christ is the covenant. "I [the Lord] will keep You [Christ] and give You as a covenant to the people." Therefore, to receive baptism is to have God's covenant put on you. Listen to Scripture, "For as many of you as were baptized into Christ have *put on* Christ" (Gal. 3:27). When administering the ordinance of covenant baptism, as per the Directory for the Publick Worship of God, "the minister is to pray to this or the like effect:

> That the Lord, who hath not left us as strangers without the covenant of promise, but called us to the privileges of his ordinances, would graciously vouchsafe to sanctify and bless his own ordinance of baptism at this time: That he would join the inward baptism of his Spirit with the outward baptism of water; make this baptism to the infant a seal of adoption, remission of sin, regeneration, and eternal life, and all other promises of the covenant of grace: That the child may be planted into the likeness of the death and resurrection of Christ; and that, the body of sin being destroyed in him, he may serve God in newness of life all his days.[130]

---

[130] Westminster Confession of Faith, Westminster Larger and Shorter Catechisms, the Practical Use of Saving Knowledge, the Directory for the Publick Worship of God, the Form of Church Government, etc., Free Presbyterian Publications, Glasgow, First

To receive the Holy Spirit is to know for sure that you are in Christ. It is to receive the reality of which water baptism depicts. It is the putting on of Christ our covenant. What did Paul tell the Romans? He said, "You received the Spirit of adoption by whom we cry out, 'Abba, Father.' The Spirit Himself bears witness with our spirit that we are children of God, and if children, then heirs – heirs of God and joint heirs with Christ" (Rom. 8:16-17). Therefore, those to whom the Spirit has been given can know they are God's children. And they know that they will inherit those things God has promised His Son.

The Holy Spirit is given to us as the deposit of the promised inheritance. The Holy Spirit was poured out on all nations at Pentecost. He is always portrayed as being poured out, sprinkled, and being shed forth. The Holy Spirit is the One who "falls upon" people, as in the Book of Acts. The Holy Spirit is the one who cleanses, isn't He? What is the Spirit doing when He cleanses us? In short, He is doing the work of regeneration. He does this by taking that which belongs to Christ and applying it to the individual.

We're speaking of what Paul in Colossians 2:11 calls "the circumcision made without hands." In Colossians 2:11ff. Paul clearly equates circumcision with water baptism. They signify the same thing. It's a sign of what the Holy Spirit is doing in the heart of the believer. The baptism of the Holy Spirit is an invisible baptism. This is the Spirit regenerating covenant people as promised in many places of Scripture. See the promise in Ezekiel 36:25f. for

Reprinted 1976, 1985, 383.

instance, where the Lord says, "Then I will sprinkle clean water on you, and you shall be clean; I will cleanse you from all your idols. I will give you a new heart and put a new spirit within you; I will take the heart of stone out of your flesh and give you a heart of flesh. I will put my Spirit within you and cause you to walk in My statutes, and you will keep My judgments and do them. Then you shall dwell in the land that I gave to your fathers; you shall be My people, and I will be your God" (Ezek. 36:25-28).

The Father and the Son pour out the Holy Spirit. God sprinkles the nations, "So shall He sprinkle many nations" (Isa. 52:15a), which is to say that the Holy Spirit is taking the blood of Christ, the blood of the covenant, and He is sprinkling or pouring it (i.e., applying it) to those who are in Christ at the time of their conversion. "And Moses took the blood, sprinkled it on the people, and said, 'Behold, the blood of the covenant which the Lord has made with you'" (Exod. 24:8). "Let us draw near with a true heart in full assurance of faith, having our hearts sprinkled from an evil conscience and our bodies washed with pure water" (Heb. 10:22). Hebrews 12:24 speaks of Jesus the Mediator of the new covenant, and of "the blood of sprinkling." Hebrews 13:20 speaks of "the blood of the everlasting covenant." 1 Peter 1:2 speaks of those who are "in sanctification of the Spirit, for obedience and sprinkling of the blood of Jesus Christ."

All of this is spoken of in the Old Testament. Again, Isaiah says, "So shall He sprinkle many nations" (Isa. 52:15). The Holy Spirit is the one who invisibly and spiritually applies the blood Christ shed on the cross. Baptism is a simple picture of Him doing what He promised to do. As He applies that precious blood, He is sealing the individual as a king seals the wax on a letter. Second Corinthians 1:22 says that God has "sealed us and [has] given us the Spirit in our hearts as a guarantee." Ephesians 1:13 says, "in whom having believed, you were sealed with the Holy Spirit of promise." And we are given this warning in, "And do not grieve the Holy Spirit of God, by whom you were sealed for the day of redemption" (Eph. 4:30). Says Kenneth Gentry,

> In Scripture there is established a conscious, deliberate correspondence between Holy Spirit baptism and water baptism (Matt. 3:11; Mark 1:8; John 1:33, Acts 1:4,5; 10:44-48; 11:15-16). The one is the sign of the other. Consequently, they correspond in modal representation. The Holy Spirit is always said to be poured out or sprinkled down upon the object of His sanctifying operations: Prov. 1:23; Isa. 32:15; 44:3; Eze. 36:25-28; 39:29; Joel 2 :28-29; Zech. 12:10; Acts 2:15-17, 33; 10:44-45; Titus 3:5,6.[131]

Thus, water baptism is a sign and a seal of the covenant of grace.

---

[131] Kenneth L., Gentry, *The Greatness of the Great Commission*, Institute for Christian Economics, Tyler, Texas, fn. 25 in chap. 6, 1993.

Conclusion

To be understood properly, baptism needs to be viewed covenantally. When baptism is viewed in terms of the covenant of grace, where water baptism is viewed in light of the baptism of the Holy Spirit, then you will not miss the fact that baptism is a sign and seal of God's promise, i.e., His everlasting covenant.

COVENANT MEAL

Introduction

Having seen that, since the fall, the covenant of grace has applied to believers, who are to guard their hearts, and that Christ is always present with us, past, present, and future, and that we are to worship God and keep His sabbath, and that believers and their children qualify for water baptism, let us now look at that other sign and seal of the covenant.

The following Scripture describes the smooth transition when the Lord transformed the Passover Meal into the Lord's Supper. We see that this is the Passover Meal on account of what Jesus says in Luke 22:15, "With fervent desire I have desired to eat this Passover with you before I suffer; for I say to you, I will no longer eat of it until it [i.e., the Passover] is fulfilled in the kingdom of God."

So, we ask the question: Which Passover did Jesus fervently desire to eat with His Apostles? "With fervent desire I have desired to eat this Passover with you." Thus, the action in this verse of Scripture took place during the Passover Meal.

Now, what I want us to see is the changeover, the transition from Old Testament or older covenant Passover to New Testament or newer covenant Lord's Supper that took place at this time.

The Old Covenant Meal

Passover was one of only two Old Testament sacraments. The other Old Testament sacrament was circumcision. Circumcision has now become baptism (Colossians 2:11-12). The transition period between circumcision and baptism was when Christ walked upon the earth. Indeed, the gradual transition period between Old Testament and New Testament took place at the time of Christ. Jesus was circumcised and then later underwent water baptism.

The four Gospels and the Book of Acts record the transitional period between the older administration of the covenant and the newer administration.

So, back to our text. This is most certainly the last Passover meal the Lord partook of, for, He was killed at Passover. And just as the removal of flesh in Old Testament circumcision pictured the cleansing of our sin by Christ, so Old Testament Passover pictured our being set free from our bondage to sin and Satan.

Sacraments, among other things, are simple pictures, signposts depicting where we've been, where we are, and where we're going. As He sat down to the Passover Meal, the Lord Jesus Christ knows where He's been, where He is, and where He's going. That's why He says in Luke 22:15, e.g., "With fervent desire I have desired to eat this Passover with you before I suffer." He's looking at the roast lamb and He sees a picture of Himself being roasted on a cross. For God, His Father is about to turn His fiery flame-thrower upon Him. Therefore, to paraphrase a little, Jesus could be saying, "I have desired to eat this Passover with you before I [too] suffer the same end as this roast lamb as the true Lamb of God that takes away the sin of the world."

Shortly, we shall run through the typical celebrating of the Passover Supper. But first notice that Old Testament Passover is a communion meal.

For Jesus says, "With fervent desire I have desired to eat this Passover <u>with you</u>." Jesus therefore is not just fervently desiring to eat the Passover Meal. He fervently desires to eat it *with* His Apostles who were sitting at the table with Him. Therefore, Jesus wasn't like a man on death row choosing his favourite food for his last meal before his execution. "Before I die, give me haggis, turnip, and mashed potatoes!" No, in all seriousness, Jesus wasn't thinking about His own stomach. He was thinking about Communion, i.e., fellowship with His followers. He wanted to share a meal, a special meal, *with* them.

And notice also how strong was His desire to sit and sup with them. The New International Version has Jesus saying, "I have <u>eagerly</u> desired…" The New King James Version has, "With fervent desire I have desired." The Authorized Version has, "With desire I have desired." All are trying to express the fact that it was Christ's "earnest desire" to have this meal with His apostles. He had His heart set on it. It was as if He couldn't wait to sit down with them. O that all Christians would have the same desire to sit at His Table with Him and His communicants!

Now, the first Old Testament Passover is recorded in Exodus 12. This, of course, was right before the Lord set His people free from bondage to Pharaoh in Egypt. The doorposts and lintels of their houses were anointed, sprinkled with the blood of the sacrificed lamb as a *sign* (Exod. 12:22). That night the LORD would "Passover" each house that was *signed* and *sealed* by the blood of the lamb, and spare those households, including the firstborn man and beast. This was some fourteen hundred odd years before Christ. So, during the intervening centuries the Passover Meal underwent certain refinements, but all refinements were within the requirements of the sacrament as instituted by God. William Hendriksen says at the time of Christ the main elements were as follows,

1. A prayer of thanksgiving by the head of the house; drinking the first cup of wine.
2. The eating of bitter herbs, as a reminder of the savage slavery in Egypt.
3. The son's inquiry, "Why is this night distinguished from all other nights?" and the father's appropriate reply, either narrated or read.
4. The singing of the first part of the Hallel (Psalms 113, 114), and the washing of hands. The second cup.
5. The carving and eating of the lamb, together with unleavened bread. The lamb was eaten in commemoration of what the ancestors had been commanded to do on the night when the Lord smote all the first-born of Egypt and delivered His people (Exod. 12 and 13). The unleavened bread was "the bread of haste" eaten by the ancestors.
6. Continuation of the meal, each eating as much as he liked, but always last of the lamb. The third cup.
7. Singing of the last part of the Hallel (Psalms 115-118). Fourth cup.[132]

---

[132] William Hendriksen, *The Gospel of Luke*, The Banner of Truth Trust, Edinburgh, Scotland, 1979, 959-60.

The Commentator Frederic Louis Godet gives a similar description. However, he does say that in the second step, "The father circulates a second cup..." And in the third step, "The father takes two unleavened loaves (cakes), breaks one of them, and places the pieces of it on the other. Then, uttering a thanksgiving, he takes one of the pieces, dips it in the sauce, and eats it, taking with it a piece of the paschal lamb, along with bitter herbs. Each one follows his example." Godet says that the third cup of wine was called the *cup of blessing* "Because it was accompanied with the giving of thanks by the father of the house."[133]

Now, there's absolutely no need for us to get hung up on the minutiae of specifics. But there you have a general outline of how the Passover was celebrated at the time of Christ, at least according to Hendriksen and Godet. So, when Luke says, "Then He took the cup, and gave thanks..." we take it that this is the third cup, i.e., the *cup of blessing.* It's called the cup of blessing because the Lord, as federal head as covenant representative, gave thanks.

Now, whatever you do, don't get this cup mixed up with what Jesus says later in Luke 22:20. This cup is only the third cup, not the fourth cup! This is still the Passover cup and not *yet* the Lord's Supper cup. The disciples were to take it and divide its contents among themselves. Some may see this as suggesting that Jesus Himself didn't drink of the

---

[133] Frederic Louis Godet, *Commentary on* Luke, (originally Funk & Wagnalls 1887), Kregel Publications, Grand Rapids, Michigan, 1981, 463.

Passover cup. But again, why wouldn't He, since it was His fervent desire to eat the Passover with His Apostles? Why then would He not partake of its elements? But let's just take note of the elements used in the Passover Meal. A lamb was to be killed in the forecourt of the Temple with its blood sprinkled or poured upon the altar. It was then to be taken and roasted whole, entrails intact! A salad of bitter herbs, unleavened bread, and wine were also to be provided. And since there was going to be thirteen of them present, a room large enough to accommodate them was needed, with suitable furniture etc.

So, there you have a bit of a background to what's happening in Luke 22:14: "And when the hour had come, He sat down, and the twelve apostles with Him." They sat down to eat the Old Testament sacrament meal called Passover. And it was then, during this meal, or toward the conclusion of it, that Jesus began to institute the New Testament's Lord's Supper.

The New Covenant Meal

In Luke 22:16 we see that Jesus had been eating the Passover Meal. For, He says there, "I will no longer eat of it until it is fulfilled in the kingdom of God." To say He will no longer eat of it implies that He had already been eating it.

So, we see then, that this is the Last Supper, i.e., the last Passover Meal of our Lord. Jesus was now going to do what had been pictured in the Passover Meal for over fourteen hundred years. He was no longer going to eat of it, or drink of its cup until He had fulfilled what the meal depicted, i.e., until He had brought to pass everything it had pictured. In other words, Jesus was declaring that this was His *last* supper, that it was His *final* meal before He went out the door of the room to suffer and die.

Think about it, the last meal Jesus had before His crucifixion was a meal whose design is to edify or strengthen. The Passover was to be eaten on the 14th of Nisan which used to be called the month of Abib. This was that day. "And thus you shall eat it: with a belt on your waist, your sandals on your feet, and your staff in your hand. So you shall eat it in haste. It is the LORD's Passover" (Exod. 12:11).

Jesus therefore is ready, belt on waist, sandals on feet, staff in hand, to hasten to His own holocaust. But, before He hastens off to be betrayed by one of the men at the table, He has some parting words to say, "And He took bread, gave thanks and broke it, and gave it to them, saying, 'This is My body which is given for you; do this in remembrance of Me.' Likewise He also took the cup after supper, saying, 'This cup is the new covenant in My blood, which is shed for you" (Luke 22:19-20). He is saying to His Apostles that He is giving His body for them. And that He is shedding His blood for them. Just as the Passover lamb was sacrificed by having its blood poured out and its flesh roasted on the 14th of the month of Nisan, so too was Jesus about to have the same done to Him. But He no longer wanted a roasted lamb to be the picture of Him, rather He was now (after some fourteen hundred years) replacing that picture with a simpler picture, bread and wine.

Therefore, He took down from the picture gallery the painting of the roast lamb, bitter herbs, unleavened bread, and wine, and He hung in its place the still life of the bread and the wine. Or, if you will, He painted over, or painted out of the picture, the roast lamb, and the bitter herbs. Here's how He did it. Notice the words, "after supper." It was *after* supper that He lifted the cup, i.e., after Passover Supper. Perhaps that word "likewise" would suggest that He had taken the bread "after" supper too? I believe the Lord's breaking of the bread was the point of transition between Passover and Lord's Supper. But what really matters is that we see Passover here becoming the Lord's Supper.

Let's look a bit more closely now at the instituting of the *new* sacrament. Only two elements are included in it, viz., bread and wine. First Jesus took bread (Luke 22:19) and then He also took the cup (Luke 22:20). So first off, the new sacrament is much simpler than the old.

There are no lamb and bitter herbs on the table. There is only bread and wine. Why did Jesus dispense with the lamb in the new sacrament? Well, what did the lamb point to? Or rather, whom did the lamb point to? The lamb represented the Messiah, the Anointed, i.e., the Christ. Jesus Himself is that Lamb of God who was sacrificed. As the Apostle says, Jesus is "our Passover" (1 Cor. 5:7). Our Passover Lamb, Jesus Christ has been killed. Therefore, no more need for a lamb in the sacrament.

Jesus is called the Paschal Lamb. The word *paschal* comes from the Greek word used for Passover, (πάσχα, *pasxa*). This word in turn comes from the Aramaic. But notice that Jesus says, "I have desired to eat this Passover with you before I suffer"

(Luke 22:15). Jesus Christ is the Lamb who suffered. As a Divine Person, He's the Lamb who's suffering echoes throughout all eternity.

The Passover lamb was holocausted, i.e., roasted in a fire. Like burning oil and pitch is poured upon those who try to storm a medieval castle, so the fiery wrath of God was poured upon the Paschal Lamb on the cross. The Paschal Lamb suffered the *everlasting* torments of hell as He hung on the cross. Like the rich man He had spoken about in the parable, who "cried and said, 'Father Abraham, have mercy on me, and send Lazarus that he may dip the tip of his finger in water and cool my tongue; for I am tormented in this flame'" (Luke 16:24). In the prophetic words of the psalmist, "My strength is dried up like a potsherd, and My tongue clings to My jaws; You have brought Me to the dust of death" (Psa. 22:15). As recorded by John, "I thirst!" (John 19:28). Christ's suffering stretched out into eternity as He suffered everlasting torments in His body and His soul, in His humanity, on a cursed tree.

Here He is having His final meal with His beloved brethren before He suffered. He was about to go and anoint the doorposts and lintel of the Kingdom of God with His own blood. He was about to go and pour His own blood upon the altar of God. That's what He did, and that's why there's no roasted lamb in the New Testament sacrament. That's why there are no bitter herbs. There is only bread and wine.

The bread represents Christ's body, given for you. And the wine in the cup represents the new covenant in His blood. In the old sacrament the lamb represented what was going to happen to the Christ.

In the new sacrament the bread represents what has happened to the Christ. So, the idea is that you look at the bread and know that what the roast lamb could only point to has been done. The lamb is gone from the plate, but the bread remains as the reminder of what He has done. But it is no longer the *bread of affliction* (Deut. 16:3). And the cup, the cup of wine, is the *cup of blessing*. For Paul the Apostle says, "The cup of blessing which we bless, is it not the communion of the blood of Christ? The bread which we break, is it not the communion of the body of Christ?" (1 Cor. 10:16).

The bread and wine is the communion, the fellowship, of the body of Christ. Christians are one spiritual body, which is to say that they are His, whose physical body, as pictured by the bread, was given for them, and whose blood, symbolized by the wine in the cup, was shed for them.

All that had represented curse and affliction is gone from the sacrament. All that remains is that which represents blessing. That's why Jesus says, "This cup is the new covenant in My blood, which is shed for you." His blood has now been shed, past tense. It is finished.

The covenant spoken of throughout the whole of Scripture has been sealed in Christ's blood, i.e., the blood you see represented by the wine in the Communion cup. Every other covenant to do with God mentioned anywhere in Scripture is united as one by Christ's blood. His shed blood is the fulfilment, the completion of every other administration of the covenant. But it is not the cancellation of every other covenant. The truth be known is that every other covenant belonging to the Lord in Scripture is simply just various administrations at various times of the one eternal covenant.

Because of Christ's shed blood, the rainbow in the clouds when God sprinkles the earth with rain, means God is promising blessings and not just that He won't send another global flood to destroy us. The sprinkling of water in our baptism is the application of God's rainbow promise. It means God's poured out blessings upon us, and not just that He won't cut us off as depicted in the bloody sacrament of circumcision. The broken bread in the Lord's Supper is a picture of our blessing, not our affliction, as pictured in the Old Testament sacrament of Passover. The cup at the Lord's Table contains the poured out gospel blessings, the blessings that were promised in the Old Covenant or Testament have arrived with Jesus Christ. These blessings are to be taken out a shared with the whole world.

Keeping in mind the blessings and curses involved in the Lord's Supper, pointing us to the cultural mandate, and reminding us of its connection with the Great Commission, Ray Sutton says,

> The covenantal design of the cultural mandate is unmistakable. Had Adam obeyed, he would have completed his covenantal commission. But the Fall interrupted everything. The seventh day, the day of special blessing, again a sanction word, was turned into a day of cursing. The Day of the Lord became a day of judgment. Ironically, "curse" not only judged the world's rebellion to God's first covenantal

mandate, it also provided a means for redemption to emerge, ultimately of course in the death of Christ. His death accomplished the original cultural mandate by receiving the curse-sanction and introduced the blessings back into the World. This appears in a special way at a final meal He conducts, just before His ascension. It is here that He gives a new cultural mandate, the Great Commission.[134]

Scripture says the life is in the blood, even as represented by the blood of grapes, or the fruit of the vine, i.e., the wine in the cup. Jesus is the true vine. He placed Himself in the winepress for believers. The cup of wine in the Lord's Supper is from His overflowing vat of blessing. Everywhere we cast our eyes in God's Kingdom we see blessings. All bitterness is gone. The God of all the earth has been propitiated by one Man on a cross. That Man is Jesus Christ our Lord, our Saviour, our Redeemer, our Blessing, our Covenant. There are great blessings to be had from sitting at His Table and supping with Him and His beloved bride. But, let it also be known that there's also judgment for him who lays a wicked hand of betrayal upon His Table.

Eleven Apostles ate and drank blessings. Judas Iscariot ate and drank judgment to himself, not discerning the Lord's body. His hand on the Table was still grubby from counting the thirty pieces of blood money he had received to betray Christ. "But behold, the hand of My betrayer is with Me on the

---

[134] Ray R Sutton, *That You May Prosper*, Institute For Christian Economics, Tyler, Texas, 1987, 127.

table. And truly the Son of Man goes as it has been determined, but woe to that man by whom He is betrayed" (Luke 22:21). William Van Doren calls Judas, "A grave in a garden!"[135] The Apostles said, "Judas by transgression fell, that he might go to his own place" (Acts 1:25b).

Judas didn't belong to the Lord. So, he ended up in the place where he did belong. He did what was in his heart. For the love of money, (the root of all evil), he betrayed the Lord of Glory, with the glad blessing of others, "And they were glad, and covenanted to give him money" (Luke 22:5). Here one is reminded of the verses, "We have made a *covenant* with death, and with Sheol we have an *agreement*" (Isa. 28:15), "And your covenant with death shall be disannulled, and your agreement with hell shall not stand; when the overflowing scourge shall pass through, then ye shall be trodden down by it" (Isa. 28:18).

Judas betrayed the Paschal Lamb who was then led to the slaughter. Jesus then had both His hands and His feet pinned to the doorway of God's Kingdom, Christ's cross. "I am the door. If anyone enters by Me, he will be saved" (John 10:9). The blood of the Paschal Lamb was smeared on the lintel as He was pinned to the wooden cross. The cherubim turned their flaming swords upon Him as He entered through the gate to Paradise. As the angel of the Lord struck down the first-born sons of Egypt, so He also struck down His first-born, His only begotten, as He

---

[135] William H. Van Doren, *The Gospel of Luke, Expository and Homiletical Commentary*, Kregel Publications, Grand Rapids, Michigan, 1981, 930.

hung on the cross. But the bitterness of God's fury is now gone. The curse has been removed from those who belong to Him.

No bitter herbs in the new sacrament, only bread and the cup of blessing. Paul the apostle refers to this as, "The cup of blessing which we bless" (1 Cor. 10:16). He says it's the communion cup of the blood of Christ. It's the cup of sharing or fellowship. That's what we see Jesus do with the cup here. He shared the communion cup with His disciples.

The eternal God sits down in our midst. He is Immanuel. He is communicating with us by His Spirit in the Lord's Supper. This new sacrament is a picture of the great wedding feast of the Lord in Paradise, the Feast of Eden if you will. "Blessed are those who shall eat bread in the kingdom of God" (Luke 14:15b). "Blessed are those who are called to the marriage supper of the Lamb!" (Rev. 19:9).

Conclusion

Your partaking of this new sacrament on the Christian Sabbath, the Lord's Day, is a picture of what you'll be doing when you enter into God's heavenly and eternal Sabbath rest. For the institutional church is a picture of the Kingdom of God on earth. In fact, the church is the kingdom of God on earth. The bread is the picture of Jesus. He is the Bread of Heaven. It is the picture of God's provision for you. And the wine, the blood of the grapes (Gen. 49:11), also pictures Jesus. He is the vine, the true vine (John 15:1). He is the life, even the tree of life. We drink the fruit of His vine and receive life.

And we've to keep on eating the new covenant bread until all is fulfilled in the kingdom of God. We are to do this in remembrance of Him. And we've to keep on drinking of His new covenant cup until the kingdom of God comes. Thus, we are proclaiming the Lord's death until He comes.

COVENANT REMEMBRANCE

Introduction

Having seen that from the fall, the covenant of grace has applied to believers, who are to guard their hearts, and that Christ is always present with us, past, present, and future, and that we are to worship God and keep His sabbath, and that believers and their children qualify for water baptism, and that baptism and the Lord's Supper supersede Old Testament circumcision and Passover respectively as the signs and seals of the covenant, let us now consider how we are proclaiming in the Lord's Supper the Lord's death until He comes.

In the army, every couple of years or more, each unit in the home barracks does a hand-over take-over, a.k.a. a HOTO. Sometimes they have a parade ground ceremony, with everyone dressed in their finest formal uniforms, witness the outgoing Commanding Officer handover authority to the incoming Commanding Officer or CO.

I was involved in one of these regarding an infantry battalion. I was part of a bagpipe band as a drummer. I got to do some solo rhythmic rat-a-tat drumbeats, keeping in time with a high-ranking individual as he marched across the parade ground to face another high-ranker, stop, and then salute. I was supposed to keep in perfect time with all their actions. Which, apparently, I did! I drummed in time with his footfalls and hit my last beat when he saluted!

We have a handover takeover, a HOTO, going on in New Testament Scripture. In fact, there are a few handovers taking place. In 1 Corinthians 11:23,

Paul received something, i.e., the Lord Jesus had handed over to him what Paul in turn was handing over to the Corinthians. And Paul reminds the Corinthians that what was handed over to him and that he is now handing over to them, took place on the night that Jesus was handed over to the authorities.

And what is the Lord's Supper if it is not Jesus handing over Himself to all who partake of it. That is why we need to be careful with the Lord's Supper. Partakers need to know what they are doing. Therefore, we need to march to the rhythm of the Scriptures. Otherwise, we will make a mess of it. The Corinthians were making a mess of it. That is why the Apostle Paul was laying out clear instructions.

> For I received from the Lord what I also passed on to you: The Lord Jesus, on the night he was betrayed, took bread, and when he had given thanks, he broke it and said, "This is my body, which is for you; do this in remembrance of me." In the same way, after supper he took the cup, saying, "This cup is the new covenant in my blood; do this, whenever you drink it, in remembrance of me." For whenever you eat this bread and drink this cup, you proclaim the Lord's death until he comes. (1 Cor. 11:23-26).

Remembering the Christ

The instructions come from Jesus, through His apostle Paul. Twice Jesus says, "do this in remembrance of Me." Once with the bread, and next with the cup. Why are the Corinthians and the rest of the Lord's church on earth to do this? Remembrance. But notice who and what it is in remembrance of: "in remembrance of Me."

So, the Lord's Supper is a memorial service for Jesus. It is to remember Jesus. And, to jog our memory, we are to eat the bread and drink the cup. Therefore, the bread and the cup are prompts, memory prompters. Who are we to remember? Jesus! Who is Jesus and what is He famous for? Ah, the bread and the cup. His body was broken for us. And His blood was shed to bring in the new covenant.

The NIV omits the word broken in the following, "This is My body which is broken for you", rendering it, "This is my body, which is for you." Whether the word broken should be in the verse or omitted, we'll let the Bible scholars argue about. However, it seems to me that the word broken, even if it ought to be omitted, is at least implied. For surely Jesus breaking bread in front of His Disciples, which bread represents His flesh, suggests that Jesus's body was broken.

Sure, not one bone of His was broken. That's what the Scriptures say (Psa. 34:20; John 19:36). However, His flesh was torn beyond recognition through the beatings, the crown of thorns, the nail prints in His hands and His feet, and the spear that cut open His side. Speaking as Christ on the cross, Psalm 22 says, "All My bones are out of joint ... They pierced My hands and My feet" (Psa. 22:14,16).

And Isaiah says of Him, "His visage was marred more than any man, and His form more than the sons of men" (Isa. 52:14). And, "He was wounded for our transgressions, He was bruised for our iniquities; the chastisement for our peace was upon Him, and by His stripes we are healed" (Isaiah 53:5). That all sounds like a broken body to me, even though none of His bones were broken. And, if we keep in mind that the Hebrew word for covenant has to do with cutting (as clearly demonstrated in the covenant God cut with Abraham where God had him cut the animals in half), then we won't have any trouble whatsoever understanding what Jesus meant in the following, "The Lord Jesus on the *same* night in which He was betrayed took bread; and when He had given thanks, He broke *it* and said, 'Take, eat; this is My body which is broken for you; do this in remembrance of Me.' In the same manner *He* also *took* the cup after supper, saying, 'This cup is the new covenant in My blood. This do, as often as you drink *it,* in remembrance of Me.' For as often as you eat this bread and drink this cup, you proclaim the Lord's death till He comes" (1 Cor. 11:23-26). Thus, the Lord's covenant is a conditional promise involving bloodshed, His bloodshed to inaugurate His last will and testament, i.e., the new covenant.

Also, apparently, the unleavened bread used at the Passover had scorch-marks on it and holes in it from baking, perhaps resembling stripes, you know, whiplash and pierce marks. Be that as it may, but we do know that Jesus knew exactly what lay ahead of Him.

Remembering the Covenant

The Lord's Supper is the New Covenant meal. The Old Covenant meal was the Passover meal.

As we have seen, the Passover meal consisted of roast lamb, accompanied by unleavened bread, bitter herbs, and all washed down with wine. In short, this meal and everything in it, all pointed to the Anointed, the Promised Messiah, Christ Jesus.

In the Old Covenant meal, there was a remembering of the past. However, there was also a present and future aspect to the Passover meal. It's just as you would expect from the eternal God, who always was, always is, and always will be. The Old Covenant meal pointed to God, the God who set Israel free from her captivity, the God who provides for His people's present needs, and the God who will provide in the future.

The Old Covenant promise was of an uncountable number of God's people living in their own land, the Promised Land. Which is a promised people and a promised land all brought about by the guiding and sovereign providential hand of God. This was God's promise made to Abraham, the father of all believers.

As you know, God killed the firstborn of the Egyptians in the first Passover. But keep in mind that Jesus is God's firstborn. More on this later. However, here's a little of what the Old Testament has to say about the Old Covenant meal, the Passover Feast. Exodus 12:24-29,

> "Obey these instructions as a lasting ordinance for you and your descendants. When you enter the land that the LORD will give you as he promised, observe this ceremony.

And when your children ask you, 'What does this ceremony mean to you?' then tell them, 'It is the Passover sacrifice to the LORD, who passed over the houses of the Israelites in Egypt and spared our homes when he struck down the Egyptians.' Then the people bowed down and worshiped. The Israelites did just what the LORD commanded Moses and Aaron. At midnight the LORD struck down all the firstborn in Egypt, from the firstborn of Pharaoh, who sat on the throne, to the firstborn of the prisoner, who was in the dungeon, and the firstborn of all the livestock as well" (Exod. 12:24-29).

The Israelites were to dress a certain way as they partook of the meal, dressed for a hurried exit. They were to put the lamb's blood on the sides and tops of the doorframes wherever they were to eat the Passover meal. Of course, all of this in every way, shape, and form pointed to the Messiah, the Christ, the Lamb of God that takes away the sin of the world.

For their own safety, the Israelites had been given the following command for the first Passover, the time when the Angel of Death would strike at midnight, "Not one of you shall go out of the door of his house until morning" (Exod. 12:22b). But what happened the night when Jesus was transitioning the Old Covenant meal into the New Covenant meal? "As soon as Judas had taken the bread, he went out. And it was night" (John 13:30). Yes, it was night!

We don't know if Judas Iscariot was a firstborn. We are only told that he was the son of

Simon Iscariot (John 6:71; 13:26). We do not believe that Simon Iscariot was Simon Peter. Therefore, we do not believe, as do some, that Judas was the apostle Peter's son. I'm sure the Scriptures would have made it plain if that had been the case. However, we do know that Judas Iscariot was the one that Jesus called "the son of perdition" or, as the NIV puts it, "the son of destruction" or "the one doomed to destruction" (John 17:12). Therefore, we know that Judas was not covered by the blood smeared on the doorposts of the building they were eating Passover in, or by the blood that was later smeared on the posts of the cross to which it pointed.

To be without the blood of Christ as illustrated in the Passover, is to be open to the LORD's destruction. For, "By faith he [Moses] kept the Passover and the sprinkling of the blood, lest He who destroyed the firstborn should touch them" (Heb. 11:28).

Judas trampled the blood of the covenant. He handed over the Christ, the Lord of Glory, to the powers of darkness. And Judas went to his own place, he "left to go where he belongs" (Acts 1:25). Yes, Judas went out, and it was night indeed! But so did Jesus...

Jesus is the Son of God, "the firstborn over all creation" (Col. 1:13). He partook of the Passover meal, then took the Apostles up to the Mount of Olives, to the place where Judas was going to betray Him.

It was the LORD who killed the firstborn on the night of the first Passover. And it was the LORD who killed His own firstborn on the night of the last

Passover. It wasn't Satan who poured out his wrath of Christ. No, it was God the Father who poured out His wrath on His Son Jesus as He hung on that cross. It was God's justice that was being propitiated. It was His righteous anger at sin that was being assuaged. And it was our sin that was being expiated. It was all our transgressions of God's law that were being covered, covered by the shed blood of Jesus, which blood is represented by the cup of wine, i.e., the new covenant in His blood.

We see then that God has handed over to Jesus all our sins. And God has handed over to us all of Jesus's righteousness. Therefore, we must march to the beat of Scripture. We must keep in step with God speaking in His Word.

And, if the unleavened bread represented bread without the yeast of sin, then Christ's body on the cross was a body without any sin, sin of His own. He died for our sins, the sins which God imputed to Him before He holocausted His Son by pouring out His fiery wrath on Him. And it was the righteousness of His Son's perfect Commandment keeping that the Father imputed or accredited to us. Therefore, the bread represents His body broken for us, and the cup represents His shed blood, the blood on the doorposts and the blood on the posts on the cross.

As we march across the Lord's parade ground, and approach that final salute where the handover takeover, the HOTO, will be complete, let recap and apply what we've learned.

The "Last Supper" is a misnomer. The Last Supper, if anything, should be called the Last Passover. It was the Last Passover that became the

Lord's Supper, which actually was, not the last but the first supper, if you follow my meaning. The Old Covenant became the New Covenant with the death and resurrection of Christ.

Notice that Jesus says, "This cup is the *new* covenant". It's the new covenant. But notice that He doesn't leave it at that but adds what's new about it, "in my blood." "This cup is the new covenant in my blood." The Old Covenant was in the blood of bulls, lambs and goats etc. But the New Covenant is in Christ's blood. Moses, as it were, held the fort until One greater than Moses arrived.

Here at the first Lord's Supper is the great handover takeover, the HOTO, from the Old Testament to the New Testament. Well talk about the words Testament and Covenant in a moment, but, "By calling this covenant 'new.' He has made the first one obsolete; and what is obsolete and outdated will soon disappear" (Heb. 8:13).

Right, of the two Koine Greek words for covenant, i.e., *suntheke* and *diatheke*, the writers of the New Testament could have used to translate the Old Testament Hebrew *berith*, as in "to cut a covenant", the writers in the New Testament opted for the latter, *diatheke*.

A "last will and testament" is where a person has to die before his or her estate is divided, handed over, to those who were listed in the will. That's what *diatheke* has to do with. Whereas the word *suntheke* speaks more of a bilateral agreement, the word *diatheke* is more unilateral.

It's kind of like the covenant God cut with Abraham. Only God walked through the valley of the shadow of death, i.e., the divided pieces of animals and the birds. It all makes better sense to you if you keep in mind that all earthly administrations of God's covenant have their source in the heavenly administration of the eternal covenant, i.e., the covenant between the Father and the Son as our representative, wherein the Son is, as Revelation 13:8b refers to Him, "the Lamb slain from the foundation of the world." The blood of that slain Lamb is the blood of the everlasting covenant" (Heb. 13:20).

When the kids play the blindfold game of piñata at a birthday party or whatever, the piñata needs to be whacked and broken open by a stick before it contents will spill out. God whacked His Son on the cross and all the covenant blessings poured out. I merely seek to illustrate, not mutilate, a point, but Jesus said, "This is My body which is broken for you." All the benefits contained in the conditional promise, i.e., the everlasting covenant, could not be given until Christ had died. But moreover, not until He had been raised again.

For look at this wonderful piece of Scripture in Hebrews 9:16-18, "In the case of a will [will here is the same word for covenant], it is necessary to prove the death of the one who made it, because a will [same word] is in force only when somebody has died; it never takes effect while the one who made it is living. This is why even the first covenant was not put into effect without blood" (Heb. 9:16-18). Says Palmer Robertson,

Particularly, the integral relation of death to a 'covenant' escapes the modern reader. Yet death is as inseparably to 'covenant' as to 'testament.' If the present study of God's covenant with Abraham establishes anything, it indicates the vital relation of death to covenant. Essential to the inauguration both of the Abrahamic and Mosaic covenants was the symbolic representation of the death of the covenant-maker. The long history of God's terminal judgments on Israel finds prophetic interpretation in light of God's execution of the death-curse on covenant breakers.

Death and covenant clearly relate. They relate concretely in two ways. First, the death of the covenant-maker receives symbolic representation at the time of the inauguration of the covenant. The covenant-making procedure is not complete without this pledge-to-death aspect. Secondly, the death of the covenant-violator receives historical actualization when covenantal judgment is executed. Once a transgression of covenantal commitment has occurred, death is inevitable.

So both 'testament' and 'covenant' involve death. Death activates a testament. Death inaugurates and vindicates a covenant.[136]

Whether made pre-fall with Adam, or post-fall with Noah or Abraham or Moses or David, all God's covenants throughout the Bible beginning to end are

---

[136] O Palmer Robertson, *The Christ of the Covenants*, Presbyterian and Reformed Publishing, New Jersey, 1980, 139.

ultimately made with Christ. Look at Christ. How so? "For no matter how many promises God has made, they are "Yes" in Christ" (2 Cor. 1:20a). The preincarnate Christ began writing His last will and testament when He covered the fallen Adam and Eve with skin from the slain animal (Gen. 3:21). And by breaking the bread in the Lord's Supper, He was as it were walking between the halved animal pieces. He signed His last will and testament with His own blood at the cross.

If we hold the view as put forth by the Presbyterian theologian Charles Hodge that "A covenant is a promise suspend upon a condition," or as I summarise it, that "a covenant is a conditional promise," we'll see that the words covenant and testament, as in last will and testament, are interchangeable. How so? Well, again, "A will is in force only when somebody has died; it never takes effect while the one who made it is living."

What are we doing when we partake of the Lord's Supper? "For whenever you eat this bread and drink this cup, you proclaim the Lord's death until he comes" (1 Cor. 11:26).

Everything Jesus has bequeathed to us is now ours! How so? Well, it's because He died, that's how! But, I hear you say, He is risen! He's alive! Yes, but He actually died, didn't He? But because He was crucified, died, and was buried, but rose from the dead, does this mean that we have to hand back to Him whatever He handed over to us? God forbid!

Jesus perfectly kept the conditions of the old covenant by His works, and we perfectly keep the conditions of the new covenant by our gift of faith.

But whether Old Testament or New Testament, the elect of God were saved the same way. In the Old Testament it was by grace through faith in the Promised Messiah, i.e., the Christ to come. And in the New Testament we are saved by grace through faith in the Christ who has come.

Jesus closed the old covenant by fulfilling its conditions, i.e., by the death of the Testator. Look at Hebrews 9:16-18 once more, only this time from the New King James Version. It'll drive home what we're on about: "For where there is a testament [same word as covenant], there must also of necessity be the death of the testator [or covenanter]. For a testament is in force after men are dead, since it has no power at all while the testator lives. Therefore not even the first covenant was dedicated without blood" (Heb. 9:16-18).

Conclusion

The Lord's Supper is the New Covenant meal that replaces the Old Covenant meal of Passover. The HOTO is complete. It is complete because of the death of Jesus our Covenant (see Isaiah 42:6; 49:8 where Jesus is called our "covenant", i.e., "a covenant for the people").

The broken bread represents His torn and pierced flesh, and the cup His shed blood, i.e., His death. The LORD struck down His firstborn on the cross. Christ is our Passover. The shed blood of the Lamb who takes away our sins, is represented by the wine. We eat and drink at His Table in remembrance of Him and what He did.

We are so quick to forget. What used to be called Armistice Day is now more popularly known as Remembrance Day. It is a day when we remember the fallen, the death and mayhem of WWII and the toll it took on humanity. Like ANZAC Day, it's "Lest we forget."

The Lord's Supper is the remembrance of the One who died to save us from death, the Lord of Life and the Prince of Peace.

COVENANT CITY

Introduction

Having seen that the covenant of grace applies to all believers since the fall, and that as such, we are to guard our hearts knowing that Christ is always present with us, and that we are to worship God corporately on His sabbath, and that believers and their children qualify for water baptism, which along with the Lord's Supper supersede Old Testament circumcision and Passover respectively, and that by partaking of the Lord's Supper we are proclaiming the Lord's death until He comes, let us now consider where we are heading as Christians.

One of the great things about being a Christian is a sense of belonging. We, who have been purchased by the precious shed blood of Jesus Christ, belong to Him. And, because of this, whatever belongs to Him now belongs also to us. We now own heaven and earth because heaven and earth belong to Jesus Christ. This sounds like a grand sweeping statement, but it's nevertheless true.

Now, what we see in the following passage of Scripture is the passing away of heaven and earth as we now know it, "And I saw a new heaven and earth, for the first heaven and earth had passed away … Then I, John, saw a holy city, New Jerusalem, coming down out of heaven from God" (Rev. 21:1-2). This is what the Apostle John over 2,000 years ago was seeing in a vision on a high mountain. And, because it has been recorded in Scripture, we today can see the same vision. Part of this vision is that of seeing God dwelling with His people in this new heaven and earth. "And I heard a loud voice from heaven, saying, 'Behold, the tabernacle of God is with men, and He will dwell with them, and they shall be His people. God Himself will be with them and be their God'" (Rev. 21:3). Then in the following verse we see that in this new heaven and earth there will be no tears, no death, no sorrow, no crying, for the former things have passed away.

This is the Kingdom to which all true Christians belong. This is our home! This is where we long to be. This is where we belong. But where is this city? And what kind of a city is it? Is it on the planet Mars? Jupiter perhaps? Is it on one of those little planets that scientists claim to have recently discovered in another universe? Can it be seen through a telescope? What is it made of? Is it real? These are the types of questions we'll seek to answer in the following.

The City's Location

Where, at this very moment in time, is the City of God? Well, consider again what John has written, "Then I, John, saw the holy city, New Jerusalem, coming down out of heaven from God, prepared as a bride adorned for her husband" (Rev. 21:2). Then up ahead it says, "'Come, I will show you the bride, the Lamb's wife' And he carried me away in the Spirit to a great and high mountain, and showed me the great city, the holy Jerusalem, descending out of heaven from God, having the glory of God" (Rev. 21:9-11a). So, let us ask, Where is this city coming from and where is it coming to? It's descending from

God, from heaven, and it's coming upon the earth, this earth.

Now then, which heaven is John speaking of here? The word "heaven" is used in three senses in the Bible. It's used of the upper air through which the birds fly. Jesus in Matthew 8:20 speaks of "the birds of the air." Literally it's "birds of the heaven" And there's the heaven through which the stars revolve. Hebrews 11:12 speaks of "the stars of the sky [lit, heaven]." Then there's the third heaven Paul the Apostle speaks of. He was "caught up to the third heaven" (2 Cor. 12:2). He calls this third heaven "Paradise." Jesus took the repentant thief on the cross to this very same "Paradise" the day they died. "Today you will be with Me in Paradise" (Luke 23:43). Therefore, the heaven mentioned by John in Revelation 21 is a real place. But it's not the place where the birds fly, nor the place where the stars twinkle. The heaven spoken of there is simply the place where the LORD God Almighty and the Lamb (i.e., Jesus Christ) dwell.

The location of the "holy city" is above and beyond even the most distant star. Yet, this third heaven has a location. Heaven is more than a state of bliss. Heaven has a location. If you will, Paradise has a post or zip code. First off, we know that it's the place where God and the Lamb dwell. It's the place where Jesus, the Lamb of God ascended to bodily after His resurrection. It's the place where the soul of the thief on the cross went. But where is it then? Well, bear with me, and we'll all get there! David Chilton helps us to understand what we're dealing with here where he says,

The truth is that the Bible tells us very little about heaven; just enough, in fact, to let us know we're going there. But the primary concern of Scripture is this present life. Of course, the blessings of the final chapter of Revelation *do* refer to heaven. It is not really an "either/or" kind of an issue. But what is important is that these things are true *now*. Heaven is a continuation and perfection of what is true of the Church in this life. We are not simply to look forward to these blessings in an eternity to come, but to enjoy them and rejoice in them here and now. John was telling the early Church of present realities, of blessings that existed already and would be on the increase as the gospel extended and renewed the earth.[137]

We see in Revelation 21:10 that John had to stand on a great and high mountain in order to see the City of God descend out of heaven. So, the idea is that special revelation of God is required before this City of God can be seen. The apostle Paul was caught up to the third heaven. John received a vision on a mountaintop. Therefore, we can conclude that Paradise, the City of God, cannot be seen by the naked eye. But in Scripture we have an accurate and infallible record of what the apostle John saw. Therefore, we have something much better than a telescope for looking into heaven, better than a

---

[137] David Chilton, *Paradise Restored, A Biblical Theology of Dominion*, Dominion Press, Fort Worth, Texas, 1985, 203.

Hubble telescope, or even the James Webb Space Telescope! We have the special revelation of God before our very eyes.

What then can we see of the City of God, of Heaven? Well, we can see clearly that the City of God is the place where God dwells with His people. Jesus is there, as is the thief who died on the cross, the apostle Paul, and all the saints who have died. We see that this holy city, the New Jerusalem, is prepared as a bride adorned for her husband. And we see that the City of God is synonymous with the bride, i.e., the Lamb's wife. In other words, the City of God is the place where the Lamb dwells with His bride. This is the "New Jerusalem" which is heavenly (Gal. 4:26). It is not the earthly Jerusalem in Palestine (Gal. 4:25).

You'll remember in Old Testament times that God "dwelt" between the cherubim on the Ark of the Covenant in the Temple in the earthly Jerusalem. But we see the following, "But I saw no temple in it, for the Lord God Almighty and the Lamb are its temple" (Rev. 21:22). The Temple at Jerusalem was destroyed in 70 AD. In other words, after the Lamb was slain, there was no longer any use for the Temple in Jerusalem. The Temple at Jerusalem was merely a picture of heaven, i.e., the place where God dwells. So, if we can locate the new place where God and the Lamb dwell, we can locate the City of God.

God had His dwelling place, i.e., the Temple, and indeed Jerusalem, destroyed. But He didn't just leave a void. He built a New Jerusalem, which is the one that we are looking at now. But, more importantly, He built a New Temple, which is Jesus Christ, the chief cornerstone of His Church. Said

Jesus, speaking of Himself, "Destroy this temple, and in three days I will raise it up" (John 2:19). Note also these words, "Behold, I lay in Zion a chief cornerstone, elect, precious" (Isa. 28:16; 1 Pet. 2:6) says the Lord God Almighty. So, to cut the long story short, the Temple at Jerusalem (where God used to dwell) gave way to the church, the bride of Christ (in whom God now dwells by His Spirit). William Hendriksen, says,

> This Jerusalem is called "new" in contradistinction to the earthly, Palestinian Jerusalem. It is called "holy" because it is separate from sin and thoroughly consecrated to God. This new and holy Jerusalem is clearly the Church of the Lord Jesus Christ, as is also plainly evident from the fact that it is here and elsewhere called the bride, the wife of the Lamb (Isa. 54:5; Eph 5:32; *etc*.). Even in the Old Testament the Church is represented under the symbolism of a city (Isa. 26:1; Psa. 48; *etc*).[138]

Isaiah says, "For your Maker is your husband, the LORD of Hosts is His name; and your Redeemer is the Holy One of Israel; He is called the God of the whole earth" (Isa. 54:5). The apostle Paul says to the Ephesians, "For we are members of His body, of His flesh and of His bones. 'For this reason a man shall leave his father and mother and be joined to his wife, and the two shall become one flesh.' This is a great

---

[138] William Hendriksen, *More Than Conquerors*, Baker Book House, Grand Rapids, Michigan, Tenth Printing 1995, 199.

mystery, but I speak concerning Christ and the Church" (Eph. 5:30). Christ, then, is our Husband. His church therefore is His bride, which dwells in the holy city, the New Jerusalem. This is where Righteousness Himself dwells, i.e., in His people and in His City. New Jerusalem, then, is the church of the Lord Jesus Christ. Says Nigel Lee,

> This "Holy City" indeed represents the Members of the Christian Church as such (both the Church Militant and the Church Triumphant). However, one can hardly divorce the Saints from their everlasting abode. Hence, it seems transparently clear that the "Holy City" of the future – includes both the Saints and the place where they shall dwell. For the Holy City is not itself the bride, but is prepared like a bride adorned for her husband. And a bride's adornments, even though they surround the bride, are not the bride herself. "The bride, the Lamb's wife," is not just "that great city" alias "the Holy Jerusalem" itself. The bride herself consists of the saved "Nations" and the "Kings" who bring their honour and glory into the Holy City.[139]

It should now be clear that the New Jerusalem is the place where God and the Lamb dwell. This is in heaven. However, because God dwells by His Spirit in the midst of His people on earth (Matt. 18:20),

---

[139] Francis Nigel Lee, *John's Revelation Unveiled*, Ligstryders, Lynnwoodrif, South Africa, 1999, 294.

there is a sense in which the City of God is located in the heart of every believer, whether, at the moment, in heaven or on earth. Or better, because of every Christian's spiritual connection to Christ and Christ's with them, the City of God extends from heaven to earth. It encompasses heaven and earth, which is to say that the location of the City of God is from here to eternity! Spiritually or invisibly, it's right here in our midst, and it extends all the way up to the third heaven. Or better still, the third heaven extends all the way down into our midst today. The New Jerusalem in a word, then, is the church both visible (i.e., Militant) and invisible (i.e., Triumphant), which is one and the same church. Therefore, though the City of God is presently in heaven, where Jesus is making preparations for His bride (John 14:1-4), an aspect of it is located wherever the true church is on earth. Remember the covenant promise: a people and a place.

Where is the true church? There are three marks by which the true church may by identified on earth,

1. The preaching of the gospel.
2. The proper administration of the two sacraments.
3. The proper exercise of church discipline.

Therefore, we should expect to see these three marks of the true Church here on earth where the gospel is faithfully proclaimed each Lord's Day/Christian Sabbath, where the two sacraments (baptism and the Lord's Supper) are properly administered, and where the church elders are encouraging their congregations to live disciplined lives to the glory of God alone.

Only when Christ comes again will His church be perfect on earth. But all true believers (whether already in heaven or presently here on earth) are part of the City of God. The church is the bride of Christ, and as such, dwells in the City of God. Let me put it another way, Christians already are in God's Kingdom. Therefore, they already are members of the City of God on account of the finished work of Christ. This is the same city that Abraham was yearning for, "For he was looking forward to the city that has foundations, whose designer and builder is God" (Heb. 11:10).

Well then, if you are already a citizen in good standing, we have to conclude that (at least in a certain sense) the new heaven and earth has already come! In other words, the New Jerusalem, the City of God, has already begun its descent to earth. Says J.V. Fesko,

> Our redemption is all by God's grace in Christ, the last Adam, but he accomplished this salvation entirely by his works. Christ fulfilled the covenant of works so that we take a step into the new heavens and earth the moment we believe. We receive a foretaste of the eternal eschatological rest each and every Lord's Day as we celebrate the completed work of Christ – we first rest – and enter the remainder of the week in the knowledge and hope that the work has been done. We can

only begin to enter this eternal rest solely by the completed work of Christ – His obedience alone – not our own. To try to mix our good works with Christ's as the means by which we enter God's eternal rest is an alchemy doomed to failure.[140]

Make sure you've got your feet firmly planted on this earth. For, as we can see clearly in Revelation 21, the City of God is descending upon *this* earth.

The City's Locals

By the locals of the City of God, we mean those who are its citizens, (more properly, subjects of King Jesus). Or, put another way, by locals we mean those who in fellowship or communion with God through Jesus Christ. The Lord's Supper is this fellowship or communion visualized. The Lord's Supper is Jesus, the Husband, sitting down to dine with the church, His bride. The Lord's Supper is Christ's Wedding Feast, the feast of Eden – to use that play on words again. Marriage, as we've seen, is a covenant. It is God's covenant with His people visualised. Thus, the Lord's Supper is the covenant meal.

In Revelation the New Jerusalem is to come down out of heaven as "a bride adorned for her husband" (Rev. 21:2). If this is to take place in the future, how can we say that it is already happening? Again, communion is the token celebration of our

---

[140] J.V. Fesko, *Adam and the Covenant of Works*, Mentor Imprint by Christian Focus Publications Ltd., Geanies House, Fearn, Ross-shire, 2021, 375-76.

marriage or covenant with Christ. Yet there are three dimensions to the Lord's Supper, viz. past, present, and future.

At the Lord's table we are remembering that Christ has come, while at the same time we are acknowledging that He is present at His table, and also that He will come again. It is what the theologians refer to as the" already but not yet." Christ is here. He is present already but not yet. Or we might say that Christ is with us but not in all His glory. This "real presence", I believe, is what the church today needs. She needs more of a sense of Christ's presence in her midst. The church on earth has not been abandoned by her husband. The children of God have not been left as orphans. Therefore, we should never neglect our duties toward Him. Christ is busy at work in our midst preparing us for the mansions that He is preparing in heaven for us. The meek are to inherit the earth (Psa. 37:11; Matt. 5:5; Rom. 4:13). Their inheritance shall come in full when Christ lowers the City of God into place.

A long time ago I was holidaying in Scotland at the place where I grew up, and, as I drove toward my dad's home at the southern end of Loch Lomond, I could see two large cranes on the skyline. I thought to myself, "What are they doing to my loch?" I discovered that they were building a huge tourist complex. The two cranes were being used to lower giant pieces of concrete and so forth into place as they built the complex on the southern end of Loch Lomond. Till then, the town's economy had been in a depressed state. Illicit drug use had become widespread, rampant. But now business was booming. Jobs were again becoming available. The depressed community had regained some of its lost dignity. Those two giant cranes on the shore of Loch Lomond were symbols, pillars of a new prosperity.

The church in any community is or should be the symbol of prosperity, spiritual prosperity. The church is used by God as the giant crane as it were to lower the City of God into place upon this depressed earth. Christians are not in the ranks of this earth's unemployed. We are the workers. We are being employed by Christ. We are the ones with all the spiritual wealth. We are the ones who should be injecting health into our community's spiritually bankrupt economy. This is the way we should see ourselves. We need to see ourselves as the City of God on earth, the city with all its gold and precious stones. Says Nigel Lee (quoting Klaas Schilder's *John's Revelation and Social Life*),

> "When God's New Jerusalem, His city of peace, comes down from God out of Heaven – culture, then divested of its sinful stains, shall surrender its fruits to God's Kingdom. The glory and the honour not only of the Kings but also of the Nations – yet not only of the masses but also of that in which the individual brilliance of the style-formers and the pace-setters is to be seen – will all be brought into God's "New Paradise" of the future…
>
> "Thus it is precisely the Calvinistic life and world view which accepts a life's task; which arouses the highest attention of the soul – in the knowledge that there is a vocation in

respect of the entire Cosmos which rests on that man who hears creation sigh ... and who hears God's voice calling him to enter into the Sabbath of God. For God's Sabbath arrives when the Cosmos is renewed and the Universe is regenerated [Matt. 19:28] ... Our building up the house of the Universe is in vain [Psa. 127] unless God Himself is put first in that construction..., to undertake the conquest of the World!"

It should be noted that the wicked breakers of God's Covenant and His Commandments shall never disturb the peace of the City of New Jerusalem in the Church Triumphant. They will, of course, even then continue to exist – and probably even then continue to break God's Commandments. But that existence, as miserable as it will be everlasting, will never even be seen from the New Earth and its heavenly City of God.[141]

Yes, our heads should be in heaven, the third heaven, but our feet should be planted firmly on terra firma. Think about it, Christ's feet, like those two giant cranes that were at Loch Lomond, so to speak, are firmly planted upon this earth. Christ is carrying us, His bride, in His arms. His two strong legs, as it were, are standing upon the earth and He's lowering His bride down into her new home. Wherever He sets her down, there is His church, the City of God, the blessing of God from heaven.

---

[141] Francis Nigel Lee, *John's Revelation Unveiled*, Ligstryders, Lynnwoodrif, South Africa, 1999, 303.

If we remember what we've already looked at regarding the pillars of fire and cloud in relation to the Old Testament theophanies, the Angel of the Covenant, covenant rainbows from the time of Noah's flood, and Christ coming with the clouds of judgment, etc., we shouldn't have any trouble seeing Jesus's future return to earth in the following,

> Then I saw another mighty angel coming down from heaven. He was robed in a cloud, with a rainbow above his head; his face was like the sun, and his legs were like fiery pillars. He was holding a little scroll, which lay open in his hand. He planted his right foot on the sea and his left foot on the land, and he gave a loud shout like the roar of a lion. When he shouted, the voices of the seven thunders spoke (Rev. 10:1-3).

Herman Hoeksema comments on these verses,

> And who can read this description of the angel's being arrayed in a cloud without thinking of the so often repeated assertion that Christ shall come with the clouds of heaven to judge the quick and the dead? In the second place, we read that a rainbow was upon his head. In other words, the rainbow is his crown. A rainbow we found thus far only above the throne of God Almighty in heaven. It is the symbol of the grace and the faithfulness of God in keeping his covenant, especially in view to all creation. And

therefore also this detail of the description could hardly be fitted in with the picture of a common angel. It makes us think of the Angel of the Covenant, of Jesus Christ Himself.[142]

Those who are alive at Christ's physical coming to earth with the City of God will rise to meet Him and the saints (who have gone before) on the way down.

> For the Lord Himself will descend from heaven with a shout, with the voice of an archangel, and with the trumpet of God. And the dead in Christ will rise first. Then we who are alive *and* remain shall be caught up together with them in the clouds to meet the Lord in the air. And thus we shall always be with the Lord. Therefore comfort one another with these words (1 Thess. 4:16-18).

Here is the direct reversal of the curse of covenant dismembering illustrated in the Abrahamic covenant (Gen. 15:17). For then shall our disembodied souls be reunited with our resurrected bodies when Christ returns with His kingdom. And body, soul, and spirit we shall live with Him on the renewed earth forever as per His everlasting covenant. Says Nigel Lee,

---

[142] Herman Hoeksema, *Behold, He Cometh! An Exposition of the Book of Revelation*, Reformed Free Publishing Association, Grand Rapids, Michigan, (1969), Second Printing 1974, 337.

The faithful 'alive-in-Christ' and the wicked 'alive-in-Satan' are both to be transformed at the same time. For, at Christ's Visible and Final coming in power and great glory, all of their bodies will be raised to unannihilatable and unchangeable everlasting continued existence. And those bodies will thenceforth spend all future eternity – either on the heavenly New Earth yet-to-come – or else in the everlasting Lake of Fire and Brimstone.[143]

"Now may the God of peace Himself sanctify you completely; and may your whole spirit, soul, and body be preserved blameless at the coming of our Lord Jesus Christ" (1 Thess. 5:23).

Conclusion

Let us be mindful that the Lord's church should be a blessing to our community. We should be hard at work in our community. We should be acting as citizens of the City of God. We should be obedient to our husband and king, Jesus Christ, in all areas of our lives. Therefore, we should assert, maintain, and defend His crown rights on earth. We do this by serving Christ faithfully in every sphere of our lives, be it religion, politics, business, family, leisure or whatever. Put Christ first in all these realms. In other words, be a good citizen of the City of God.

In the words of that great hymn-writer, John Newton, who, alluding to the City of God, wrote,

---

[143] Francis Nigel Lee, *John's Revelation Unveiled*, Ligstryders, Lynnwoodrif, South Africa, 1999, 287.

Glorious things of thee are spoken,
Zion, city of our God;
He whose word cannot be broken
Formed thee for His own abode.
On the Rock of Ages founded,
What can shake thy sure repose?
With salvation's wall surrounded,
Thou mayst smile at all thy foes.

Develop a sense of belonging, a sense of belonging to the City of God. Once you have developed a sense of belonging to the City of God, then it will begin to develop itself before your very eyes. You'll begin to see the beautiful blessings Christ is even now lowering into place on earth. Again, commenting on the Book of Revelation, says Nigel Lee,

> The saints will not stay in that 'merely heavenly' condition forever. No. After the Final Judgment, the time will come when Heaven itself and all of its inhabitants will come down onto the (then re)new(ed) Earth. For even God's Temple of Heaven – shall yet be brought down to Earth. And when God's saints get their bodies back, they will serve Him for ever in those bodies here on Earth (after its renewal). Meantime, right now, 'they are before the throne of God, and serve Him day and night in His Temple' in Heaven. But on the New Earth yet to come, 'He Who sits on the throne shall dwell among them. They shall hunger no more, neither thirst any more.

Neither shall the sun [cast] light or any heat upon them. For the Lamb Who is in the midst of the throne, shall feed them – and shall lead them to fountains of living water. And God shall wipe all tears from their eyes. Then the Lamb will consummate everything. Indeed, 'when He had opened the seventh seal, there was silence in Heaven.' For the Cosmic Sabbath then arrives – the saints' Everlasting rest here on Earth; in Heaven-on-Earth.[144]

Catch the vision, the vision that has been set before our eyes. Be part of the true City of God to the glory of God.

---

[144] Ibid., 65-66.

COVENANT CONSUMMATED

Introduction

Having seen that the covenant of grace applies to all believers since the fall, and that as such, we are to guard our hearts knowing that Christ is always present with us and that we are to worship God corporately on His sabbath, and that believers and their children qualify for water baptism, which along with the Lord's Supper supersede Old Testament circumcision and Passover respectively, and that by partaking of the Lord's Supper we are proclaiming the Lord's death until He comes while knowing where we are heading as Christians, let us consider something of what it means now that God's eternal covenant has been consummated.

The eternal covenant was sealed in blood when Christ died on the cross at Calvary. "When He had by Himself purged our sins, [He] sat down at the right hand of the majesty on high" (Heb. 1:3b), and "This Man, after He had offered one sacrifice for sins forever, sat down at the right hand of God, from that time waiting till His enemies are made His footstool" (Heb. 10:12-13). After He was resurrected from the dead He ascended into heaven (Acts 1:9-11; Dan. 7:13-14). The consummation of the eternal covenant began with the outpouring of the Holy Spirit from heaven by the Father and the Son (Acts 1:5; 7-8; 2:14; Luke 24:49).

The church received the Holy Spirit at Jerusalem. It is from there that the church and kingdom began to spread throughout the whole world as Christians took the gospel with them. The Spirit works with the Word (two witnesses), and it is through the proclamation of the Good News that people are converted by the Spirit who effectively works within their hearts.

Whole communities and cities and even whole nations are transformed as the gospel, like leaven spreading through the whole batch of dough, influences people's lives for good. This is in line with Psalm 110:1 where we read the words king David wrote under inspiration of the Holy Spirit, "The LORD said to my Lord, sit at My right hand, till I make Your enemies Your footstool." This verse is alluded to by the writer to the Hebrews where he says of Christ (as already mentioned above and restated here), "This Man, after He had offered one sacrifice for sins forever, sat down at the right hand of God, from that time waiting till His enemies are made His footstool" (Heb. 10:12-13).

Those who have been redeemed by Christ also need a place to dwell. That is what is meant by the meek inheriting the earth. It speaks of a people and a place. See this alluded to in the following portion of Scripture in which the Son speaks of what the Father said to Him, "I will declare the decree: The LORD has said to Me, You are My Son, today I have begotten You. Ask of Me, and I will give You the nations for Your inheritance, and the ends of the earth for Your possession" (Psa. 2:7-8). The gospel presently going out to all nations is the outworking of this eternal decree. While looking at the impact of the gospel in the world, says Loraine Boettner

The redemption of the world is a long, slow process, extending through the centuries, yet surely approaching an appointed goal. We live in the day of advancing victory, although there are many apparent set-backs. As seen from the human viewpoint it often looks as though the forces of evil are about to gain the upper hand. Periods of spiritual advance and prosperity alternate with periods of spiritual decline and depression. But as one age succeeds another there is progress. Looking back across the two thousand years that have passed since the coming of Christ we can see that there has indeed been marvelous progress. This process ultimately shall be completed, and before Christ comes again we shall see a Christianized world. This does not mean that all sin ever will be eradicated. There always will be some tares among the wheat until the time of harvest – and the harvest, the Lord tells us, is the end of the world. Even the righteous fall, sometimes grievously, into temptation and sin. But it does mean that Christian principles of life and conduct are to become the accepted standards in public and private life.

That a great spiritual advance has been made should be clear to all. Consider, for instance, the awful moral and spiritual conditions that existed on earth before the coming of Christ, – the world at large groping helplessly in pagan darkness, with slavery, polygamy, the oppressed conditions of women and children, the almost complete lack of political freedom, and the ignorance, poverty, and extremely primitive medical care that was the lot of nearly all except those who belonged to the ruling classes. Today the world at large is on a far higher plane. Christian principles are the accepted standards in many nations even though they are not consistently practiced. Slavery and polygamy have practically disappeared. The status of women and children has been improved immeasurably. Social and economic conditions in almost all nations have reached a new high plateau.[145]

In the following I'd like to draw your attention to a verse of Scripture that perhaps has been one of the most overlooked verses of God's infallible Word. This verse of Scripture follows directly after that most well-known of all verses, i.e., John 3:16. John 3:16, as practically everyone knows, goes, "For God so loved the world that He gave His only begotten Son, that whoever believes in Him should not perish but have everlasting life." John 3:16 is an awesome verse of Scripture, isn't it?

Let me just spend a moment by giving a reminder of what it means before we look at the verse that follows it. John 3:16 tells us that God does not *hate* the world but *loves* the world. John 3:16 tells us that God gave the world His only true Son. God gave to the world His only begotten Son as an act of His goodness and mercy. John 3:16 tells us *why* God gave

[145] Loraine Boettner, *The Millennium*, Presbyterian & Reformed, USA, Thirteenth printing, 1984, 38.

His eternally begotten Son. God gave the world His only begotten Son as Saviour of the world, which is to say that God the Son became also *a man* to save the world as a man. Why? Because God loves the world!

And John 3:16 tells us that His Son is Saviour of all those who, by His grace through faith, believe in Him as Saviour, which is to say that all those who gladly receive God's gift of His eternally begotten Son (who became also a human being in the womb of the Virgin) will never perish. In John 3:16, to perish doesn't mean to disappear or vanish forever as in being annihilated. But rather the kind of perishing spoken of here is to remain forever in a state of mental and emotional and physical torment. You can see why John 3:16 is often called "the Good News in a nutshell." It is telling us that God gave His Son to save sinners from the everlasting torments of Hell.

And John 3:16 also tells us that those believing in His only begotten Son will have everlasting life. This means that all those who receive the gift that God is giving the world will enter into a state of mental and emotional and physical and spiritual bliss that lasts forever and ever. There's a lot in John 3:16. So, it's little wonder that John 3:16 is often referred to as the gospel, i.e., the Good News of Glad Tidings, in one verse.

Let me repeat John 3:16 so that you can see the gospel in a nutshell one more time, "For God so loved the world that He gave His only begotten Son, that whoever believes in Him should not perish but have everlasting life." So, we see then that God is not hiding Himself on the planet Mars. We can see that

He isn't trying to avoid spaceships by hiding Himself behind rocks on the dark side of the moon. We see that God has revealed Himself to man. We see that He has revealed Himself to humankind in the Person of Jesus Christ. God has given the world His only begotten Son Jesus Christ. Why did God give the world His only begotten Son Jesus Christ? God has given His only begotten Son to the world because He does not hate the world, rather He loves the world. If God hated the world, He wouldn't have sent His Son into the world.

So, the world that God loved, the world that God sent His Son into the world to die for, is the same world that God covenantally promised to Abraham, the father of the faithful, "For the promise that he would be the heir of the world *was* not to Abraham or to his seed through the law, but through the righteousness of faith" (Rom. 4:13). Like Abraham, those who believe in God's Son shall not perish but have everlasting life in God's redeemed world.

The Saviour of the World

Why did God the Son leave His glory in heaven and enter into this world by becoming also a man? Well, that's where John 3:17 comes in. Many people overlook John 3:17 because they're too enamoured with John 3:16. But John 3:17 helps us to understand John 3:16 more fully. And it also helps us to understand why God gave the world His Son.

Now, if you think God gave the world His Son just to make it possible for people to be saved then you really need to read John 3:17. Somehow over the years the attention has been taken off the fact that it was God who gave the world His Son by sending His Son into the world. God is no longer the centre of attention nowadays. For, when it comes to the gospel, i.e., the Good News, the attention nowadays is all on man not God. It's as if man has become his own saviour, and not God. That's why it's good to look at John 3:17.

God did not send His only begotten Son into the world to make it possible for some people to be saved from God's justice of everlasting torment. For if you believe that then you are believing that a person can be his or her own saviour. But that's not what the Good News is all about. The Good News is all about God sending His Son into the world as the Saviour of the world. If you don't believe me then grab a Bible and just look at John 3:17, "For God did not send His Son into the world to condemn the world, but that the world through Him might be saved." How is the world saved? The world is saved through Him, not through you or me, or you plus Him, or me plus Him. No! The world is saved through the One God has sent into the world to save the world.

Now, I'll grant you that that little word "might" might cause some people to misunderstand what this verse is actually saying. Let's say you asked me why I wheeled my wheely-bin out to the kerb. I might say to you that I wheeled my wheely-bin out to the kerb so that the garbage-man might collect it. Do I mean to say that the wheely-bin-man might perhaps just possibly collect my garbage? Or do I mean that I did it so that the bin-man would definitely take away my garbage? So, God did not send His Son into the world just so that He might perhaps just possibly take away the sins of the world as a bin-man might take away our garbage. No! God sent His Son into the world so that the world through Him would definitely not perish like so much rotting garbage, but rather be saved.

When viewed properly, i.e., when viewed from God's perspective, the focus is back on the action of God, isn't it? God is the One who has entered into the muck and rotten filth of sinful humanity. Why? He became also a man to take away the sins of the world. This is what the world is reminded of each Christmas. The eternally begotten Son of God was miraculously conceived by the Holy Spirit and the power of the Highest in the womb of a virgin by the name of Mary (Luke 1:35). And nine months later He is born in the usual manner, but in an unusual place. He was born in a place ordinarily where animals are kept. And He was laid in a manger, i.e., a trough from which animals eat.

God the Son has entered into the muck and filth of sinful humanity. Why? He came to take away the sin of the world, which is to say that He came so that the world through Him might be saved. "For God did not send His Son into the world to condemn the world, but that the world through Him might be saved."

Now, a number of years ago a congregation had this verse of Scripture printed on many sheets of paper, along with an invitation for the recipients to come along to church. We then placed those many sheets of paper (with this verse written on it) into over five hundred letter boxes around the community. When I was delivering my lot of leaflets, I was pondering that verse over and over in my mind. Notice that John 3:17 begins with the word "for". This tells us that it is attached to the verse that comes before it, i.e., the famous John 3:16. Therefore John 3:17 is given to explain John 3:16, which is to say that God's action of sending His Son into the world should not be seen as God's condemnation of the world.

Sometimes a person's actions can be misread and taken as hostile. But God's action in sending His Son into the world should be viewed as the expression of His love for the world. But most importantly His action of sending His Son into the world ought to be seen by all the world as His actual saving of the world. So, why wouldn't God save the world, seeing as He is the One who created it? The very first verse of the Bible says, "In the beginning God created the heavens and the earth" (Gen. 1:1). And we know that the God who created the heavens and the earth is triune, which is to say that God is the Trinity, i.e., the Father, and the Son, and the Holy Spirit. These three Persons are One God. So, God the Father sent God the Son into the world. How did the Son come into the world? He came into the world by clothing Himself in flesh in the womb of the Virgin Mary. And He was born in a stable in Bethlehem.

Now, notice that John 3:17 does not say that God sent Santa Claus from the North Pole to bring the world presents. No! It says that God sent His Son into the world that the world through Him might be saved. Now, as we've already noted, this saving of the world is contrasted with condemning the world. Put negatively, God did not send His Son into the world to condemn the world. Put positively, God did send His Son into the world that the world through Him might be saved.

What does it mean to be condemned? And what does it mean to be saved? Well, to be condemned means that you are as good as being in the wheely-bin at the kerbside. To be condemned is to be awaiting transportation to the world's dump. "Hell" the Bible calls it. But the Good News is that that's not what God's Son Jesus Christ came into the world to do. No! He has come into the world to salvage, i.e., to save the world!

The World Needs a Saviour

Now then, this is where we need to find our thinking caps and put them on. If God sent His Son into the world to save the world, then God must believe that the world needs saving? So, let me ask you, Are you with God on this? Do you believe the world needs saving? If you look through the eyes of the same God who, in the beginning created the heavens and the earth and all therein and declared it to all be *very good*, then you'd agree with Him.

The world is no longer very good. Therefore, the world is in need of saving. Well, that's what the birth of Jesus Christ is all about. It's about God sending His Son into the world to save it because it's no longer very good. And when something is not very good, then what is it good for? What is a broken toy good for? What is a broken lawnmower good for? A dead goldfish? A rotten apple? What are human beings who won't stop sinning good for? What is a world full of sin, misery, and death good for? After all the Christmas presents are opened, all the wrappers go into the wheely-bin, don't they? And so do all the broken bits and pieces of toys. So do all the apple cores and half chewed chocolate bars, leftover turkey bits and bones. Well, John 3:17 is saying that God did not send His Son into the world to throw the world in the cosmic wheely-bin like so much broken and rotting rubbish. But rather God sent His Son into the world to repair and restore and renew the broken and rotting world.

The big picture is that the world was already in the cosmic wheely-bin sitting at the side of the road with all of us in it. But God has sent His Son into the world to save it, to salvage it, to rescue it, yes, to redeem it from final destruction. So, this must mean that the world was condemned already, mustn't it? And that's exactly what the verse following John 3:17 says, "He who believes in Him is not condemned; but He who does not believe is condemned already, because he has not believed in the name of the only begotten Son of God" (John 3:18). So, it's simple then, isn't it? If you want to know whether you're still in the cosmic wheely-bin or not, you just ask yourself whether you believe in God's only begotten Son or not.

By not believing in the God's only begotten Son you are proving you are condemned already. But if you are believing in God's only begotten Son, then you are no longer condemned. As the Scriptures say elsewhere, "There is therefore now no condemnation for those who are in Christ Jesus" (Rom. 8:1). You're either in Christ Jesus where you're saved and safe or you're in the cosmic wheely-bin where you're condemned and ready for the cosmic dump.

The cosmic dump is Hell. It is a real and permanent place. It is a place where real people keep on perishing forever. But the Good News is that "God so loved the world that He gave His only begotten Son, that whoever believes in Him should not perish but have everlasting life."

The sad fact is that some would rather perish than believe in Jesus Christ. But I would urge you to give glory to God by thanking Him for sending His only begotten Son into the world, not to condemn it, but as Saviour of the world.

This World Belongs to God

This is where we test what we've learned by reading this book. We stated the following at the outset:

> At its simplest, covenant theology is about the New Adam doing what the Old Adam failed to do, how He did it, and the promised reward He then received from God for a job well done. In short, before the foundation of the world (1 Pet. 1:20), God the Father promised God the Son (i.e., Christ) an uncountable amount of people (Psa. 2:8; John 17:9), and a place (i.e., the world, as in the renewed Heavens and the renewed Earth) for them to live in along with Him (Rev. 21:1).

We ask then why God sent His only begotten Son? Well, what do we know about the covenant of redemption? We know that there was an agreement between the Father and the Son from in eternity past. What was that agreement? Again, as per our quote above, God the Father promised God the Son (i.e., Christ) an uncountable amount of people (Psa. 2:8; John 17:9), and a place (i.e., the world, as in the renewed Heavens and the renewed Earth) for them to live in along with Him (Rev. 21:1).

Who is this uncountable amount of people? As per John 3:16 they are all those who believe in Him and therefore do not perish, i.e., those whom the Father has chosen to give His Son. And what is the world that God so loves? It is the renewed creation that He is giving His Son. He and they shall dwell therein forever. And why is God giving His Son His promised people and place? It is because Jesus as the second Adam perfectly kept the covenant of works and even paid the penalty for breaking it. At what stage are we in the history of the covenant of grace? Says Nigel Lee,

> The kingdom of this world even now already belongs to God – namely in principle – because Christ created and redeemed it. Therefore it is – progressively – to become His in practice too.[146]

In order for Christ's kingdom on earth to grow like the proverbial mustard seed, Satan's false

---

[146] Francis Nigel Lee, *John's Revelation Unveiled*, Ligstryders, Lynnwoodrif, South Africa, 1999, 93.

kingdom needs to be demolished. The cross of Christ demolished it in principle. That principle needs to be fulfilled in practice. As I've stated elsewhere,

> There are three major things that the Son of God came into the world to do. The first is twofold: Jesus came into the world to take away and pay for the sins of His people. The second is also twofold: Jesus came to destroy the Devil and to destroy the works of the Devil. And the third is that He came to set up His kingdom. So, we could put those three things together and say that Christ's Kingdom is established, sins are forgiven, Satan and his works are destroyed, by the preaching of the gospel of Jesus Christ.[147]

So, in terms of the covenant of redemption and of the covenant of works, victory! Christ has won the war. However, just as God's Old Testament people conquered the Promised Land with the edge of the sword, so God's New Testament people will conquer the promised earth with the sword of the Spirit, i.e., through the proclamation of the gospel. Have all of Christ's enemies been put under His feet yet? "Then *comes* the end, when He delivers the kingdom to God the Father, when He puts an end to all rule and all authority and power. For He must reign till He has put all enemies under His feet. The last enemy *that* will be destroyed *is* death" (1 Cor. 15:24-26).

---

[147] Neil Cullan McKinlay, *The Gospel: Simple yet Profound*, Tulip Publishing, Lansvale, NSW, 2021, 8.

Right now, the Holy Spirit is in the process of preparing Christ's bride by working with the Word in their hearts, and He is preparing a place where they will live by working with the Word in the world. Working with the bride "to make her holy, cleansing her by the washing with water through the word, and to present her to himself as a radiant church, without stain or wrinkle or any other blemish, but holy and blameless" (Eph. 5:26-27), and working in the world "till He has put all enemies under His feet" (1 Cor. 15:25).

The Cultural Mandate meets the Great Commission only when Christians in the power of the Spirit become obedient to Christ in all the things their hands find to do. As the apostle Paul says, "Therefore, whether you eat or drink, or whatever you do, do all to the glory of God" (1 Cor. 10:31), "And whatever you do in word or deed, *do* all in the name of the Lord Jesus, giving thanks to God the Father through Him" (Col. 3:17).

Conclusion

Do *you* believe in God's only begotten Son? Is Jesus *your* Saviour? If He is, then rejoice in the good news that "God so loved the world that He gave His only begotten Son, that whoever believes in Him should not perish but have everlasting life. For God did not send His Son into the world to condemn the world, but that the world through Him might be saved" (John 3:16-17).

Now we know why God sent His Son into the world. It was to fulfill the covenant of redemption, first expressed as the covenant of works with Adam, and then more fully in the covenant of grace with Christ as the second Adam.

Bibliography

Ames, William, *The Marrow of Theology*, Translated from the third Latin edition 1629 by John Dykstra Eusden, Baker Books, Grand Rapids, Michigan, *reprint* 1983

Bannerman, James, *The Church of Christ*, Still Waters Revival Books, *reprint* 1991

Bavinck, Herman, *The Doctrine of God*, Translated by William Hendriksen, Banner of Truth, Reprinted 1991

Bavinck, Herman, *Reformed Dogmatics: Sin and Salvation in Christ*, Vol. 3, Baker Academic, Grand Rapids, Michigan, 2006

Belcher, Jr., Richard P., *The Fulfillment of the Promises of God: An Explanation of Covenant Theology*, Mentor Imprint by Christian Focus Publications Ltd., Geanies House, Fearn, Ross-shire, 2020

Berkhof, Louis, *Systematic Theology*, Eerdmans, Edinburgh

Boettner, Loraine, *The Millennium*, Presbyterian & Reformed, USA

Brown, David, *Jamieson, Fausset, and Brown, A Commentary Critical, Experimental, and Practical on the Old and New Testaments, Volume Three*, Eerdmans Publishing, Grand Rapids, Michigan

Calvin, John, *Calvin's Commentaries, John-Acts*, Associated Publishers and Authors, Wilmington, Delaware, (no date)

Calvin, John, *Genesis*, The Banner of Truth Trust, London, England, (1554) 1965

Calvin, John, *The Institutes of the Christian Religion*, Battles Edition

Calvin, John, *Institutes of the Christian Religion*, Beveridge Edition

Calvin, John, *Institutes of the Christian Religion*, Translated from the first French edition of 1541 by Robert White, The Banner of Truth Trust, Edinburgh, U.K., reprinted 2017

Chilton, David, *Paradise Restored, A Biblical Theology of Dominion*, Dominion Press, Fort Worth, Texas

Clowney, Edmund P, *Preaching Christ in All of Scripture*, Crossway Books, Wheaton, Illinois

Clowney, Edmund P. *Preaching, The Preacher and Preaching in the Twentieth Century*, Edited by Samuel T Logan, Presbyterian & Reformed Publishing, Phillipsburg, New Jersey, 1986

The Confession of Faith, The Larger and Shorter Catechisms, with the Scripture Proofs at Large: together with The Sum of saving Knowledge, Free Presbyterian Publication, Glasgow

Dabney, Robert Lewis, *Systematic Theology*, first published 1872, Banner of Truth, Edinburgh, Scotland

Dickson, David, *Matthew*, The Banner of Truth Trust, Edinburgh, (First published 1647), 1981

Dooyeweerd, Herman, *The Christian Idea of the State*, Craig Press, Nutley, New Jersey,1968

Fairbairn, Patrick, *The Typology of Scripture: Viewed in Connection with the Whole Series of The Divine* Dispensations, Volume 1, Fourth Edition, T & T Clark, Edinburgh, Scotland, 1864

Fesko, J.V., *The Trinity and the Covenant of Redemption*, Mentor Imprint by Christian Focus Publications Ltd., Geanies House, Fearn, Ross-shire, 2016

Fesko, J.V., *Adam and the Covenant of Works*, Mentor Imprint by Christian Focus Publications Ltd., Geanies House, Fearn, Ross-shire, 2021

Fisher, Edward, *The Marrow of Modern Divinity*, Christian Focus Publications, Tain, Ross-shire, 2009

Geldenhuys, Norval, *The New International Commentary of the New Testament: The Gospel of Luke*, Eerdmans Publishing, Grand Rapids, Michigan, 1979

Gentry, Kenneth L., *The Greatness of the Great Commission*, Institute for Christian Economics, Tyler, Texas, 1993

Gleason, Ron, *The Death Penalty on Trial, Taking a Life for a Life Taken*, Nordskog Publishing Inc., Ventura, California, 2008

Godet, Frederic Louis, *Commentary on* Luke, (originally Funk & Wagnalls 1887), Kregel Publications, Grand Rapids, Michigan, 1981

Green, Jay, *The Interlinear, Hebrew/Greek/English Bible*, Volume Three, Associated Publishers and Authors, Inc, Evansville, Indiana, 1978

Hendriksen, William, *The Gospel of Luke*, The Banner of Truth Trust, Edinburgh, Scotland, 1979

Hendriksen, William, *The Gospel of Matthew*, The Banner of Truth Trust, Edinburgh, Scotland

Hendriksen, William, *More Than Conquerors*, Baker Book House, Grand Rapids, Michigan\

Henry, Matthew, *Matthew Henry's Commentary on the Whole Bible: Complete and Unabridged in One Volume*, Peabody, Hendrickson, 1994

Hodge, Charles, *Ephesians*, (1856. Banner of Truth, Edinburgh, 1991), Hodge, *Ephesians*, (1856), Banner of Truth, Edinburgh, 1991

Hodge, Charles, *Systematic Theology*, Eerdmans, Grand Rapids, Michigan

Hoeksema, Herman, *Behold, He Cometh! An Exposition of the Book of Revelation*, Reformed Free Publishing Association, Grand Rapids, Michigan, (1969), Second Printing 1974

Horton, Michael, *The Christian Faith, A Systematic Theology for Pilgrims on the Way*, Zondervan, Grand Rapids, Michigan, 2011

Hosking, E.B., *The Covenants in Creation: The History of Salvation and the Continuing Significance*, Coral Coast Printers, Bundaberg, Australia

Jamieson, Fausset, and Brown, *A Commentary Critical, Experimental, and Practical on the Old and New Testaments, Volume Three*, Eerdmans Publishing, Grand Rapids, Michigan, Reprinted 1989

Keil and Delitzsch, *Old Testament Commentaries*, Vol. 1, Associated Publishers, Grand Rapids, Michigan, no date

Kline, Meredith G., *Images of the Spirit*, Eugene, OR, Wipf and Stock Publishers, 1999

Kuyper, Abraham, *God's Angels: His Ministering Spirits*, (Translation by Rev. Richard Stienstra), Kindle Edition

Lee, Francis Nigel, *The Covenantal Sabbath*, The Lord's Day Observance Society, London, 1966

Lee, Francis Nigel, *Creation, Flood, and Conquest*, E-book

Lee, Francis Nigel, *Jahweh – Jehovah* (On-line)

Lee, Francis Nigel, *John's Revelation Unveiled*, Ligstryders, Lynnwoodrif, South Africa, 2000

Logan, Samuel T, *Preaching, The Preacher and Preaching in the Twentieth Century*, Presbyterian & Reformed Publishing, Phillipsburg, New Jersey, 1986

Lloyd-Jones, D. Martyn, *Romans, Exposition of Chapter 1, The Gospel of God*, The Banner of Truth Trust, Edinburgh, Scotland, 1985

Lloyd-Jones, D. Martyn, *Romans, Exposition of Chapter 5, Assurance*, The Banner of Truth Trust, Edinburgh, Scotland, (1971), Reprinted 1988

Lloyd-Jones, D. Martyn, *Romans, Exposition of Chapter 9, God's Sovereign Purpose*, The Banner of Truth Trust, Edinburgh, Scotland, 1991

Machin, J. Gresham, *The New Testament – An Introduction to its History & Literature*, Banner of Truth, Edinburgh, Scotland, first published 1976, 1981

MacLeod, John, *Scottish Theology*, Knox Press & Banner of Truth Trust, 1974

Murray, John, *Christian Baptism*, Presbyterian and Reformed Publishing Co, Phillipsburg, New Jersey, 1980

Pink, Arthur, *Gleanings in Genesis*, Moody Press, Chicago, Illinois, 1978

Poole, Matthew, *A Commentary on the Holy Bible*, Banner of Truth

Robertson, O Palmer, *The Christ of the Covenants*, Presbyterian and Reformed Publishing, New Jersey, 1980

Schwartz, D. Rudi, *The Lord's Day: Does it Really Still Matter?*, Ark House Press, Australia, 2021

Sibbes, Richard, *Commentary on 2 Corinthians Chapter 1, Works of Richard Sibbes*, Edinburgh, Banner of Truth, 1981 reprint

Sproul, RC, *Truths We Confess: A Layman's Guide to the Westminster Confession of Faith*, Volume 1, P&R Publishing, Phillipsburgh, New Jersey, 2006

Strong, James, *The New Strong's Exhaustive Concordance of the Bible*, Thomas Nelson Publishers, Nashville, Tennessee, 1984

Sutton, Ray R, *That You May Prosper, Dominion by Covenant*, Institute for Christian Economics, Tyler, Texas, 1987

Thomas, David, *Gospel of Matthew, Expository and Homiletical*, Kregel Publications, Grand Rapids. Michigan, Reprint of 1873 edition, 1979

Van Doren, William H., *The Gospel of Luke, Expository and Homiletical Commentary*, Kregel Publications, Grand Rapids, Michigan, 1981

Venema, Cornelis P., *Christ and Covenant Theology: Essays on Election, Republication, and the Covenants*, Phillipsburg, NJ, P&R Publishing, 2017

Vos, Geerhardus, *Biblical Theology, Old and New Testaments*, The Banner of Truth Trust, Edinburgh, Scotland, 1948 (Reprinted 1985)

Ward, Rowland S, *God & Adam, Reformed Theology and The Creation Covenant*, New Melbourne Press, Wantirna, Australia, 2003

Ward, Rowland S, *God and Adam Reformed Theology and the Creation Covenant*, Tulip Publishing, Lansvale, NSW, 2019

Ward, Rowland S, *The Westminster Confession of Faith for the Church Today*, Presbyterian Church of Eastern Australia in Melbourne, 1992

Waters, Reid, and Muether, *Covenant Theology: Biblical, Theological, and Historical Perspectives*, Crossway, Wheaton, Illinois, 2020

Watson, Thomas, *The Art of Divine Contentment: An Exposition of Philippians 4:11*, Free Presbyterian Publications, Glasgow, Scotland, (First published 1855, republished no date)

Westminster Confession of Faith, Westminster Larger and Shorter Catechisms, the Practical Use of Saving Knowledge, the Directory for the Publick Worship of God, the Form of Church Government, etc., Free presbyterian Publications, Glasgow, First Reprinted 1976, 1985

Williamson, G.I., *The Heidelberg Catechism, A Study Guide*, P & R Publishing, Philippsburg, New Jersey, 1993

Witsius, Herman, *Economy of Covenants Between God and* Man, 2 Vols, Book I, Chapter I, VII, (First published 1677, reprinted 1822, Kindle version 2014)

Printed in Great Britain
by Amazon